THE LITERATURE OF FACT

RONALD WEBER

THE LITERATURE OF FACT:

Literary Nonfiction in American Writing

OHIO UNIVERSITY PRESS
Athens, Ohio

Library of Congress Cataloging in Publication Data

Weber, Ronald, 1934-
  The literature of fact.

  Bibliography: p. 176
  Includes index.
  1. American prose literature—20th century— History and criticism.
2. Journalism—United States. 3. Fiction—Technique. 4. Historiography.
I. Title.
PS369.W4   813'.081   80-16323
ISBN 0-8214-0558-6
ISBN 0-8214-0823-2 pbk.

FOR PAT

The art of narrative, in fact, is the same, whether it is applied to the selection and illustration of a real series of events or of an imaginary series. Boswell's *Life of Johnson* (a work of cunning and inimitable art) owes its success to the same technical manoeuvres as (let us say) *Tom Jones*: the clear conception of certain characters of man, the choice and presentation of certain incidents out of a great number that offered, and the invention (yes, invention) and preservation of a certain key in dialogue. In which these things are done with more art—in which with the greater air of nature—readers will differently judge. Boswell's is, indeed, a very special case, and almost a generic; but it is not only in Boswell, it is in every biography with any salt of life, it is in every history where events and men, rather than ideas, are presented—in Tacitus, in Carlyle, in Michelet, in Macaulay—that the novelist will find many of his own methods most conspicuously and adroitly handled. He will find besides that he, who is free—who has the right to invent or steal a missing incident, who has the right, more precious still, of wholesale omission—is frequently defeated, and, with all his advantages, leaves a less strong impression of reality and passion.

Robert Louis Stevenson: *Memories
and Portraits*

. . . it is as if History had come back to revenge itself on its upstart rival, Fiction. But not without Fiction's own techniques. . . .

Alfred Kazin: *Bright Book of Life:
American Novelists and Storytellers
from Hemingway to Mailer*

CONTENTS

Acknowledgements

Chapter 10, "Letting Subjects Grow," appeared in somewhat different form in an article in *The Antioch Review* (1978). Chapter 13, "Illuminating Recent History," and the Conclusion, "A Queer Genre," appeared in somewhat different form in an article in *South Atlantic Quarterly* (1979). A portion of the Appendix, "Literary Nonfiction at the Decade's End," appeared in an essay review in *The Sewanee Review* (1980).

Introduction: Nonfiction with a Literary Purpose

One of the noteworthy features of American writing throughout the 1960s and 1970s has been the prominence of journalistic nonfiction. This book is about one strain of nonfiction reportage in those years—nonfiction with a literary purpose. Needless to say, this category of serious writing is not well defined, and the many terms used to describe it—art-journalism, nonfiction novel, essay-fiction, factual fiction, journalit—have done nothing to clarify matters. The most widely used term has been the most confusing of all: New Journalism. Any kind of fact writing that departed from the familiar forms of journalism or recreated events, however slightly, rather than simply describing them came to be called New Journalism. The term was used to refer to so much that it soon ceased to refer with decent clarity to anything.

Here I shall be using a simple descriptive term: literary nonfiction. Above all I want to avoid any suggestion that the work I am looking at is somehow radically innovative, something that sprang to life in the sixties with the appearance of Truman Capote's *In Cold Blood* and precipitated a new wave in American letters. Literary nonfiction has a long and honorable history in our literature; and although this book is not about that history, I mean to keep it in mind.

In the first part of the book, I review some aspects of the critical context of recent literary nonfiction. It seems to me that the resurgence of interest in nonfiction in the sixties and seventies had a good deal to do with the critical debates in those years about the direction of the novel—in light of the apparent demise of realism—and the direction of journalism—in view of increasing unease with the canons of impersonality and objectivity. I do not mean to imply that some of the notable nonfiction writers of the time— Capote, Norman Mailer, Tom Wolfe, Gay Talese—produced books somehow intended to demonstrate critical positions; all of them, however, and Wolfe especially, took an active part in the critical discussion. My point is simply that the questioning of attitudes and approaches that surrounded fiction and journalism in those years provided some impetus for the renewal of interest in nonfiction as a significant literary form. I therefore describe some of that questioning as a necessary part of the background for the subsequent examination of particular works in the second part of the book.

As I go on, I give some definition to literary nonfiction as a genre, viewing it as a complex counterpointing of its two constituent elements, history and literature. In actual practice, in the sixties and seventies that combination has resulted in fact writing based on reporting that frequently employs techniques drawn from the art of fiction to create something of fiction's atmosphere or feeling and that, most important, moves toward the intentions of fiction while remaining fully factual. Excluded by this loose definition are, on the one hand, books that mix fact and invention, which consequently become works of fiction, and, on the other, that writing sometimes called the higher journalism—journalistic work written with notable care or stylishness or involving unusual kinds of research or reporting.

This last is especially difficult to distinguish from the work I call literary nonfiction. Many nonfiction writers make use of fictional techniques and try to create some of fiction's atmosphere yet do not go all the way toward a full fictionlike dramatization or reconstruction of the materials of fact, or they simply draw on a tradition within journalism of fine writing and careful construction. Such writers consider their nonfiction primarily journalistic rather than at once journalistic and literary. The line of separation here is surely faint, yet it provides a useful distinction between a form of literary journalism and the journalism as literature I take as my subject.

Another way of defining the subject is by reference to Donald Pizer's distinction between two kinds of documentary narrative—one exploring a factual event simply as an event (documentary narrative), the other exploring it as meaning (documentary narrative as art).[1] Pizer uses William Manchester's *The Death of a President* as an example of the first, Capote's *In Cold Blood* as an example of the second. Manchester piles up factual detail but does not impose on it, or draw from it, significant themes; Capote, through selection, arrangement, emphasis, and other literary devices, discovers some meaning or theme in his factual materials. The difference is the difference between journalism and art. In the one case accuracy, or at least verisimilitude, is the end, in the other it is simply a means to an end, which is meaning or the interpretation of experience. What Pizer sees as documentary narrative is what I take to be the higher journalism; in contrast, nonfiction writing with a self-conscious literary purpose, or documentary narrative as art, is a form of nonfiction in which the writer tries to draw together the conflicting roles of observer and maker, journalist and artist.

But although I give some definition to the form, I realize that literary nonfiction remains a hazy and perhaps puzzling form, one that places severe demands on reader and writer alike. Rather than attempt more abstract clarification, I want instead to see how particular examples of literary nonfiction work, how they are put together and what their effects are; I want, in other words, to talk about the work as it is, in all its variety and complexity, rather than try to set out a theory of literary nonfiction. I suspect—and Tom Wolfe has said as much—that the very openness of the form and the lack of much theorizing about it has been part of its considerable appeal during a time in which fiction and journalism alike have been subjected to heavy loads of theorizing.

In no sense do I offer a complete survey of recent nonfiction. I treat only what I take as some of the more important and interesting examples of the form, and although many of my selections are obvious ones, there are some notable omissions—for example, the work of James Willwerth or Peter Maas or Joe Eszterhas. I am especially aware of a lack of discussion of the tape-recorded book. Tape-recorded books, usually intended to give a voice to the voiceless, have rarely sought a literary level, but the pioneering studies of Oscar Lewis were conceived in self-conscious rivalry with fiction and merit study within the context of literary nonfiction.

Finally, there is a question of an appropriate tense for this study.

Although he devoted a chapter of *Bright Book of Life* to the "imagination of fact" in the work of Capote and Mailer, Alfred Kazin announced in the book that the "art-journalism" they had produced was already old and withered. "It went through a whole cycle in the Sixties," he said, "and no longer astonishes." In a *Commonweal* article Thomas Powers wondered: "Whatever happened to the New Journalism?" Contrary to earlier belief he found the novel healthy, selling well enough and once again the darling of writers, and he concluded: "So, the novel is alive and well . . . which is okay with me, and journalism . . . trapped for so long in leaden books—well, journalism, alas . . . is still journalism." And Hilton Kramer simply stated: "We hardly ever hear about the 'nonfiction novel' anymore."[2]

Of course it was not to be expected that the New Journalism—or whatever else it was called—would remain forever fresh in the eyes of critics. It was bound to end up in the dustbin of literary trends, linked to a decade past, the rebellious sixties. Predictably, the realistic novel, never dead or dying despite the attention to its health, got up a new head of steam in the seventies and gathered to itself new writers and new energies. Many of the major names tied to literary nonfiction either turned for the first time to the novel or returned to it, and their major works, as Kazin said, no longer seemed astonishing.

But writers did not abruptly abandon literary nonfiction with the passing of its trendy period. What happened in the sixties was a rather noisy revival of the tradition of literary nonfiction in American writing under the inspiration of Capote's well-publicized demonstration that documentary journalism could yield a work of art. Ambitious works of literary nonfiction continued to appear throughout the seventies, though happily accompanied by less fanfare and minus claims of literary breakthroughs; and they will surely continue to appear in the future. Some of the recent works discussed in this book, C. D. B. Bryan's *Friendly Fire* for one, seem to me as important as anything produced in the sixties.

In saying this, I do not wish to seem to side with those who have promoted literary nonfiction as *the* literary form of the time, a new hybrid kind of factual fiction that has supplanted the novel or rendered obsolete the accomplishments of the old journalism. Nothing could be further from the truth. My view is simply that a considerable amount of work of combined literary power and journalistic merit has been accomplished in recent years and that such work is a significant development within the larger framework of serious American writing.

I hope in this study to provide both a partial history of that development and a continuing exploration of the literary uses of nonfiction. The appropriate tense is at once both past and present.

Notes

1. Donald Pizer, "Documentary Narrative as Art: William Manchester and Truman Capote," reprinted in *The Reporter as Artist: A Look at the New Journalism Controversy*, ed. Ronald Weber (New York: Hastings House, 1974), pp. 207-219. A number of critical articles referred to in this volume are reprinted in that collection (hereafter cited as Weber, *The Reporter as Artist*), where the original place and date of publication of each article are to be found.

2. Alfred Kazin, *Bright Book of Life: American Novelists and Storytellers from Hemingway to Mailer* (Boston: Little, Brown, 1973), p. 240; Thomas Powers, "Cry Wolfe," *Commonweal*, 24 October 1975, pp. 497, 499; Hilton Kramer, "Beautiful Reds," *New York Times Book Review*, 2 April 1978, p. 3.

PART ONE: THE BACKGROUND

John Kouwenhoven once suggested that the "tradition of reportorial journalism which first attained literary quality more than a hundred years ago in Dana's *Two Years Before the Mast* had become, since Mark Twain's time, one of the principal shaping forces in our literature."[1] That may well overstate the matter, but it is certainly true that American fiction has been influenced in a number of still largely unexplored ways by journalism—and equally true that there has been a significant strain of literary nonfiction in our serious writing, much of which has been based on reporting or has taken the form of the journalistic report, extending from Dana and Twain through James Agee and John Hersey, Truman Capote and Norman Mailer.

The 1960s and 1970s witnessed a dramatic renewal of the nonfiction tradition against a background composed of both a shift in the nation's reading habits from fiction to nonfiction and a new interest in nonfiction films and television documentaries.[2] In turn these changes reflected and drew upon new attitudes at work in the society and especially upon deeply divided critical attitudes about what constituted a proper style of both fiction and journalism for the time. It is useful to sketch this background in broad outline in order to see recent literary nonfiction in some perspective.

Notes

1. John A. Kouwenhoven, *Made In America: The Arts in Modern Civilization* (Garden City, N.Y.: Doubleday, 1948), p. 254.

2. About film, one commentator remarked: "There was such a resurgence of creative activity and production in the nonfiction film during the 1960s that the term *rebirth* is not an exaggeration." Richard Meran Barsam, *Nonfiction Film: A Critical History* (New York: Dutton, 1973), p. 247.

1
Toward Irrealism

After World War II, magazines began shifting their editorial formulas and replacing fiction with nonfiction, especially with articles treating contemporary issues. An editor of *True* remarked that the "fact is that men don't read magazine fiction anymore. They still want good reading, good stories, but they like them better when they know they're true."[1] Editors of many women's and general circulation magazines apparently felt the same. But such a change in editorial policy was not surprising; in large part it was simply a response to a new competitive situation brought about by the rise of television and film. What *was* surprising, as the novelist Wright Morris observed, was that a large number of literary people now seemed to share the new interest in "fact."

Norman Podhoretz in his 1958 benchmark essay called "The Article as Art" argued that the magazine article was a more appropriate literary form for the time than fiction because the former fit better with contemporary notions of functionality. "I would suggest," Podhoretz wrote, "that we have all, writers and readers alike, come to feel temporarily uncomfortable with the traditional literary forms because they don't *seem* practical, designed for 'use,' whereas a magazine article by its nature satisfies that initial condition and so is free to assimilate as many 'useless,' 'non-functional' elements as it pleases." Podhoretz felt this was hardly an ideal situation for literature to be in, but nothing was gained by ignoring it. The undeniable fact was that "a large class of readers . . . has found itself responding more enthusiastically to what is lamely called 'nonfiction' (and especially to magazine articles and even book reviews) than to current fiction."[2]

In *Making It*, the account of his rise in the New York literary world published in 1969, Podhoretz recalled that the very center of American writing had seemed to shift in the fifties to nonfiction. One passage is worth quoting at length:

> I did not believe . . . that fiction was the only kind of writing which deserved to be called "creative," and I did not . . . believe that the novel was at the moment the most vital form that literature was taking in America. There were young novelists around I respected—Malamud, Bellow, Flannery O'Connor, Ellison, Donleavy, the Jones of *From Here to Eternity*, and especially Mailer—but the truth was that the American books of the postwar period which had mattered to me personally, and not to me alone either, in the large way that fiction and poetry once had mattered were not novels . . . but works the trade quaintly called "nonfiction," as though they had a negative existence: *The Liberal Imagination, The Origins of Totalitarianism, Notes of a Native Son,* and a host of still uncollected pieces. . . . Whether or not such writing merited the honorific "literature"—and I thought they did—they, and even lesser than they, had made an impact upon my mind, imagination, and soul far greater than anything I had experienced from reading even the best of the younger American novelists. Theirs was the company I would have wished any book I might write to join. The center, I thought, had shifted to them.
>
> But where exactly was that? I would not have been able to say. Vaguely it all came together in my mind as "society" in opposition to the privatized universe of most current American fiction. . . . "Society" was *out there*; it was where everything after all was really going on; it was where *history* was being made.[3]

Similar comments popped up everywhere, all more or less following Podhoretz's line of reasoning: current nonfiction was as interesting as fiction and certainly more important because it dealt with the real world, the world of society and history, while fiction by comparison seemed indrawn, private, trivial. The critic John Thompson, reviewing the *O. Henry Prize Stories of 1961* in *Partisan Review*, querulously asked:

> I wonder, who reads short stories? When you pick up a magazine, do you turn to the short story? What is it doing there, anyway? It looks as boring as a poem, and probably it is. Maybe if you yourself write short stories, yes, you take a quick slice at it, to see who's doing it now, is he one up on you or not, what's he copying?

The fictional story seemed so annoyingly archaic to Thompson because, as he said elsewhere, "Every form of our literature is turning more and more to direct statement, to autobiography, to confession, to forms of the essay."[4] In a world consumed by problems, the indirections of storytelling seemed an indefensible luxury, wholly at odds with a pragmatic, issue-oriented new sensibility.

Theodore Solotaroff, editor of the *New American Review*, putting together a collection of essays by literary figures, saw the characteristic tone of expression of the time emphasizing "immediacy, relevance, involve-

ment, or, in the idiom of the day, 'being where it's at,' 'telling it like it is,' "
interests that now found their natural home in magazine journalism.[5]
When *Esquire* put out a collection of its best work from the sixties, it
omitted fiction entirely; and Harold Hayes, the magazine's editor,
explained that events during the period "seemed to move too swiftly to
allow the osmotic process of art to keep abreast." Hayes also noted that
when *Esquire* turned up a good novelist during the sixties, it "immediately
sought to seduce him with sweet mysteries of current events."[6]

Little seduction seemed necessary, however, for even committed fiction
writers like Herbert Gold were saying that novelists who "no longer want to
leave to others the formal judging and measuring of experience," feel
compelled instead to speak out in their own voices in articles and essays, as
well as through character and situation in fiction.[7] For Gold and others the
appropriate literary models for the time were not so much Joyce or
Hemingway or Faulkner, but George Orwell and James Baldwin, who—
although both were novelists—were now singled out for their passionate
and personal journalism.

By the middle sixties such critical statements were commonplace. In a
time of change, with the word itself seeming to struggle for survival against
McLuhanesque assaults, fiction appeared to many to be a nineteenth-
century diversion, historically valuable but no longer offering the voice
needed to address the times adequately. There was frequent reference to the
death of the novel; and even though most critics denied the bad news, the
feeling was widespread that fiction was not in the best of health. If the novel
was not dead, the *age* of the novel might be, the genre nearing exhaustion,
coming to the end of its historical period, the circumstances that called it
into being now vanishing. Of course literature in all its forms, fiction and
nonfiction, seemed to count for less in relation to the intellectual life as a
whole, but if any kind of writing could compete with film and television, to
say nothing of history and popular sociology and psychology and even the
daily newspaper, it seemed to be nonfiction writing. For one of its earliest
and most zealous advocates, Seymour Krim, nonfiction had become by the
middle sixties "the *de facto* literature of our time."[8]

*

Coupled with heightened interest in direct writing through nonfiction
forms was a debate in literary circles about the direction of fiction in a post-
realistic period. Although the fictional effort to portray common
experience and render the world through realistic detail still had its critical
defenders and a good number of important practitioners, there was
widespread feeling that the novel of social realism was no longer a viable
literary form. *That* novel was indeed dead—so the argument went—its
function usurped by nonfiction and film. When critics like Podhoretz called

attention to the apparent irrelevance and uselessness of fiction, they were addressing themselves to an outmoded representational fiction that still sought to bring news or information of the world; there was wide agreement, as Warner Berthoff put it, that it was in its "function of news-delivering entertainment—seeking to hold our attention by transforming the formless data of contemporary circumstances and moral consciousness into a significant narrative progression—that the novel is in trouble."[9] The realistic novel, or that part of the novel that was realistic, had been preempted by visual and verbal forms that brought us the world more directly and with greater immediacy.

Another problem with the fiction of social realism was that even when a writer believed the novel could still hold its own as a realistic medium, he was apt to think himself overwhelmed by the chaos of contemporary life. To impose a "significant narrative progression" on social events could seem beyond his powers at a time, as Norman Mailer said, when "History inhabits a crazy house" and day-to-day reality dwarfs the imagination.[10] Realistic fiction has to be plausible but life does not, and in the sixties life often seemed bent on being as implausible as possible, resisting surface description let alone the attempt to find the figure in the carpet, the threads of meaning or symbolic design.

Philip Roth, in an often-quoted 1961 essay called "Writing American Fiction," complained that the "American writer in the middle of the 20th century has his hands full in trying to understand, and then describe, and then make *credible* much of the American reality. It stupifies, it sickens, it infuriates, and finally it is even a kind of embarrassment to one's own meager imagination." Roth asserted, "It is the tug of reality, its mystery and magnetism, that leads one into the writing of fiction," but what was one to do when one was "not mystified, but stupified? Not drawn but repelled?" At the time, Roth thought the fiction writer might turn to the historical novel or satire—or stop writing. Certainly he had no choice but to withdraw from "some of the grander social and political phenomena of our times," subjects that could no longer be treated within the familiar imaginative confines of realistic fiction.[11]

But in a sense the realistic writer's problem with contemporary subject matter was even larger than Roth allowed. Put simply, the problem had to do with the essential reality of those grander social and political phenomena of the times; were they indeed real in the sense of being true reflections of present reality? Podhoretz, defending Mailer's controversial novel *Barbary Shore*, argued that to write realistic fiction, one had to believe that "society is what it seems to be and that it reveals the truth about itself in the personalities it throws up, the buildings it builds, the habits and manners it fosters; all the writer need do is describe these faithfully . . . and the truth will be served." But Mailer's point in the novel was just the opposite. American society seemed prosperous and purposeful when in fact it was empty, confused, and gripped by invisible forces it neither recognized nor controlled. The only hope of making literary sense of such a society was through the indirect, nonrealistic means Mailer had chosen, for "invisible forces" could not be described but only "talked about abstractly and pictured allegorically."[12]

Contemporary reality was not only incredible then but untrue. It might offend and even embarrass the fictional imagination, but the more penetrating point was that it failed to reveal in its surface detail the true state of society. The forms of the society, its manners and morals, masked confusion, deceit, and spiritual disintegration. Flannery O'Connor had talked about fiction as the movement through manners into mystery, a traditional view, but to many writers manners seemed to lead away from mystery toward deception rather than toward revelation. The alternative was to pursue fictional forms that gave scant attention to social realities of the more public sort and sought through various indirect means to touch the hidden, inner, essentially private truths of how we lived now.

The result of all such talk was to put realistic fiction in a vulnerable position, seemingly attacked from all sides. Some still retained the view of Lionel Trilling's classic essay "Manners, Morals, and the Novel" that the primary purpose of the novel was the investigation of social reality. Alfred Kazin, for example, defended the merits of Saul Bellow's realistic fiction against the critical onslaught:

> The novel, whose essential genius as a medium has always been the utter free-dom it has given, since the eighteenth century, to the individualization and concretization of experience, has by its very freedom and plasticity in dealing with matter of fact become an embarrassment to those over-impressionable intellectuals . . . . who have no natural love for the unmediated facts of existence, thus no longer think of the novel as the indispensable free form most bountifully expressive of life.[13]

But the dominant feeling, articulated by such influential critics as Richard Poirier, Richard Gilman, Robert Scholes, and Ihab Hassan, was that realism was no longer a vigorous literary mode and that the pressing question was where fiction should go, if it was to continue at all, in a decidedly post-realistic period.

There was no lack of answers. Two strains of fiction have long been distinguished, the novel and the romance, realism and fantasy, and now many critics called for a self-conscious return to the tradition of the romance, to a "fabulous" fiction that had its source in myth, fable, and fantasy. Fabulation offered a fictional world that was clearly, even stridently, discontinuous from this world—and therefore a world in which the writer, freed from discredited and ultimately futile efforts to record and chronicle the world, might be able to engage the real issues of his time.

Fabulation in contemporary fiction took many forms and had a variety of notable practitioners—Kurt Vonnegut, Jr., Robert Coover, Thomas Pynchon, Donald Barthelme, John Barth—but found a critical center in a broad opposition to the conventions of realistic fiction, the effort to record life, to freeze it. The up-to-date writer was now seen not as recorder but constructor, and what he constructed was a version of the world, not an imitation of it. This was the problem at the heart of literary realism—a new awareness that literature can offer only models of reality, not descriptions of it. Thus Barth predicted that "irrealism" would characterize the fiction of the 1970s, replacing a descriptive realism that, Barth added, now seemed only "a kind of aberration in the history of literature." [14]

Some criticism, however, also called into question the movement toward fabulation as a response to an abandoned realism. It was pointed out that if the world could not be recorded by the realist, neither could it be escaped by the fabulist; the construction of worlds totally elsewhere was as impossible as transcriptions of this one, the creation of genuine fantasy no more possible than genuine reality. The only truly authentic territory for fiction therefore was fiction itself, and the truly up-to-date writer was one who self-consciously exploited this resource. Insofar as such "metafictions" could be said to be "about" anything, they were about fiction itself, its history, achievements, processes; they were fictions about fiction—which is, it was pointed out, what fiction is really all about anyway. Among the chief practitioners of such self-reflective art were Jorge Borges, who Barth praised as one who "confronts an intellectual dead end"—meaning the possibility of creating new and original works of fiction—"and employs it against itself to accomplish new human work," and Barth himself, who characterized his own work as "novels which imitate the form of the Novel, by an author who imitates the role of Author." [15]

Another solution to the demise of literary realism, offered by such critics as Scholes and Leslie Fiedler, was science fiction, or at least fiction set in the future. Scholes pointed out that science fiction did not try either to record reality, since the future obviously cannot be recorded, or to deny its reality. Since all future projection was actually model making, "future-fiction" thus accepted what we now understood as the nature of fiction—that it can never be chronicle, only construction—and so was free of what Scholes called the "solipsistic problem that has proved so crucial for modern fiction." [16] As a fictional form, future-fiction could therefore develop as it would.

*

The merit of all such talk about fiction is not the issue here. Rather the point is to note that the renewal of interest in literary nonfiction took place against a background of this kind of discussion of serious writing. Literary nonfiction, like fabulation, metafiction, and future-fiction, was in part a response to the loss of confidence in literary realism and to a widespread feeling that realism was no longer a viable mode for serious writing.

An anthology of contemporary short fiction devoted to the principle, as the editor put it, that fiction now expressed "radical new doubts about the nature of 'reality' and the validity of the fiction-making process in relation to 'reality,' " grouped the work into five decidedly post-realistic categories: Fantasy-Fabulation-Irrealism; Neo-Gothic; Myth-Parable; Metafiction— Technique as Subject; Parody and Put-On.[17] Critics of course acknowledged that serious treatments of modern life in the realistic manner were still produced, but such work no longer seemed at the center of things. Indeed, serious writers who continued the realistic tradition often seemed embarrassingly close in manner to popular best-selling writers who invariably produced works of realistic fiction that drew in fairly literal fashion on historical accounts or the lives of well-known people.

At the very least, the remaining realists seemed distinctly old fashioned, stubbornly maintaining a tradition that had been passed by. Young writers and many readers, it was argued, even if unaware of the critical attack on realism, were simply fed up with the accumulated baggage of the form, with its omniscience and characterization and plottedness, especially with its overall effort to chronicle the world. This was the heart of the problem. "It is because reality cannot be recorded," Scholes explained, "that realism is dead." And he went on: "All writing, all composition, is construction. We do not imitate the world, we construct versions of it. There is no mimesis, only poiesis. No recording. Only construction."[18]

Again, it is against such a background that recent literary nonfiction must be seen. Like fabulation, metafiction, and future-fiction, the work was in some degree a response to an erosion of faith in literary realism, though a response that took a quite different direction. Rather than abandoning realism in favor of more insistently fictional fictions, recent work continued it within the forms of nonfiction and sought to become a nonfiction fiction or a factual fiction—retaining many of the technical devices and effects of realism while directly recording or reporting on the world rather than re-creating it as fiction. In other words, if one response to the critical questioning of realism was in one way or another to abandon it, another was to pursue it all the more—but pursue it outside the troubling critical questioning that afflicted fiction in favor of neglected nonfiction forms. Seymour Krim said that his intention as a nonfiction writer was "an extension of the realistic novel in the only direction it could logically go— into real, quotidian, actual, scary life itself."[19]

Tom Wolfe maintained that one of the most compelling things about nonfiction or journalism was that it had no conventions to speak of, whereas the novel had too many. Since little critical attention had been visited on nonfiction, the writer was free to explore the form without the debilitating self-consciousness that now attached to fiction. Wolfe said about journalism: "It's a low-rent form—always has been a low-rent form—and there's always been room for a lot of brawling about and a lot of mistakes."[20] In particular, it afforded the freedom to continue, and with relish, the realistic impulse to chronicle the world. This function critics seemed willing to concede to nonfiction writers. We would, Scholes said, "turn to the new journalists if it is chronicle we want" whereas we expected conscious construction from fiction if it was to be true to its nature.[21]

Of course nonfiction did not really escape the philosophical issue raised by critics. As the argument went, nonfiction could no more chronicle reality than fiction since all forms of writing offer models or versions of reality rather than actual descriptions of it; consequently, nonfiction was as inherently "irrealistic" as fiction. But as a low-rent form, nonfiction had been allowed to go its way without much critical questioning. The practical result was the availability of the form for continuing the traditions of literary realism at a time when serious fiction, for some of the reasons already indicated, had supposedly separated itself from those traditions.

Notes

1. Quoted in *Magazines in the Twentieth Century* by Theodore Peterson (Urbana: University of Illinois Press, 1964), p. 314.

2. Norman Podhoretz, "The Article as Art", reprinted in Weber, *The Reporter as Artist*, pp. 136, 129.

3. Norman Podhoretz, *Making It* (New York: Random House, 1967), pp. 261-262.

4. John Thompson, "Plot, Character, Etc.," *Partisan Review*, 28 (September-October 1961), 715; "Other People's Affairs," *Partisan Review*, 28 (January-February 1961), 124.

5. Theodore Solotaroff, Introduction to *Writers and Issues*, reprinted in Weber, *The Reporter as Artist*, p. 163.

6. Harold Hayes, Introduction to *Smiling Through the Apocalypse: Esquire's History of the Sixties,* reprinted in Weber, *The Reporter as Artist*, p. 160.

7. Herbert Gold, "How Else Can a Novelist Say It?" reprinted in Weber, *The Reporter as Artist*, p. 152.

8. Seymour Krim, "The Newspaper as Literature/ Literature as Leadership," reprinted in Weber, *The Reporter as Artist*, p. 183.

9. Warner Berthoff, *Fiction and Events* (New York: Dutton, 1971), p. 106.

10. Norman Mailer, *The Armies of the Night* (New York: New American Library, 1968), p. 54.

11. Philip Roth, "Writing American Fiction," *Commentary*, 31 (March 1961), 224, 225.

12. Norman Podhoretz, "Norman Mailer: The Embattled Vision," *Doings and Undoings* (New York: Noonday, 1964), pp. 188, 189.

13. Alfred Kazin, Introduction to *Seize the Day*, by Saul Bellow (New York: Fawcett Books, 1968), p. vi.

14. Joe David Bellamy, *The New Fiction: Interviews with Innovative American Writers* (Urbana: University of Illinois Press, 1974), p. 4.

15. John Barth, "The Literature of Exhaustion," *The Atlantic*, August 1967, pp. 31, 33.

16. Robert Scholes, *Structural Fabulation* (Notre Dame, Ind.: University of Notre Dame Press, 1975), p. 18.

17. Joe David Bellamy, ed., *Superfiction, or The American Story Transformed* (New York: Vintage Books, 1975), p. 6.

18. Scholes, *Structural Fabulation*, p. 7.

19. Seymour Krim, "The Enemy of the Novel," *Iowa Review*, 3 (Winter 1972), 61.

20. Bellamy, *The New Fiction*, p. 78.

21. Scholes, *Structural Fabulation*, p. 23.

2

Like a Novel

Tom Wolfe emerged in the late 1960s as the major spokesman for literary nonfiction as well as one of its more visible practitioners. He first offered his views in interviews, in the introductions to collections of magazine pieces, *The Kandy-Kolored Tangerine-Flake Streamline Baby* (1965) and *The Pump House Gang* (1968), and later in a long introductory essay to an anthology of the new nonfiction called *The New Journalism* (1973). The argument developed by Wolfe was that (1) modish fiction writers and literary critics were all wrong about realism, but (2) their obtuseness was fortunate in that it offered a remarkable opportunity for journalists like himself.

Wolfe held that realism was not one among many technical strategies available to the fiction writer but *the* strategy, the one that brought the novel in the work of Dickens and Balzac to its highest point of artistic power and public acceptance. The introduction of realism into fiction was a fundamental aesthetic breakthrough that elevated the novel to its dominant literary status and had an impact like the introduction of electricity into machine technology. Although Wolfe's faith in the enduring power of literary realism was clear enough, his reasoning was obscure beyond the historical assertion that fiction was at its best when it was powered by a straight-out realism that simply recorded the social scene without the baggage of higher meaning or deeper insight that cluttered up later artistic versions of the genre.

What his view appeared to rest on was a belief that realistic elements in fiction trigger the memory of the reader to fill out a characterization or situation, and in this way involving the reader in the fiction and producing emotion, the kind of emotion expressed when we say we are "absorbed" or "lost" in a work. It is realism that best produces this shock of recognition and the consequent emotional involvement of the reader, and this is accomplished not so much by extensive recording of the world but by jogging the reader's experience of the world through indirect suggestion.

Whatever the exact psychological process, the result was an emotional experience—and for Wolfe the stimulation of emotional response was the unique power of realistic fiction. "No one," he observed, "was ever moved to tears by reading about the unhappy fates of heroes and heroines in Homer, Sophocles, Molière, Racine, Sydney, Spenser, or Shakespeare. But even the impeccable Lord Jeffrey, editor of the *Edinburgh Review*, had cried—actually blubbered, boohooed, snuffled and sighed—over the death of Dickens' Little Nell in *The Old Curiosity Shop.*"[1] For Wolfe the creation of such feelings in the reader was fiction's highest achievement; to try to improve on it was pointless. Yet this improvement was exactly what many contemporary writers, with strong critical prodding, had attempted to do. While searching about for a more sophisticated, critically up-to-date, artistically correct fiction, they had in fact worked themselves back to the dim days before the rise of realism, to the misty period when myth and fable reigned in fiction. They had given themselves over to a "Neo-Fabulism" that might have been personally satisfying but had totally separated them from the ordinary reading audience.

Wolfe did not directly address the argument that realism springs from a false view of literature since literature can never chronicle the world, only construct versions of it. Rather he rested his case on the psychological effectiveness of realism; it works for the reader, and this effectiveness, not ideological purity, was what mattered. On another issue, however, the old-fashioned quality of realism, Wolfe met the critics directly. He argued that the form itself could never be outdated or used up due to the great work already produced in it because the material, the content, was always changing. To think that "Because Proust did this much, and Henry James did this much, and James Joyce did this much, I can't do *those* things" was to paint oneself into an aesthetic corner through too much self-consciousness about literary history and too much stress on literary form. Current novelists were simply "strangling themselves on what is now a very orthodox conventional aesthetics based on form."[2] What was needed was a redirection of interest from form to content with the realization that content was always changing.

One could write in exactly the same realistic forms as Balzac and Thackeray and Dickens and still be fresh because the material, the social world, would be different. Every age, and especially the present one, offered immensely rich material. "There's so much *terra incognita*," Wolfe maintained, "that novelists should be getting into that they could easily be wholly concerned with the social fabric, the social tableau. Forget the ersatz psychology that they get into." Wolfe did not wholly dismiss the importance of form but called for a new concern with content, especially the social world of manners and morals, and less absorption with inventing new forms based on rarified aesthetic principles. For Wolfe, form was narrowed from elaborate technical schemes to simply the writer's "priceless, unique way of looking at things."[3] The exercise of the writer's special sensibility, yoked to a concern with the changing conditions around him, could result in continually fresh and compelling work.

Although Wolfe was swift to diagnose the novelists' problems, he held out no hope of cure. They were all "crowded into one phone booth," all bent on discovering new forms or inventing new worlds. "They're just all in there. It's like some kind of stunt. It's a shame."[4] Of course it was not really a shame since it opened the territory for Wolfe and other literary-minded journalists. Wolfe's darts sent in the direction of contemporary novelists and critics were really intended to explain the rise of nonfiction rather than resurrect fiction. A "journalist's bonanza" opened up in the middle 1960s because of the mistaken ventures of novelists, and Wolfe and a fellow band of journalists were quick to take advantage.[5]

In Wolfe's version of the brief history of what he insisted on calling the New Journalism, the movement began innocently enough with a handful of feature writers in a few metropolitan newsrooms, especially the newsroom of the *New York Herald Tribune*. When Wolfe went to work for the newspaper in 1962, he discovered another kind of journalistic competition in addition to the usual "scoop" competition—an effort among feature writers to achieve in various "soft" news areas literary effects. The feature writers had freedom from rhetorical and space restrictions ordinary reporters did not have, and those working for the faltering *Herald Tribune* had the additional freedom to experiment with methods and materials in the hope that something would rescue the paper. In the hands of such feature writers as Dick Schaap, Charles Portis, Jimmy Breslin, and Wolfe himself, this relatively open journalistic situation led to a discovery, as Wolfe put it, that "it just might be possible to write journalism that would . . . read like a novel."[6] The crown the feature writers were competing for was the novel, and many of them were only in journalism until they could write one; in the meantime the best they could do was write a form of journalism that read like fiction.

But here in Wolfe's history an irony set in. In the effort to emulate the novel in artistic effect by applying fictional techniques to nonfiction materials, the feature writers actually supplanted it. In their journalistic work, especially as it appeared in Sunday supplements and in longer pieces appearing in magazines like *Esquire* and *Harper's*, they made the discovery that journalism could not only be like fiction but it could be better. The edge came with a style of reporting the New Journalists mastered together with basic literary techniques drawn from realistic fiction: saturation reporting, Wolfe called it, reporting that went to the bottom depths of the material and sought out not only what was said and done but what was thought and felt, reporting that got inside character and scene the way novelists did but without the invention they employed. The result was a factual fiction that provided all of fiction's pleasures while paying the added dividend of being true.

In its rise to power the New Journalism was, once again, helped by the retrograde state of serious fiction. While magazine editors and book publishers were crying for writers to tackle the great social concerns of the 1960s, the typical novelist, in Wolfe's history, was "sailing off to Lonesome Island on his Tarot boat with his back turned and his Timeless cape on, reeking of camphor balls." But the New Journalism was not just a case of opportunism; for Wolfe it was solidly based on the mastery of the techniques of literary realism—the manipulation of point of view, scenic telling, use of dialogue, and the recording of symbolic details—together with the application of in-depth reporting and the curious power of fact. This last, Wolfe concluded, was the New Journalist's major advantage— the reader's knowledge that what was written about actually happened, that it was real in a way even realistic fiction could never be real. The "screen is gone," Wolfe insisted. The writer is "one step closer to the absolute involvement of the reader that Henry James and James Joyce dreamed of and never achieved."[7]

The result was that by the end of the sixties, the New Journalists had "seized power" by doing what the novelists had once done but by doing it better. A new literary style had arisen out of feature-story journalism, and the novel was no longer king. And so Wolfe was able to write his capsule history of the New Journalism to show how it had come about "that the most important literature being written in American today is in nonfiction, in the form that has been tagged, however ungracefully, the New Journalism."[8]

*

This, surely, was not the case—as even Wolfe himself seemed to know. His description of what happened to both fiction and nonfiction in the sixties was laced with a hyperbole that seemed intended to infuriate almost everyone; consequently, his description inspired attacks that brought the New Journalism and Wolfe himself to public attention. But beneath the razzle-dazzle style and sweeping claims there was a narrower argument that was harder to dispute.

Near the end of his short history of the New Journalism Wolfe wrote:

> When we talk about the "rise" or "death" of literary genres, we are talking about status, mainly. The novel no longer has the supreme status it enjoyed for ninety years (1875-1965), but neither has the New Journalism won it for itself. The status of the New Journalism is not secured by any means. In some quarters the contempt for it is boundless . . . even breathtaking. . . . With any luck at all the new genre will never be sanctified, never be exalted, never given a theology. I probably shouldn't even go around talking it up the way I have in this piece. All I meant to say when I started out was that the New Journalism can no longer be ignored in an artistic sense. The rest I take back.[9]

This seemed the basic claim: the new nonfiction could not be ignored in an artistic sense. It had gained some literary status and the novel had lost some; it had shown itself, as the novel once had, an effective device for dealing with social reality. This did not mean that the New Journalism had replaced the novel, but it did mean that the serious writer now had a choice of mediums. The difference between the two was not one of artistry or of literary effect but a matter of weighing certain advantages.

"The novel as a form," Wolfe said, "no longer has any fascination for me as something that is a superior literary form. It's just a way of dealing with reality." The main advantage of the fictional way of dealing with reality lay in its allowing the writer to be more compact, in the sense of combining external detail and psychological characteristics, and so create a taut texture of material that might be hard to match in actual life. The novelist also had certain freedoms in dealing with real people that libel laws denied to the journalist. The greatest advantage of nonfiction, however, was the reader's sense that it was real. Wolfe said:

> Nonfiction has the advantage of the reader knowing that it's real. Now this is a tremendous thing—it sounds like nothing—but it's a tremendous thing to know that you're reading something that actually happened. That's why memoirs have always been so popular. You get all the advantages of a novel, and yet you know, or you assume, that it's true.[10]

So in Wolfe's view of the literary situation of the time, the serious writer could now take his choice of fiction or nonfiction. Wolfe himself of course pressed the advantages of nonfiction, especially at a time when fiction writers had supposedly abandoned realistic techniques and subjects, but the basic thrust of his various arguments was an insistence on the equal artistic possibilities of fiction and nonfiction.

Wolfe was not alone in this view of an enlarged literary situation. Capote said that *In Cold Blood* was based on a theory he had held for some twenty years that "journalism, reportage, could be forced to yield a serious new art form: the 'nonfiction novel,' as I thought of it." Gay Talese insisted that "reporting is an art form, can be an art form, and that people who really care about reporting are artists, can be artists as much as a novelist can be an artist." Neither Capote nor Talese felt their emphasis on the artistry of nonfiction denied the importance of the novel. Capote said that "reporting can be made *as* interesting as fiction and done *as* artistically—underlining those two 'as'es. I don't mean to say that one is a superior form to the other."[11] Talese still found the novel "great when it works." But both were agreed, as Talese said, in opposing the view that the novel alone "is the form we have to strive for."[12]

Notes

1. Tom Wolfe, *The New Journalism, with an Anthology Edited by Tom Wolfe and E. W. Johnson* (New York: Harper & Row, 1973), pp. 34-35.

2. Bellamy, *The New Fiction*, pp. 78, 79.

3. Bellamy, *The New Fiction*, pp. 79, 80.

4. Bellamy, *The New Fiction*, p. 80.

5. Wolfe, *The New Journalism*, p. 30.

6. Wolfe, *The New Journalism*, p. 9.

7. Wolfe, *The New Journalism*, pp. 30-31, 34.

8. Wolfe, *The New Journalism*, Preface.

9. Wolfe, *The New Journalism*, p. 35.

10. Bellamy, *The New Fiction*, p. 83.

11. George Plimpton, "Truman Capote: An Interview," reprinted in Weber, *The Reporter as Artist*, pp. 188, 190.

12. John Brady, "Gay Talese: An Interview," reprinted in Weber, *The Reporter as Artist*, p. 110.

3

Personal Journalism

When Wolfe referred to an artistic excitement in journalism, he was viewing the new nonfiction of the 1960s and 1970s as essentially a literary phenomenon, an attempt to render literature from reporting, art from fact, and so discussed nonfiction in relation to the novel and the use of fictional techniques to create fictionlike effects. But there was another side to nonfiction writing, one more strictly journalistic. This aspect of the work drew less attention than the literary side because it lacked both a spokesman of Wolfe's zeal and central attention-getting works like Capote's *In Cold Blood*. Nonfiction of this sort, more journalistic in form and intention than literary though drawing on a long tradition in American journalism that has honored finely crafted and emotionally forceful writing, is not my subject here. But it is necessary to take note of some of the influences on literary nonfiction coming from journalism if the full background of recent work is to be seen.

Wolfe's history of the New Journalism starts with a handful of writers trying to extend the boundaries of journalism in the direction of fiction. Considering the New Journalism in a more narrowly journalistic sense, one sees that the history could also have been written by concentrating on a number of other reporters in the same period who were interested in widening the scope of journalism, although they did not have fiction in mind so much as a more evocative, interpretive, and personal kind of reporting. In the introduction to an anthology of articles from the "Style" section of the *Washington Post*, Thomas R. Kendrick made a distinction between using "facts to make art" and using "art forms to extend journalism," his point being that the kind of New Journalism practiced by the writers in the anthology was of the latter sort. What the *Post* writers were attempting to do, he went on, was more journalistic than literary in that, rather than try to turn journalism into art, they sought instead to "mesh traditional reporting disciplines of research, accuracy, moral objectivity and clear thinking with a new freedom of literary expression."[1] On occasion this sort of New Journalism resulted in work of evident literary quality, but for the most part it remained a distinguished journalistic rather than literary nonfiction.

In this freer, enlarged journalism the role of the personal was especially important. In the 1960s many reporters—often better trained than their predecessors, more professional in their attitudes, and consequently more self-conscious about themselves as professionals—grew notably restive with the detached, impersonal, seemingly objective point of view that dominated journalistic writing. They argued that in reality the reporter was never a totally neutral figure, that inevitably something of the personal crept into his work. Furthermore, to deny the shaping presence of the reporter because of theoretical demands of detachment and objectivity was to be fundamentally dishonest with the reader as well as oneself. Impersonal journalism implied that detachment was accuracy, that whatever was stripped of individual feeling and judgment was therefore to be trusted and relied upon. Professional newsmen increasingly offered evidence that this was not the case.

In 1966 Dan Wakefield published a book that effectively captured the reporter's unease with the traditions of impersonal journalism—*Between the Lines: A Reporter's Personal Journey Through Public Events.* Wakefield said the book was for readers "who have grown increasingly mistrustful of and bored with anonymous reports about the world, whether signed or unsigned, for those who have begun to suspect what we reporters of current events and problems so often try to conceal: that we are really individuals after all, not all-knowing, all-seeing Eyes but separate, complex, limited, particular 'I's."[2] To demonstrate the point, he reprinted several magazine pieces done in an impersonal manner and added to them personal information about what was happening to him at the time of the writing, how what he gathered and wrote was affected by people and circumstances. The effect he intended was the revelation of what was hidden between the lines in the reports all along—the presence of the writer and the pressure of his personality and consciousness on what was finally written.

Wakefield argued that impersonal writing was a kind of code that could deceive the reader who was not fully aware of the limitations of the convention. His book was an attempt to "hold those official coded reports [the previously printed pieces] over a flame and allow the warmth to bring out the other, more interesting words that were there in the white space, written in the invisible ink of personal experience."[3] Only in this way, with the reporter fully acknowledged as a functioning presence in the work, could the reader be certain of his ground and so in a position to make accurate judgments about news events.

Other journalists offered similar arguments. Seymour Krim insisted that the reporter must "declare his credentials [to the reader] by revealing the concrete details and particular sweat of his own inner life; otherwise he (or she) will not have earned the right to speak openly about everything or be trusted."[4] Gloria Steinem, describing the ideal newspaper of the future, saw the journalist in a clearly personal role, openly interacting with subjects and readers:

> I would like to see it [the daily newspaper] broken down into community sections internally, so that you get the international news . . . but with some kind of human mind's work trying to make sense of all this stuff, and questioning what the President says and not just reporting, not just accepting the State Department news releases. But then, inside the paper I'd like to see more community emphasis with people, reporters who live in the community and cover that exclusively, and who are visible to the community, so they have to be responsible.[5]

Jack Newfield found direct "participation and advocacy" on the part of the reporter the touchstones of new and encouraging developments in journalism. Giving up his neutrality for personal involvement, the journalist became for Newfield "a free man, relying on his instincts, intelligence, and discipline, liberated from all the middlemen who try to mediate between the writer and reality."[6]

Timothy Crouse's account of journalists on the presidential campaign trail in 1972, *The Boys on the Bus*, conveyed the yearning of some political reporters for more personal freedom in their work, including freedom from what Crouse called the "time-honored techniques of objective journalism" and the "restraints of formula writing."[7] Crouse maintained that Hunter Thompson, a personal journalist with a vengeance, became a grudgingly admired figure among his fellow journalists during the campaign because his freedom from journalistic constraints as a correspondent for *Rolling Stone* allowed him to make direct, passionate, and—at least in retrospect— insightful comments about the candidates that more staid publications would not allow.

The kind of personal journalism Wakefield called for and that Newfield, Thompson, and many others practiced was by no means new. Personal reporting has long been a feature of journalism in America, especially literary journalism, with James Agee's *Let Us Now Praise Famous Men* the celebrated example. The difference now was that personal writing was often urged as a central feature of journalism and not merely a minor element. Wakefield's view was that the "admission and use of the first singular is the most exciting, challenging, and potentially fruitful course for modern journalism" because, as Thoreau had noted long before, "It is, after all, always the first person that is speaking."[8]

To journalists of deep social concern, personal writing seemed a moral as well as technical issue. Newfield pointed out that certain topical concerns that had drawn the attention of journalists—racism, prison conditions, poverty, the Vietnam war—were morally charged issues that could not be written about in morally neutral fashion. As an advocate of truth, the journalist could not hide behind the impersonal conventions of journalism but was required to take an open stand in favor of what he thought to be true. Newfield approvingly quoted Andrew Kopkind's assertion that "Objectivity is the rationalization for moral disengagement, the classic cop-out from choice-making." In Newfield's view the most distinctive feature of current nonfiction was the challenge of personal advocacy it threw at journalism's "central myth of objectivity." He added: "The new journalist does not call the anonymous source or the official expert for a quote. He does not try to speak for an institution, only for his own conscience. He does not take into account 'the national interest,' but only what he sees and thinks."[9]

One of the more extreme ways of describing the kind of personal, committed journalism Newfield called for was to label it "existential journalism." John Merrill, a journalism educator, distinguished two basic tendencies in journalism, one rationalist and the other existential, and ardently urged the latter. The existential journalist tended to be subjective, emotional, and judgmental while the rational journalist leaned toward the neutral, the objective, the impersonal. "Existential journalism," Merrill wrote, "is mainly a *subjective* journalism—subjective in the sense that it puts special stress on the *person* of the journalist himself" while retaining a "firm foundation of reasonableness."[10] Merrill offered professional newsmen like Tom Wicker of the *New York Times* and Daniel Schorr of the Columbia Broadcasting System as examples of the existential journalist.

*

Although there were two quite different strains in recent nonfiction writing, one coming from a literary quarter and the other from journalism, they found common ground in an emphasis on the personal. The stress on the person of the journalist himself, as Merrill put it, was evident enough in the center-stage participatory manner of Thompson's journalism, in the direct advocacy of Newfield, and in the efforts of Wakefield to give authenticity to earlier pieces through addition of personal material. It also was evident in the highly personal literary nonfiction of Mailer and even in the more detached work of Capote, Talese, and Wolfe.

In books like *In Cold Blood* and *Honor Thy Father*, the "I" was sternly avoided in favor of the omniscient "eye" of the writer; yet in the obvious meticulousness of the reporting and in the novelistic artistry of scene and characterization, the writers made their presence and shaping consciousness felt. The absence of the "I" in such work was often largely a matter of appearance since the presence of the writer was distinctly felt in the re-creation of events and in the selection and arrangement of the material. In books like *The Electric Kool-Aid Acid Test*, the "I" was acknowledged from time to time but vividly felt throughout the work in Wolfe's breathless prose style.

In both the enlarged journalism of the time and in literary nonfiction, there remained, of course, wide variation in how personal the writer chose to be and how openly he figured in his finished work. But it was here, in its emphasis on the personal, that both strains of nonfiction writing in the sixties and seventies found a common center. At the same time it was to this center that much of the criticism of the work was directed.

Notes

1. Thomas R. Kendrick, Introduction to *Writing in Style*, ed. Laura Longley Babb (Washington: The Washington Post Co., 1975), p. x, iv.

2. Dan Wakefield, *Between the Lines: A Reporter's Personal Journey Through Public Events* (New York: New American Library, 1966), p. 1.

3. Wakefield, *Between the Lines*, p. 2.

4. Seymour Krim, *Shake It For the World, Smartass* (New York: Dial Press, 1970), p. 22.

5. "Gloria Steinem: An Interview," reprinted in Weber, *The Reporter as Artist*, p. 78.

6. Jack Newfield, "Journalism: Old, New and Corporate," reprinted in Weber, *The Reporter as Artist*, p. 65.

7. Timothy Crouse, *The Boys on the Bus* (New York: Random House, 1973), p. 306.

8. Dan Wakefield, "The Personal Voice and the Impersonal Eye," reprinted in Weber, *The Reporter as Artist*, p. 46.

9. Newfield, "Journalism: Old, New and Corporate," p. 61. For an essay discussing the critique of the convention of objectivity in American journalism in the 1960s, see *Discovering the News: A Social History of American Newspapers*, by Michael Schudson (New York: Basic Books, 1978), ch. 5.

10. John C. Merrill, *Existential Journalism* (New York: Hastings House, 1977), p. 50.

4

A Bastard Form

Criticism of the new literary nonfiction came both from literary and journalistic quarters. Literary figures took it to task for remaining too journalistic, too tied to fact. As a way of expressing literary disapproval, the work was often dismissed as "mere reportage." At the same time journalistic figures faulted it for its literary aspirations, for appearing to take liberties with the facts or treating them in ways intended to create artistic or emotional effects. A common term of dismissal on this side was "parajournalism."

In effect, both literary and journalistic criticism concentrated on the personal quality of the new nonfiction. On the one hand, the work was not personal enough—that is, in its adherence to fact it did not fully utilize, or utilize as fully as great literature, the artist's individual imprint on the work, the stamp of his special imaginative sensibility. On the other hand, it was much too personal—that is, it drew on the writer's individual sensibility to an extent that seemed to threaten the sovereign authority of the facts as well as journalistic canons of objectivity and neutrality.

The point can be illustrated another way. Serious literature, realistic as well as fabulistic, never holds up an entirely accurate mirror to the world. That is the aim of journalism. Literature, as opposed to journalism, is always a refracting rather than reflecting medium; it always to some degree distorts life, if only in giving it a shape or clarity that otherwise cannot be detected. And the roots of literary distortion are always located in the writer himself, in the deflection and refraction of the material in the filter of the self. In literature it is really distortion we prize—the distortion of the uniquely individual. We prize the writer's ability to draw us into *his* realm of reality, to persuade us of *his* vision of the world, a world that is always, in Richard Poirier's apt phrase, a "world elsewhere."[1] This is exactly literature's magic charm. No one, as Philip Young has pointed out, "really wants to read about life precisely and exactly as he knows it"—which helps explain why we celebrate tragedy in literature though not in life, why we find happy endings suspect in fiction while totally desirable in life.[2]

Journalism is another matter. If art is not about life, journalism is supposed to be. It is supposed to bring us news, not of worlds elsewhere, but of this world. Likewise, if literature seeks out the distortion of the uniquely individual, journalism attempts to minimize it. If the aim of the fiction writer is to get us to view his material in his terms, the aim of the journalist is to get us to view the material as it is, in its own terms. An account of reality itself, not the journalist's private version of it, is what is desired. As the historian Peter Gay has remarked, "what is not required of art is required of history: to discover, no matter how shocking the discovery, what the old universe was like rather than to invent a new one."[3]

Once again, it was here, in the conflicting roles of the personal in journalistic and literary writing, that critical attacks on literary nonfiction were centered. Some critics argued that the work missed literary quality because it remained bound to fact, inhibiting the full play of artistry that the imaginative writer could bring to bear. But at the same time, the argument went on, the work lacked real journalistic quality because in the very imaginative artistry it *did* employ, it left itself suspect as solid reporting.

Criticism coming from the journalistic quarter was perhaps the strongest attack mounted against the new nonfiction. Its literary aspirations could be dismissed with cavalier disdain, but its journalistic aspirations had to be treated more seriously, if only because the work often came billed as a New Journalism with claims of extensive reporting. The lines of journalistic criticism were established by Dwight Macdonald when in a 1965 review of Tom Wolfe's first book, *The Kandy-Kolored Tangerine-Flake Streamline Baby*, he called Wolfe's brand of New Journalism "parajournalism"—that is, "a bastard form, having it both ways, exploiting the factual authority of journalism and the atmospheric license of fiction."[4] Parajournalism appeared in the guise of journalism and claimed itself as journalism, but in fact it was not journalism since its aim was not to convey information but create entertainment. Its tendency to personalize issues and events and to dramatize situations through fictional techniques of scene setting and character building made for lively reading but dubious history. The result of Macdonald's criticism was widespread doubt about literary nonfiction as serious journalism, let alone serious literature, and the tendency to see it as yet another branch of the entertainment industry.

Writers countered with impassioned claims of factual accuracy. They insisted, as Capote said of *In Cold Blood*, that their works were "true" accounts. Extended scenes, long stretches of dialogue, interior monologues—all of it was derived from the arduous reporting they did, from months and even years spent with their subjects. "One doesn't spend almost six years on a book," Capote said in defense of the minute factual truth of his book, "the point of which is factual accuracy, and then give way to minor distortions."[5] Wolfe said he expected readers "to allow me a certain leeway *if* it leads towards a better grasp of what actually took place," but that leeway was to be found in stylistic touches and some sophistication about point of view and did not involve "the right to make up anything. . . . Because part of the impact is the fact that you're telling the reader *this happened*. This is not a short story. This is not a novel. This is not fiction."[6]

The aspect of literary nonfiction that raised the most doubt about accuracy was the revelation of interior states of mind. Reporters who took us inside the heads of people they wrote about, the argument went, had clearly stepped over the line into *creative* writing, and so forfeited any claim to journalism as it is usually understood. But here again writers held their ground. They maintained that the portrayal of interior states, while a dramatic device drawn from fiction, could be harmonized with the factual basis of journalism since the material was derived from reporting. The writer simply interviewed the subject about thoughts and emotions as well as everything else and then reconstructed his response in dramatic form. To get such material required intense reporting and the full cooperation of subjects, but writers like Talese were convinced that it was possible, "by asking the right question at the right time, to learn and to report what goes on within other people's minds."[7]

Writers like Talese and Wolfe in fact found the reporting of interior states the real frontier in nonfiction writing and that aspect of nonfiction that brought it closest to fiction and hence to literary art. Wolfe held that film and television had usurped many of the functions of stories and novels, but one thing they had not been able to handle was interior monologue, the sense of being inside the consciousness of a character. This was still the province of fiction—and now of nonfiction, as he thought he had demonstrated in his own work, and especially in *The Electric Kool-Aid Acid Test*. Wolfe admitted to the validity of one type of criticism of interior reporting: that it might be hard for a subject to remember what he was thinking even just a moment ago, let alone in the distant past. Still he found it possible through careful reporting to get an "approximation of the mood" and thought it "justifiable to do it to at least try to get inside of the psyche somehow, and to be able to report on the interior of the skull in some way."[8]

The use of interior monologues in nonfiction was usually combined with the re-creation of scenes—and this was another device drawn from fiction that raised doubts about factual accuracy. Wolfe admitted that when he first saw the device used in nonfiction, in an *Esquire* article done by Talese in 1962 on Joe Louis, he assumed it was all invented. The article was approached largely as a series of scenes that drew on physical detail, dialogue, and interior thought which gave the reader the impression of being inside a situation rather than being told about it from without. Scenic telling was deeply associated with fiction and that was the problem with it when adapted to nonfiction: it did not seem that it could be accurate because it departed so sharply from the methods of external description associated with journalism.

But here again nonfiction writers maintained that scenes were available to writers if they got close enough to their subjects and stayed with them long enough to allow, as Wolfe said, "things to happen in front of your eyes."[9] This involved a fundamental change in journalistic reporting, with the reporter as eyewitness rather than the gatherer of secondhand accounts. Talese described the usual manner of reporting this way:

> . . . you go out, at two o'clock in the afternoon, you get your quotes or whatever it is of the alleged happening, most of which you didn't see, incidentally. The old journalism was never eye-witness, except in sports writing. . . . But most of us went out, and we got the police sergeant's version of the thing, together with the social worker's, or the bombardier's, or the press agent's or the PR man's. And in any case, we were not able to report how things changed, because the newspaper business is just a one-shot business.[10]

Saturation reporting was much more than a one-shot business. It meant seeing things for oneself, which in turn meant involvement with subjects for long durations.

"The initial problem," Wolfe said, "is always to approach total strangers, move in on their lives in some fashion, ask questions you have no natural right to expect answers to, ask to see things you weren't meant to see, and so on."[11] It also involved, Capote added, the capacity to "emphathize with personalities outside his [the writer's] imaginative range, mentalities unlike his own, kinds of people he would never have written about had he not been forced to by encountering them inside the journalistic situation."[12] Such reporting, in other words, required the total involvement of the writer, drawing him deeply inside his material, making demands on him that surpassed anything experienced in the ordinary journalistic situation.

*

But even if nonfiction writers were able to persuade their critics that, despite the use of fictional techniques, their work was based on careful reporting, another problem remained. This was the strongly personal element in their work, especially in accounts in which the writer was a participant or wrote in the first person. Michael Arlen, while conceding that many of the writers were careful with the facts, was troubled by the tendency to draw everything toward the writer himself, to present reality as embedded in the writer's own ego. An example was Mailer's *Of a Fire on the Moon*, which seemed less about the moon landing itself than about Mailer's effort to generalize about it. Much nonfiction seemed, like this work, an attempt to control and confine a subject within a writer's own temperament and vision—and it was here, Arlen felt, that analogies between fictional practice and the techniques of literary nonfiction broke down.

The novelist's control of his creations was based on the fact that they were *his* creations. But the journalist's subjects had a reality beyond him; they were "real people whose real lives exist on either side of the journalist's column of print."[13] He did not mean, Arlen said, that writers should present the totality of someone's life, because that could not be done, but that the writer of nonfiction must allow his subjects their own breathing room, some possible reality beyond the writer's particular version of it.

Wilfrid Sheed made a similar point. He wondered whether the new nonfiction's "natural tendency to personalize issues and to overvalue the reporter's own experience" limited its usefulness to fairly trivial materials rather than substantial subjects. He discussed the question in relation to David Halberstam's *The Best and the Brightest*, in his view an example of personal journalism even though the "I" was carefully avoided in the book. Halberstam personalized the issues at stake in his discussion of the Vietnam war, centering the book on the actions and motives of a handful of highly placed characters—with the result, for Sheed, that his book made for lively reading but possibly doubtful history. Throughout the book, Sheed said, echoing Arlen, "we are at the author's mercy, depending on his omniscience, psychological accuracy and personal honor . . . a heavy burden even for a priest."[14]

The burden was especially heavy because of the nature of Halberstam's subject; he treated not celebrities or an exotic bit of national subculture but a convulsive war whose roots and development were of vital concern. Sheed felt Halberstam had avoided the major pitfalls of personal journalism, but his book illustrated the limits of the form for handling delicate tasks of historical analysis that demanded both massive scholarship and a more objective historical sense.

Herbert Gold agreed with both Arlen and Sheed, and for the same reasons. "To make oneself larger is an impulse legitimately gratified through the magnifying vision of the fictive imagination," he wrote, but in nonfiction the emphasis on the self can be simply "spoiled self-display." A "delight in the self" could involve a "lack of delight in subject matter," in the world beyond the confines of the writer himself.[15] A little objectivity about that world, Gold added, was not necessarily a bad thing, and neither was an emphasis on subject matter rather than on the creative self.

The media historian John Tebbel lashed out at the tendency toward personal journalism as a "kind of perpetual ego trip or literary paranoia."[16] He described Mailer's work as simply a case of asking the reader to believe that the writer's psyche had more importance than public events, a predictable assumption for a generation turned in upon itself and believing that external events were important only when they affected one's life. This focus on the writer was a serious matter for Tebbel because he felt the rise of interest in personal writing—together with the other literary inclinations of the New Journalists—was damaging the credibility of the press in a vulnerable period and obscuring the many accomplishments of the old journalism. He insisted that for writers like Mailer, Talese, and Wolfe, "style is everything and substance is a nuisance."[17]

To complaints such as these, nonfiction writers simply pointed to what they considered the evident merits of personal journalism—its lively, engaging quality and its establishment of a more honest relationship with the reader. Wakefield, arguing against Macdonald's charge of parajournalism, said he did not think that "recent journalism with its freer style is any more guilty of distortion than the older, more traditional forms." He went on: "The important and interesting and hopeful trend to me in the new journalism is its personal nature—not in the sense of personal attacks, but in the presence of the reporter himself and the significance of his own involvement."[18] If nothing else, Wakefield added, in personal journalism the writer was always acknowledging the truth—as Thoreau had observed—that after all it is always the writer himself that is speaking.

Notes

1. Richard Poirier, *A World Elsewhere* (New York: Oxford University Press, 1966).

2. Philip Young, *Three Bags Full* (New York: Harcourt Brace Jovanovich, 1972), p. 166.

3. Peter Gay, *Style in History* (New York: Basic Books, 1974), p. 194.

4. Dwight Macdonald, "Parajournalism, or Tom Wolfe and His Magic Writing Machine," reprinted in Weber, *The Reporter as Artist*, p. 223.

5. Plimpton, "Truman Capote: An Interview," p. 202.

6. Bellamy, *The New Fiction*, p. 96.

7. Brady, "Gay Talese: An Interview," p. 36.

8. Leonard Wallace Robinson, "The New Journalism: A Panel Discussion with Harold Hayes, Gay Talese, Tom Wolfe and Professor L. W. Robinson," reprinted in Weber, *The Reporter as Artist*, p. 71.

9. Robinson, "The New Journalism: A Panel Discussion," p. 71.

10. Robinson, "The New Journalism: A Panel Discussion," p. 72.

11. Wolfe, *The New Journalism*, p. 50.

12. Plimpton, "Truman Capote: An Interview," p. 189.

13. Michael J. Arlen, "Notes on the New Journalism," reprinted in Weber, *The Reporter as Artist*, p. 253.

14. Wilfrid Sheed, "A Fun-House Mirror," reprinted in Weber, *The Reporter as Artist*, p. 296, 297.

15. Herbert Gold, "On Epidemic First Personism," reprinted in Weber, *The Reporter as Artist*, p. 285.

16. John Tebbel, "The Old New Journalism," *Saturday Review*, 13, March 1971, p. 96.

17. John Tebbel, *The Media in America* (New York: Crowell, 1974), p. 441.

18. Wakefield, "The Personal Voice and the Impersonal Eye," p. 46.

5

Zero Interpretation

Despite the varied critical attacks it drew, and no doubt partly because of them, literary nonfiction also drew a sizable audience. The nonfiction books of Capote, Wolfe, Talese, and Mailer were among the best sellers of the sixties. *In Cold Blood* and *Honor Thy Father* were turned into movies. Mailer, whose reputation took a sharp upswing with his entry into nonfiction, became one of the best-known writers of the time, a candidate for mayor of New York and a frequent performer on TV talk shows. How does one account for such popularity? There were several answers, ranging from the sheer quality of the work to shrewd huckstering by the authors, from cultural and historical explanations to the functioning of fad and fashion.

A common view was simply that the contemporary sensibility found itself more at home with nonfiction than with fiction. Some felt this had to do with the dislocations of the time, the sense of flux and change and spiritual upheaval, that encouraged writers to speak directly to events and issues and readers to turn to such material. James M. Cox put it this way:

> For when politics and history become dominant realities for the imagination, then the traditional prose forms of the essay and the autobiography both gain and attract power and the more overtly "literary" forms of prose fiction—the novel and the short story—are likely to be threatened and impoverished.[1]

Podhoretz, in his claims for nonfiction, also pointed to something in the spirit of the times that responded to the "usefulness" of nonfiction and found itself impatient with the indirections of fiction. He offered an analogy with architecture: because our sense of beauty is tied today to a sense of practicality, we admire functionalism in modern design and functionalism in literature, a sense that the product is designed for use, stripped of superfluous qualities. For Podhoretz nothing qualified on the grounds of practicality, simple use, so much as the magazine article.

If the article was practical, it was also timely, and this was another way of accounting for its appeal. Edward Hoagland, both a novelist and nonfiction writer, saw nonfiction's timeliness as its special edge in relation to fiction. "The task of explaining ourselves to ourselves," he argued, "which is the textbook function of novel-writing, is beyond the range of anyone in the profession at the moment, but journalists at least enjoy the front-line privilege of being first to announce each new phantasmagoria that heaves in sight and then remains to be explained." Journalists escaped the irritating sensation afflicting the novelists of being left behind in a tumultuous world—and likewise escaped the "old-fashioned, time-consuming obligation to invent a certain proportion of what they write."[2] Hoagland found an irony in the novel's meaning "new" when it was journalism that really dealt with the new, and today it was the new, the topical, the up-to-date that was demanded. As a result it was to journalism that the young with literary ambition now inclined.

Another way of accounting for the popularity of literary nonfiction was to focus on it as personal writing and see it in relation to the contemporary appeal of the personal—to see it, in other words, as "I" writing for an "I" time, personal writing for an age of personalism. Wolfe wrote that the exploration of *me*—my life, my needs, my uniqueness—was the great frontier of recent times, giving rise to a new growth industry called the human potential movement. "Fifteen years ago," Wolfe said, "it was popular among historians to say that the great 19th-century wave of individualism was over and that America was now in the era of the 'mass man.' Thirty years from now historians will record the widespread discovery of the Self in the 1960s and 1970s as one of the most extraordinary developments in American history."[3] It was observed that literary nonfiction was simply another aspect of the re-emergence of the self, the writer unmasking his shadow (whether previously journalistic or fictional) and speaking directly at a time when everyone else was doing the same.

Brock Brower reflected in a similar vein. He found the old journalism routinely mindless and voiceless but the new just the opposite; it allowed the writer the opportunity to come through his work as a "vividly experiencing 'I,'" to apply his intelligence directly to his subject matter, and to cultivate a personal and natural voice.[4] And this, the writer speaking directly and in his own voice, was what the time found congenial, what rang true for the modern sensibility. A case in point was James Baldwin, a writer whose voice seemed constrained and even false in fiction but was set free in the nonfiction form of the personal essay to discover its true range and depth.

Morris Dickstein saw a connection between the new subjectivity in nonfiction writing and the overall cultural style of the sixties that challenged all forms of impersonal authority in American life. In literature the challenge had its roots in the personal display of the Beat generation; here the line between fiction and autobiography grew dim and a confessional mode of writing became dominant. Likewise, the New Journalism, whether Wolfe's literary variety or the more journalistic kind of the underground and advocacy press, challenged the conventions of the old journalism in the name of individual assertion. But such developments were simply part of a broad cultural movement that resisted appeals to tradition and authority in all realms of life.[5]

Another way of thinking about the popularity of nonfiction writing was to see it as a literary response to the emergence of a new kind of mass audience. In his review of Wolfe's first book, Dwight Macdonald, taking note of the book's broad sales, suggested that it was not so much addressed to the nonreading young, as the title might have indicated, but to "a large and growing public that feels it really should Take an Interest and is looking for guidance as to what is, currently, The Real Thing."[6] This was not the old middlebrow public but a liberally educated public that had been through the required surveys of literature yet was caught up in a contemporary fascination with the new and topical.

With the new nonfiction, the audience received information but received it entertainingly, with familiar literary trimmings. It received an up-to-date factual fiction that abandoned the dreariness of day-to-day journalism yet did not fly off in the strange and complex ways of Barth, Borges, Barthelme, and other fabulists. What the audience was offered, in other words, had both the authority of literature and the authority of fact, and so had broad appeal for a new mass audience with college-trained tastes that sought "culture" yet wanted to be in on what was happening now. From this perspective, it was suggested that nonfiction had begun to function in something of the same way for an educated middle class as the realistic novel had for an emerging economic middle class—it brought the news and brought it engagingly.

To think of literary nonfiction in this way was to reduce its status, to drop it down from competition with the serious novel to the level of popular literature, here to compete not so much with Bellow or Updike as with the best-selling historical fictions of Leon Uris and Herman Wouk or the "contemporary narratives" of Cornelius Ryan and Theodore H. White.[7] At the height of media talk about the New Journalism, *Harper's* magazine carried a house ad that sought to describe with a geographic metaphor the appeal of the work:

> Somewhere west of journalism and this side of history . . . there is a place where reporting became literature. There are those—namely one million readers—who think Harper's Magazine is the place.
>
> For Harper's Magazine is dedicated to the idea that fine writing need not buckle under the pressure of a deadline, nor should literature be solely confined to the dim distant past or the recent inventions of a novelist's mind. It can deal with *now*—with the angers of our time, the beautiful beginnings of a changed society and the sad vestiges of a violent past.

The ad linked the appeal of the new nonfiction to its capacity to be "literature" and yet to "deal with *now*" at one and the same time. Even allowing for the inflated advertising prose, the suggestion was offered that the place where "reporting becomes literature" was really in the category of popular literature and that the rise of literary nonfiction could best be considered in relation to new developments in popular culture.[8]

But this was a line of thought hard to pursue because of an increasingly faint distinction between high culture and popular culture, or at least an increasing unwillingness to insist on any clearcut demarcation. Most attempts to account for the popularity of nonfiction treated it in relation to general trends in the culture—for example, an inclination toward functionalism—or in relation to the kinds of developments in serious literature sketched earlier. The most provocative argument in the latter vein was offered by Mas'ud Zavarzadeh. In articles entitled "The Apocalyptic Fact and the Eclipse of Fiction in Recent American Prose Narratives" and "A Typology of Prose Narrative," he developed the view that the thrust of all modern writing is away from efforts to interpret the human condition and toward a "zero degree of interpretation" and that literary nonfiction—or what he called the nonfiction novel—came closer than current fiction to realizing this intention. The view was later set out in a book, *The Mythopoeic Reality: The Postwar American Nonfiction Novel*, that expanded the theory and argued it in relation to such works as *Hiroshima*, *In Cold Blood*, *The Armies of the Night*, and *The Electric Kool-Aid Acid Test*.

The contemporary resistance to literary interpretation had its roots, Zavarzadeh believed, in the complexity of modern society and the tendency of fact and fiction to fuse into baffling existence. In this confused situation the traditional novel, based on shaping fragmented human experience into significant wholes, found itself confronted with a task that defied its customary aesthetic ordering of reality; it was simply no longer a uniquely effective means for exploring reality because reality itself was shot through with fictions, the actual with artifice. "The traditional function of the novel," Zavarzadeh declared, "thus has been canceled in technetronic cultures," though interpretive fictions were still produced by such old-fashioned "neo-escapist" novelists as Saul Bellow, Bernard Malamud, John Updike, and Joyce Carol Oates.[9]

The most significant literary response to this failure of function on the part of the traditional novel had been twofold, and both, in Zavarzadeh's thick terminology, were "acknowledgements of the impossibility of formulating an interpretive frame of reference which can decode the bizarre realities of today in aesthetic idioms without falsifying and reducing their density." One way in which the writer sought to "trace his way back out of the labyrinths of distorting commentaries" was through what Zavarzadeh called "transfiction," a form of fiction which tried to "shatter the illusion of reality which is the aesthetic foundation of the totalizing novel." Within transfiction Zavarzadeh located such sub-types as metafiction, surfiction, and science fiction. A second way bypassed fiction altogether and attempted to get back to the "experiential realities" through the form of the nonfiction novel.[10] In either case, transfiction or nonfiction, Zavarzadeh saw the writer as constructing a narrative that was noninterpretive and consequently an authentic response to the contemporary situation.

In one of the irrealistic modes of fiction Zavarzadeh discussed, metafiction, interpretation was eliminated through forms of baroque over-interpretation, the effect being a parody of all "straight" efforts to supply fictional meaning. The point of such work (in, for example, the fictions of Thomas Pynchon or Donald Barthelme) was to demonstrate the confusing variety of reality and thus the absurdity of offering a single unified vision of life in a work of fiction. In Zavarzadeh's language,

> By substituting parody of interpretation for straight interpretation, the metafictionist demonstrates the confusing multiplicity of reality and thus the naiveté involved in attempting to reach a total synthesis of life within narrative. The metafictionist's over-totalization, consequently, creates a work with low-message value at the zero degree of interpretation, thus freeing the narrative from an anthropomorphic order-hunting and insuring that, as Barthelme says, there is nothing between the lines but white spaces.[11]

The nonfiction novel, in Zavarzadeh's view, took just the opposite tack, eliminating interpretation not by parody of it but by avoiding it altogether through the accumulation of neutral facts of a fantastic world. It refused to apply any interpretive scheme to the facts but simply transcribed them, thus in effect—and properly for Zavarzadeh—rejecting any notion of art as the creation of order or the concept of the artist as seer or visionary. Indeed, the noninterpretive stance of nonfiction was far more complete than that of metafiction because in the very attempt at over-interpretation, there remained "echoes of a judgmental voice" still seeking to order experience. As a result the nonfiction novel was a "more authentic reaction" to the present literary situation because it more nearly approached the "zero-interpretive stance" demanded by fantastic reality.[12]

Zavarzadeh observed that works of literary nonfiction often had the shapeliness and aesthetic control associated with the traditional novel, but he insisted this configuration was not the same as the interpretive metaphysics of the traditional novelist. The nonfiction writer inevitably had a viewpoint and he had to make selections of reality, but his work did not spring, as did the work of the traditional novelist, from a private reading of reality. He did not choose a viewpoint and a principle of selection that was meant to persuade the reader to accept a vision of the ultimate meaning of life—and for the very good reason that such meaning was no longer available. "The nonfiction novel," Zavarzadeh maintained, "is the 'fiction' of people who have lost faith in any single interpretation of reality. For them the only authentic 'fiction' is the fiction of facts."[13]

Zavarzadeh emphasized that the nonfiction novel was a *fiction* of facts and not simply a straightforward nonfiction. It was work written *about* facts, he said, but not *in* them, by which he meant not that the work searched beyond fact to meaning, but that it combined a concern with the verifiable external world with the internal aesthetic completeness of fictional art. It was a kind of narrative that was "bi-referential" in that it referred both to its internal coherence and to an external correspondence to actuality; as such it was a form of narrative uniquely equipped to deal with the "elusive fusion of fact and fiction which has become the matrix of today's experience."[14]

*

Zavarzadeh's ideas about the nature of contemporary narrative were far from new. They were rooted in the familiar anti-interpretation ideas that Alain Robbe-Grillet formulated in *For a New Novel*, as well as in a broad critical reaction in recent years against interpretation in all the arts. Robbe-Grillet called for the new novel to avoid the tendency of the old novel to impose "signification" upon the world, the tendency to impose a meaning upon the world that does not belong to the world but to man himself. The world, he proclaimed, "is neither significant nor absurd. It *is*, quite simply."[15] The old novel's search for signification, its insistence on seeing the world in light of the human need to explain and understand, had obscured that simple reality, blinded us to the world's objective presence. The task of the new novel was to restore that reality, to allow the presence of the objects and figures of the world to prevail over explanatory theories that tried to classify or order them.

For Robbe-Grillet the old novel was devoted to assigning meaning to the world and hence controlling it, bringing it within human range, but it was now clear that this effort had been merely an "illusory simplification." Rather than make the world clearer, the novel had limited it, made it less alive. Since it was "chiefly in its presence that the world's reality resides," its objective surfaces, that presence had to be taken into literary account if the world was to be restored to full life. The serious writer therefore had no choice but to move in this direction. The effort to draw significance from the world assumed a stable universe that could be intelligently comprehended; the very notion of telling a story in familiar linear ways, of moving from beginning to middle to meaningful conclusion, was based on an "innocence" about a continuous, coherent, decipherable universe. But now we knew that such a sensibly "human" world did not exist, so now to "tell a story has become strictly impossible." The writer's necessary response was to move from a storytelling "realism" of imposed signification to a "reality" of objective concern for the actualities of the world, the world of confusing multiplicities, the world that simply existed.[16]

Lionel Trilling observed a similar contemporary resistance to the significations of storytelling. In modern literature, he noted, it was apparent that narration, the telling of stories, had suffered a drastic reduction—and for two reasons. One was the contemporary suspicion of narrative's capacity to draw the reader out of himself, to suspend his sense of disbelief, to hold him spellbound with the fate of another. To the modern sensibility, there seemed something inauthentic in allowing oneself to be taken over by literature's magic spell.

The other reason had to do with the assumption of rationality and control in the act of telling a story. "A chief part of the inauthenticity of narration," Trilling said, "would seem to be its assumption that life is susceptible of comprehension and thus of management." It was in the very nature of narrative to explain, to give counsel, to provide signification. The tale is never told by an idiot, Trilling went on, but by a "rational consciousness which perceives in things the processes that are their reason and which derives from this perception a principle of conduct, a way of living among things." And he asked: "Can we, in this day and age, submit to a mode of explanation so primitive, so flagrantly Aristotelean?"[17]

The answer—at least the answer given by a broad segment of contemporary culture—was apparently no. And no because of a modern sense of the confusion of existence and a consequent uncertainty about what counsel to give, what principle of conduct to assert. Narrative's mode of explanation was primitive, and consequently inauthentic for a sophisticated age, because it rested on the assumption that blueprints for life were available, an assumption that could no longer be easily maintained.

Inauthentic was the key word. The broad reaction against interpretation in the contemporary arts rested on the feeling that there was something inauthentic in art's ancient effort to wring order from chaos, especially the order of rational understanding or coherent statement. To be authentic, fully attuned to the modern sensibility, the modern arts needed to move toward Zavarzadeh's zero degree of interpretation. Evidence of such movement was everywhere in a concern with the surface: in *cinéma-vérité*, in pop-art renditions of Brillo boxes and soup cans and photographs of Marilyn Monroe, in a new hard-edge realism in painting, in the silent music of John Cage. In this sense many of the arts were stridently telling us, as Richard Poirier said of literature, how little they meant. Many of them, as Susan Sontag said, could be "understood as motivated by a flight from interpretation"—a flight that led toward parody or abstraction or decoration or simply anti-art.[18] In the search for authenticity, the arts were attempting in one way or another to align themselves with a modern aesthetic that mistrusted authoritative interpretation and found congenial Oscar Wilde's comment that the mystery of the world is the visible, not the invisible.

Zavarzadeh's view of literary nonfiction was, then, drawn from a larger argument about appropriate directions for the contemporary arts. And this critical perspective was in turn set against a sense of metaphysical void in contemporary life that inevitably forced the serious artist away from judgments about experience and toward re-creations of its fragmented surfaces. For Zavarzadeh the authentic literary responses to such a situation were to be found in the various forms of transfiction and in literary nonfiction—that is, in forms of modern writing that refused to "reduce the puzzling multiplicity of the contemporary experience into a monolithic fictive construct." And of the two, literary nonfiction came closer to a zero degree of interpretation, to simply mapping the "*is-ness* of the world," and so seemed the most authentic literary response to the modern condition.[19]

Notes

1. James M. Cox, "Autobiography and America," *Virginia Quarterly Review*, 47 (Spring 1971), 252.

2. Edward Hoagland, "Where the Action Is," *New York Times Book Review*, 13 October, 1974, p. 55.

3. Tom Wolfe, "The Third Great Awakening," *Chicago Tribune Magazine*, 26 November 1972, p. 76.

4. Brock Brower, "The Article," reprinted in Weber, *The Reporter as Artist*, p. 145. The quotation is drawn from a comment of Elizabeth Hardwick.

5. Morris Dickstein, *Gates of Eden: American Culture in the Sixties* (New York: Basic Books, 1977), ch. 5.

6. Macdonald, "Parajournalism," p. 229.

7. The term was used by White to describe Ryan's historical narratives. White said Ryan was "one of those who have brought to climax that particular American excellence in the Contemporary Narrative which marks our generation as distinctively as did the dominance of Hemingway, Faulkner, Fitzgerald and Wolfe over the novel in the 1920s and '30s." White described the contemporary narrative as the "most difficult, disciplined, painstaking form of the craft of story-telling—where the imagination must deal with facts as they come raw and bleeding and unsorted, with episodes which the master must weave together to tell us of the action the way it really was." Theodore H. White, "In the Matter of Cornelius Ryan," *Book-of-the-Month Club News*, October 1974, p. 4.

8. I develop this view at more length in my essay, "Some Sort of Artistic Excitement," *The Reporter as Artist*, pp. 24-26.

9. Mas'ud Zavarzadeh, "The Apocalyptic Fact and the Eclipse of Fiction in Recent American Prose Narratives," *Journal of American Studies*, 9 (April 1975), 77. The reference to "neo-escapist" novelists appears in his book, *The Mythopoeic Reality: The Postwar American Nonfiction Novel* (Urbana: University of Illinois Press, 1976), p. 224.

10. Zavarzadeh, *The Mythopoeic Reality*, pp. 37, 38, 41.

11. Zavarzadeh, *The Mythopoeic Reality*, p. 40.

12. Zavarzadeh, "The Apocalyptic Fact," p. 79.

13. Zavarzadeh, "The Apocalyptic Fact," p. 81.

14. Zavarzadeh, *The Mythopoeic Reality*, p. 57.

15. Alain Robbe-Grillet, *For a New Novel*, trans. Richard Howard (New York: Grove Press, 1965), p. 19.

16. Robbe-Grillet, *For a New Novel*, pp. 23, 32, 33, 157.

17. Lionel Trilling, *Sincerity and Authenticity* (Cambridge, Massachusetts: Harvard University Press, 1972), pp. 135-136.

18. Susan Sontag, *Against Interpretation* (New York: Noonday, 1966), p. 10.

19. Zavarzadeh, "The Apocalyptic Fact," p. 83.

6

Creative Reportage: Some Limits

I have described at some length the notion of the new literary nonfiction as noninterpretive because it was one of the most serious critical approaches to the work and also one of the most misleading. That view had the merit of seeing the work in relation to broad literary trends, but it had the serious defect of praising it for what it might have been like rather than for what it in fact was like.

To see what the actual achievements of literary nonfiction have been, one must turn to the work itself. But before doing that, I want to come back to some of the issues touched upon in the preceding pages and to set out in general terms some of my own views, views to be treated in more detail in relation to specific works.

Wolfe, Capote, and other recent apologists for literary nonfiction seem to me quite right in praising the artistic achievements of the work. The renewal of interest in nonfiction writing during the sixties and seventies amply demonstrated that work could be produced that corresponded to the events of the world and at the same time had the aesthetic unity of literature—work that indeed was "bi-referential." But it did not demonstrate that recent work in nonfiction had an aesthetic effect that equaled that of distinguished fiction or replaced it in serious writing. The point may seem too obvious to need remarking; but given the heated claims for nonfiction in recent years, it needs to be made.

Capote said it best at the beginning of the new interest in literary nonfiction when he remarked that he wanted to show that reporting could be made *as* interesting as fiction and done *as* artistically. This is exactly what *In Cold Blood* and other recent works show; they are as interesting to read as good fiction, crafted with as much skill and invention, and have many of fiction's atmospheric and thematic qualities. But that is not to say that these works have the same effect on the reader as good fiction or that they in any sense replace it.

The second point first. The nonfiction tradition in American writing has been important but in no way compares with the rich tradition of the novel, and this evaluation was as true during the sixties and seventies as in the past. Literary nonfiction did not wholly dominate the attention of writers during the period or wholly capture the reading public. Fiction, both realistic and fabulistic, remained in decent health during the period. It is simply not true to say, as Wolfe did in his more hyperbolic moments, that nonfiction wiped out the novel as literature's main event.

What happened was that literary culture in general experienced some decline under competition with other narrative forms. The novel in particular lost some of its high status with both writers and readers—and nonfiction gained some. And part of the reason for this shift in relative importance—for writers at least—no doubt had something to do with what Wolfe called the availability of journalism or nonfiction at a time when the novel was subjected to an especially heavy load of critical theory. Part of the attraction of nonfiction was that it could free the writer for a time from all the talk about new directions for fiction.

Nevertheless, the novel remained a strong if somewhat diminished form at the same time that nonfiction was drawing new interest. And at this writing, the novel—and especially the much-abused realistic novel—seems firmly back in the literary saddle, with nonfiction again taking a secondary role (a place where it is bound to be, as I will try to indicate later) though with a new generation of writers freshly aware of its artistic possibilities. Once again, Capote characterized the literary aims of the new nonfiction in relation to the novel in just the right way. "I don't mean to say that one is a superior form to the other," he said. "I feel that creative reportage has been neglected and has great relevance to 20th-century writing."[1] It is in this light, with creative reportage or literary nonfiction as simply another artistic outlet for the writer, that recent achievements in the form ought to be seen.

This leads to my other point, which is that while nonfiction can be artistically satisfying, its effects remain fundamentally different from those of fiction. There is no easy way to say what fiction does, and thus what its effects are, without slipping off into simplicity or obscurity, and surely any attempt at definition in brief space is foolhardy. But I shall mention two things.

E. M. Forster long ago distinguished between the way we perceive people in real life and in fictional life. In real life we know people only in a "rough and ready" way and largely through "external signs." In real life, in other words, people are only imperfectly seen. But in fictional life we can know people completely, if the writer wishes; their inner and outer lives can be fully exposed, and so they can seem more definite and substantial than people in real life. In the novel, Forster said, "we can know people perfectly . . . we can find here a compensation for their dimness in life. In this direction fiction is truer than history, because it goes beyond the evidence, and each of us knows from his own experience that there is something beyond the evidence, and even if the novelist has not got it correctly, well—he has tried."[2] The result of the distinction was Forster's conclusion that human beings have two sides, one appropriate to history and the other to fiction, and the side appropriate to fiction is clearly the richer—because the more complete—of the two.

Events also have two sides, or two ways of being related. Forster made a celebrated distinction between a story and a plot. A story is a narrative of events arranged chronologically: this happened and then this happened. A plot is also a narrative of events but with an emphasis on causality: this happened and then this happened and for this reason. A story requires only curiosity on the reader's part, but a plot demands intelligence and memory and so is a more elevated way of treating events.

As Forster described it, plot in fiction is also a seeking beyond the evidence toward something we know, or at any rate want to believe, is there—explanation, meaning, at the very least some design or pattern. In the writing of history the writer's task, if he is to do more than merely tell a story, is to discover the pattern apparent or implied in the facts. In other words, if the writer is to present a plot rather than a story, he must move his work in the direction of meaning—but meaning that derives from the facts. The fiction writer of course is under no such limitation. He can invent or choose "facts" that work to create any design or meaning he wishes to present.

The point I want to make by these references to Forster's distinctions between history and fiction is this: The writer of literary nonfiction, like the writer of fiction, can take us deeply inside people and events and construct works that move beyond story to plot. But in neither case can he do this to the same extent that the fiction writer can. He is finally restrained by his commitment to the facts. Literary nonfiction of course seeks to have it both ways, to be true as history and at the same time true as art, and recent work in the form shows the considerable degree to which this can be done. But it also shows the limits.

Our knowledge of nonfiction characters is never quite satisfying enough in literary terms. Likewise, the design or meaning that can be drawn from the facts is never quite satisfying enough in literary terms. In both cases the nonfiction writer is held back by his inability to move imaginatively beyond the facts or to create "facts" to fit an imagined design. This does not mean that literary nonfiction can have no literary or artistic authority; it can and does—and often to a greater degree than much routine fiction. Literature and history, art and journalism, can be joined to create work of considerable appeal and power in both realms. But the joining does not erase the differences. Nonfiction can touch the reader in ways fiction never can because of nonfiction's commitment to the truth of what can be known about the world. But fiction can touch us in ways nonfiction never can precisely because of fiction's commitment to the truth of what cannot be known about the world but only imagined—its commitment, in Forster's terms, to that "something beyond the evidence" we know is there.

It could well be argued that the view of fiction held to here is simply outmoded. The case made for literary nonfiction by Mas'ud Zavarzadeh insisted that the work was the only appropriate "fiction" for a technetronic world that had lost faith in the striving of the imagination to seek beyond the facts of experience, and especially the effort to discover, through acts of the imagination, some pattern or meaning in experience. From this perspective the literary effects of literary nonfiction are the only authentic modern literary effects, the only kind to which we can now submit without embarrassment. Even so fine a literary intelligence as Lionel Trilling's questioned the present authenticity of the fictional modes of the past.

But such questioning seems to me to reveal more about recent critics than about recent writers. Throughout the sixties and seventies many important fiction writers held fast to traditional notions of fiction, creating characters and plots and offering—in an old phrase from Cleanth Brooks and Robert Penn Warren—a "tissue of significances" that E. M. Forster would have found familiar.[3] Even fabulists and irrealists of various sorts, committed to literary construction rather than chronicle, sought to make up the world, as one admiring commentator put it, "as an indispensable way of making sense of it."[4] In one way or another writers remained dedicated to what Saul Bellow said is always the function of art: "The giving of weight to the particular, and the tendency to invest the particular with resonant meanings." We are haunted, Bellow added, by the sense that our existence is peculiarly significant—and "the business of art is with this sense, precisely."[5]

*

If Zavarzadeh's ideas effectively draw on a significant critical current of the time, they fail to conform to a close reading of some of the central works of literary nonfiction published in the sixties and seventies. For one thing, Zavarzadeh insists on thinking about literary nonfiction as a form in which distinctions between fact and fiction no longer apply; he sees the nonfiction novel as a "distinctly postmodern genre" because in its bi-referential quality, it reflects the "breakdown of the established boundaries between fact and fiction" in recent experience. Even more, he holds that the "ultimate meaning" of nonfiction novels "lies neither in their internal aesthetic shape nor in their correspondence to the actualities of the empirical world, but in the fictuality which emerges out of the counterpointing of fact and fiction."[6] But the works Zavarzadeh takes as his prime examples—*Hiroshima, In Cold Blood, The Armies of the Night,* etc.—do not fit such an easy blurring of categories. Such works may reveal a fact-fiction fusion in recent experience and may indeed be bi-referential in their concern with internal coherence as well as external correspondence, but they remain fact-books because the writers choose to be restrained by what can be demonstrably known. The books are not fictions because the writers do not choose to go beyond the facts or invent "facts" to fit their purposes.

The difference between fact writing and fiction writing is not located in the use of factual material or in the employment of novelistic techniques. Neither is it found in the "creativity" at work in one form and its absence in the other; imposing significant form on the materials of unaltered life may be a more demanding creative act than shaping them from the more orderly processes of the imagination. What matters is the fact writer's decision to stay within the confines of the evidence as it can be known—and within those confines, if he chooses to write literary nonfiction, to do many of the things fiction writers do—or the fiction writer's decision to leap in some manner beyond the evidence.

It is surely true that the line between fact and fiction in contemporary writing seems increasingly faint. This is especially so of the line between autobiography and fiction. John Gregory Dunne's "memoir" *Vegas* begins with this convoluted note from the author:

> This is a fiction which recalls a time both real and imagined. There are, for example, comics, prostitutes and private detectives in Las Vegas; there is no Jackie Kasey, no Artha Ging, no Buster Mano. I am more or less "I," he and she less than more he and she.[7]

The head spins. But if fact-fiction distinctions have grown faint, they are still apparent and still worth keeping in mind. They still define fundamentally different approaches to the writer's material and his treatments of it and equally different effects for the reader.

"The nonfiction novel," Zavarzadeh says, summing up his argument, "replaces 'interpretation' with a 'transcription' of naked facts."[8] But this seems to me a second way in which he misreads recent nonfiction. If literary nonfiction is less interpretive or judgmental than traditional fiction or even the varieties of transfiction, it is only because the writer is restrained by his commitment to the facts in offering patterns of meaning and not because of a critical decision to avoid the effort. In trying to write an artistically coherent form of nonfiction, recent nonfiction writers have sought to reveal meaning every bit as much as the most old-fashioned fiction writers. The difference is that they have sought meaning within the limits of the facts.

Capote was notably candid about the role of meaning in *In Cold Blood.* He spoke about the characters in the book as a "perfect set of symbols," about working his own "opinions" into the book, about moving toward "one view, always"—all aspects of meaning that, given his detached methods, emerge through selection and arrangement. Like a fiction writer, he said he "often thought of the book as being like something reduced to a seed. Instead of presenting the reader with a full plant, with all the foliage, a seed is planted in the soil of the mind." And he added that readers, judging by letters they sent him, were responsive to the book's symbolic or thematic intent: "About 70 per cent of the letters think of the book as a reflection on American life—this collision between the desperate, ruthless, wandering, savage part of American life, and the other, which is insular and safe, more or less."[9]

Mailer was equally candid about the purpose of his very personal methods in *The Armies of the Night.* He portrayed himself as a "good working amateur philosopher" and saw this role separating him both from ordinary journalists and ordinary storytellers because it allowed him, unlike them, to pierce through events into the realms of symbol, metaphor, and meaning.[10] Like Capote, Mailer offered his readers an interpretation of events, a judgmental voice.

In developing his theory in light of specific works, Zavarzadeh acknowledges, as noted before, that the nonfiction novelist inevitably has a viewpoint on his material, a perspective, that is a product of his personal history and sense of the world. But he insists that such subjective qualities are simply a "local reaction and interpretation rather than a global totalization" and that the writer "does not assemble his sensory impressions into a significant form in order to formulate a particular metaphysics or convey a single vision of reality as the fictive novelist does." Despite the qualification, the thrust of Zavarzadeh's argument is toward a view of literary nonfiction in which meaning or the interpretation of experience is avoided in favor of the transcription of experience. Fittingly, the last section of his book discusses tape-recorded works of nonfiction, and especially Oscar Lewis's *La Vida* which Zavarzadeh calls a "notational non-fiction novel" and admires for its absolute "refusal to totalize or comment on" the reality it transcribes.[11]

Contrary to Zavarzadeh, it is my view that the literary quality of recent nonfiction is located precisely in the capacity of the writer to find in factual experience some "tissue of significances," some "resonant meanings." Such meanings may be less "totalizing" or grandly metaphysical than they once were, but they are as nonetheless present in nonfiction that seeks the level of art as in fiction, and works of literary nonfiction can be explored by examining how writers have used fictional techniques to reveal meaning and by trying to gauge the extent to which they have been able to do so. As I try to show in the second part of the book, a number of nonfiction writers have been remarkably successful in this sense, enriching serious writing. But at the same time I think it evident that nonfiction writers cannot go as far in the direction of meaning as fiction writers can precisely because of their commitment to the authority of fact. This commitment is at once their strength, in an historical sense, and their limitation, in a literary sense. Capote said that *In Cold Blood* continued after its publication to resonate for him in the manner of a novel:

> . . . it keeps churning around in my head. It particularizes itself now and then, but not in the sense that it brings about a total conclusion. It's like the echo of E. M. Forster's Malabar Caves, the echo that's meaningless and yet it's there: one keeps hearing it all the time.[12]

The best works of literary nonfiction have exactly this quality. They churn and echo in the mind like a novel—though never quite to the same degree.

*

Capote's *In Cold Blood* and Mailer's *The Armies of the Night* represent distinctly different approaches to literary nonfiction—the one rigorously impersonal on the surface, the other stridently personal. Both works of course are personal in the sense that works of art always are, always bearing the writer's individual stamp; but in Mailer's case the personal element is open and direct, the writer coming forward in his own person—or at least as "Mailer"—and addressing the reader in his own voice. Of the two strains, that represented by Mailer was perhaps the more eagerly pursued by nonfiction writers, and the more debated by critics.

The interest in directly personal forms of nonfiction no doubt had something to do with the need writers felt in the sixties and seventies to speak out in their own voices rather than through the indirections of fictions. No doubt it also had something to do with the desire of writers turning to literary nonfiction from backgrounds in journalism to break free of the impersonal conventions of traditional journalism. But there is perhaps another and deeper sense in which directly personal forms of literary nonfiction held out strong appeal to the writer. They could seem to be a way of escaping the literary limitations imposed on the nonfiction writer by his commitment to the truth of events; by bringing himself openly into his work and speaking in his own voice, the writer could remain within the facts yet at the same time seek beyond them through the play of mind, imagination, and language to touch that area of literary meaning that

Mailer called metaphor. In other words, through directly personal methods, the writer might seem to fuse, and at the highest level, the roles of observer and maker, true both to the exploration of event as event and event as meaning.

I understand Robert Fitzgerald to be saying something like that in this passage about the nonfiction of James Agee:

> He was after the truth, the truth about specific events or things, and the truth about his own impressions and feelings. By truth I mean what he would chiefly mean: correspondence between what is said and what is the case—but what is the case at the utmost reach of consciousness. Now this intent has been delicately and justly distinguished from the intent of art, which is to make, not to state, things; and a self-dedication to truth on the part of Shakespeare or Mozart (Ageean examples) would indeed strike us as peculiar. On the other hand, with philosophy dethroned and the rise of great Realists, truth-telling has often seemed to devolve almost by default upon the responsible writer, enabling everyone else to have it both ways: his truth as truth if they want it, or something else if they prefer, since after all he is merely an artist. Jim Agee, by nature an artist and responsive to all the arts, took up this challenge to perceive in full and to present immaculately what was the case.[13]

Agee sought to bridge the gap between journalism and art, between stating things and making them, by combining the effort to tell the truth about specific events with the effort to tell the truth about his own impressions of those events. If Agee's aim was essentially still that of correspondence between event and statement, it was an enlarged sense of correspondence— one that embraced, as Fitzgerald says, the "utmost reach of consciousness." The challenge Agee took up was to perceive and present "what was the case"—but what was the case equally involved the artist's open dedication to the truth of "his own impressions and feelings."

There are no recent examples of literary nonfiction that compare with Agee's exhaustive effort in *Let Us Now Praise Famous Men* both to state things and to make them through direct concentration on the self. But there have been many attempts in this direction, by Mailer and others, and some of them will be discussed in the following pages. To my mind, directly personal methods have indeed permitted some recent nonfiction writers to reach beyond the literary limitations of more detached methods and more nearly match the effects of distinguished fiction. C. D. B. Bryan's *Friendly Fire* is the best example I know of such work.

But if the directly personal can be an especially fruitful course for the writer of literary nonfiction, it can also be a notably hazardous one. The problem is always that the emphasis on the self will imprison the writer rather than free him, narrow the effects of his work rather than enlarge them.

The primary task of nonfiction is always to deal with the real world, and the "I" can easily get in the way, becoming the subject itself rather than a way of apprehending the subject. The "I" can become a substitute for the world and leave the writer with nothing more than a narcissistic form of self-revelation. Some of the most telling criticisms of literary nonfiction pointed to this tendency. "It used to be," Herbert Gold observed, "that journalists buried themselves like cynical monks, telling who-what-where-when-how, and leaving out the why. Now, trying to give the meaning of it all, the playful parajournalists lie down like puppies, howling operatically, their four paws in the air, scratching their own bellies." [14]

Nevertheless, there are times when the nonfiction writer, through the means of a directly personal narrative, intertwines with his subject in a way that renders the subject fully and yet throws over it the meaningful resonance of fiction. Such work does not become fiction in any sense, nor does it finally erase the distinction between fiction and nonfiction. But it perhaps enables the writer of literary nonfiction to come as close as he possibly can to reconciling his opposed roles.

*

There are several built-in difficulties with nonfiction writing that are too little discussed, difficulties that prevent it from being much of a rival of fiction even in a simple quantitative sense.

For one thing, there is the extraordinary amount of time, effort, and sheer good luck demanded of the writer. The writer of nonfiction is forced away from the desk and his own imagination and into an untidy world in which he must deal with events and people as they come to him. He must become involved in the lives of others, all sorts of others, and he must accept the inevitable tedium of waiting for things to happen, of waiting for the scenes to unfold so that he can then reconstruct them in fictional fashion. And there is no guarantee that after the effort and the waiting, after weeks or months of it, anything much will result. A key subject may be unwilling to talk. A scene necessary for aesthetic shapeliness refuses to take place. Or a whole story, once so compelling, evaporates into the haze of yesterday's news.

The time demanded of the writer in pursuit of a piece of literary nonfiction is also a matter of expense. It is not the sort of work the writer can toss off after working hours, or the sort of thing likely to land him a Guggenheim or a summer at Yaddo. And for a magazine or a publisher to pick up the expense is a considerable gamble. So there is always a question of who is going to pay for the plane tickets and the motels and the rented cars that field work requires. If a magazine or publisher is to do it, then the writer must already have some reputation—he must already be a Mailer or Capote or Wolfe. And if the writer has funds of his own to gamble with, then it is likely he has already made a name for himself. The point is that literary nonfiction has some clear economic disadvantages for the new writer or the writer without a substantial reputation.

There is another side to the economic question that needs mention.

Nonfiction writers deal with real people and real people are easily offended and quick to seek redress in the courts. Even when the writer gets everything down with impeccable accuracy, his subjects can feel ill-treated. "People simply do not like to see themselves put down on paper," Capote noted. "They're like somebody who goes to see his portrait in a gallery. He doesn't like it unless it's overwhelmingly flattering." [15] As a consequence the nonfiction writer ordinarily gets a prior legal release from all the principal figures in his account, and getting that can be a difficult and expensive undertaking.

Joseph Wambaugh gave a revealing account of the problem with his book *The Onion Field.* Wambaugh had written two successful novels when he turned to a nonfiction account of a story he had long wanted, but had been unable, to do because the principal figure, a policeman who survived a 1963 abduction that resulted in the execution of his partner, refused to give a release. A half-dozen years or so after Wambaugh first became interested in the story, and after getting encouragement from Capote that it was indeed a good story, he persuaded the ex-policeman to let him do it. Without the man's cooperation, the story simply could not have been told. Wambaugh said:

> . . . I could *not* have written without *him*; I mean it would just be impossible. For instance, to draw an analogy, how could Capote have written *In Cold Blood* without the complete cooperation and release of Perry Smith? It would have been impossible. It would never have been *In Cold Blood.* He would have written a story about a terrible crime, and that would have been it. And that's how badly I needed *this* guy, if not worse; I needed this guy *more* than he needed Perry Smith.

The cooperation Wambaugh finally got came at a price. The reluctant ex-policeman received a lump-sum payment, as did other people mentioned in the book, all payments scaled according to each individual's importance for the writer. Wambaugh explained:

> Some people got a nominal payment just to make it legally *binding.* And some people got large amounts of money; it depended on how badly I *needed* them. A lot of the people in my book didn't get anything—they are just peripheral characters. Some who actually appear in the book weren't interviewed by me; I used other information I had and drew them in, but there were *actually* sixty-two people interviewed. And they were all paid something.

The money came not from the book's publisher but from Wambaugh himself—and it was, he said, an enormous amount:

> This book cost me a small fortune, not just in legal releases but in lawyers doing research for me. I had to retain a lawyer for most of the six months that I spent writing the book. He spent that time at the law library doing various kinds of research, giving me material on the case. I mean, I had to do all sorts of things to get in to see my two killers. To get into San Quentin I had to get the one guy's lawyer and fly him up there and go with him. And I had to get the retired

detective who handled this case and is now Chief of Police in Colorado—I had to bring him out here and go over the whole crime scene and do all that. So I had an enormous amount of money invested in this.[16]

The Onion Field became a commercial success, but only after Wambaugh invested a good deal in it, an investment he could afford to make because of the success of his earlier novels. Needless to say, not all writers are so fortunate.

Few writers have been willing or able to make a sustained career of literary nonfiction. Many of the writers discussed in the following pages came to literary nonfiction from a background in fiction, or later turned to it—and not surprisingly. Capote expressed sheer relief in talking about the novel he intended to write after the demanding experience of completing *In Cold Blood.*

> It's quite a step—to undertake the nonfictional novel. Because the amount of work is enormous. The relationship between the author and all the people he must deal with if he does the job properly—well, it's a full 24-hour-a-day job. Even when I wasn't working on the book, I was somehow involved with all the characters in it—with their personal lives, writing six or seven letters a day, taken up with their problems, a complete involvement. It's extra-ordinarily difficult and consuming.[17]

The novelist can retire to his mythical shack in the woods, there to wrestle in private with his imagination. The writer of literary nonfiction must first take a turn in the world. That involvement is at once the attraction of the form and its special burden.

*

The basic critical problem with literary nonfiction cast in the form of fiction is always credibility. Because such work reconstructs events instead of describing them and because it draws on a variety of techniques associated with fiction—dialogue, point of view, interior monologue, evocative detail—it invariably raises questions about the writer's commitment to fact.

Because of the skepticism the form naturally encourages, it would seem wise for the writer to provide some account of his methods of research and reporting. The writer of directly personal nonfiction, whether he remains within an essentially journalistic form or to some extent casts his work in the form of fiction, has an advantage here because in portraying his own involvement in events or in revealing the process of writing about them, he automatically provides some means of measuring the reliability of his work. In directly personal nonfiction we see the writer at his work to some extent, and so can gauge the depth and range of the work. Or to put it another way, since in personal nonfiction everything comes to us through the filter of the writer's self, all we need do is determine the reliability of that self to grasp the overall reliability of the work.

Impersonal nonfiction in fictional form is another matter. Here the writer is hidden, performing his work out of sight and presenting the reader with only the results of his work and none of its processes. Hence, here especially, it would seem wise for the writer to give some account of his methods either in an author's note or an explanatory afterword. Such accounts will not in themselves establish credibility, but they can help—if only as some evidence that the writer recognizes an inherent problem with literary nonfiction and is willing to address it.

Oddly enough, many writers fail to address the problem at all, perhaps feeling that explanation intrudes (in the same way that the inclusion of photographs might) on the literary intentions of the work, or that authenticity can be established by tone or by reliance on familiar documentary materials or by the kind of subtle system of internal verification apparent to careful readers of *In Cold Blood*. But some direct word from the author on the subject of methods would not seem out of order and might make him slightly less vulnerable to the familiar charge of parajournalism.

For the better the writer's detached reconstruction of events, the greater the question of credibility. Tom Wicker, reviewing Victor Villasenor's *Jury: The People vs. Juan Corona*, was troubled precisely because of the evident care that had gone into the work. "The problem with his reconstruction," Wicker wrote, "is not that it isn't good: it's *too* good to be entirely credible."[18] Faced with that kind of problem, the writer of literary nonfiction needs to gain for himself all the factual authority he possibly can.

Notes

1. Plimpton, "Truman Capote: An Interview," p. 190.

2. E. M. Forster, *Aspects of the Novel* (New York: Harcourt, Brace, 1927), pp. 74, 98, 98.

3. Cleanth Brooks and Robert Penn Warren, *Understanding Fiction*, 2nd ed. (New York: Appleton-Century-Crofts, 1959), p. 668.

4. Bellamy, *Superfiction*, p. 17.

5. Saul Bellow, "Machines and Storybooks," *Harper's*, August 1974, pp. 49, 54.

6. Zavarzadeh, *The Mythopoeic Reality*, pp. 57, 227.

7. John Gregory Dunne, *Vegas* (New York: Warner Books, 1975), Preface.

8. Zavarzadeh, *The Mythopoeic Reality*, p. 224.

9. Plimpton, "Truman Capote: An Interview," pp. 195, 196, 206.

10. Mailer, *The Armies of the Night*, p. 91.

11. Zavarzadeh, *The Mythopoeic Reality*, pp. 43, 211, 221.

12. Plimpton, "Truman Capote: An Interview," p. 206.

13. Robert Fitzgerald, "A Memoir," *The Collected Short Prose of James Agee*, ed. Robert Fitzgerald (Boston: Houghton Mifflin, 1968), pp. 24-25.

14. Gold, "On Epidemic First Personism," p. 286.

15. Plimpton, "Truman Capote: An Interview," p. 197.

16. John Brady, "Joe Wambaugh Cops from Experience," *Writer's Digest*, December 1973, pp. 20-21.

17. Plimpton, "Truman Capote: An Interview," p. 206.

18. Tom Wicker, "When Citizens Sit in Judgment," *New York Times Book Review*, 1 May 1977, p. 49.

PART TWO: THE WORK

If its credibility as journalism or history was a continuing issue in the critical response to the nonfiction of the 1960s and 1970s, its newness was another. Commentators pointed out that many others had written in a vein similar to, and with a skill equal to, that of Capote, Mailer, Wolfe, and Talese. The list of names brought forward included Joseph Mitchell, Vincent Sheean, Lillian Ross, Jimmy Cannon, Alva Johnson, Paul Gallico, and Jim Bishop, to mention a few. The new nonfiction writers were themselves willing to admit to a few predecessors. Capote allowed that Mitchell and Rebecca West had done narrative reportage and that Ross's *Picture* might be called a nonfiction novella.

Wolfe took up the issue of newness at greater length than anyone else. He argued that on close inspection, the names usually offered as having earlier done similar work fell into four categories: People who were not writing nonfiction at all, but fiction in the guise of nonfiction; traditional essayists; autobiographers; and what he called "Literary Gentlemen with a Seat in the Grandstand." The difference between what Wolfe called the New Journalism and the type of work produced in the latter three categories was to be found in reporting. The autobiographer, for example, was not really a reporter because he was simply recording his own lived experience; and the Literary Gentleman with a Seat in the Grandstand rarely did much reporting or the right type; he seldom came down from his lofty perch to grub around in the "tedious, messy, physically dirty, boring, dangerous even" business of reporting. Nevertheless, Wolfe was ready to acknowledge some "not half-bad candidates" who showed many of the characteristics of the New Journalism—among them, George Orwell, A. J. Leibling, Ross, and Richard Gehman.[1]

But to point out, as numerous critics rightly did, that the literary nonfiction of the sixties and seventies was not strictly new was only to correct some of the extravagant boosterism of the time. The correction did not provide a critical perspective on the work or an explanation of the broad interest in it. Few, if any, of the techniques of literary nonfiction were new—saturation reporting had been done in the past and the various storytelling devices of fiction had been applied to factual material—but what was different was the extent to which they were now used and the tendency to think of the work in relation to fiction, to see it as not merely extending the boundaries of journalism but doing in journalism what had heretofore been done in fiction. The claims for nonfiction were new—and especially the claim, as Capote said, that reporting could be made as interesting as fiction and could be done as artistically.

The real critical task was evaluation of such claims. In trying to do that, it is important to see that recent literary nonfiction does indeed rest on earlier developments, and at the same time to see this not as a way of dismissing the work, but simply of locating it in a continuing tradition. In talk about predecessors, two names surfaced most often, James Agee and John Hersey, and I want to begin with a discussion of the best-known work of each as it relates in craft and effect to more recent work.

Notes

1. Wolfe, *The New Journalism*, pp. 44, 45.

7

Diffidence and Dominance

I

Wolfe had an odd though understandable response to Agee's *Let Us Now Praise Famous Men* (1941). He said that finally reading it, after years of hearing it critically acclaimed, was a great disappointment. Agee seemed to him "too diffident" in his treatment of the sharecropper families he wrote about, too locked into a point of view that was strictly his own. "Reading between the lines," he said, "you get a picture of a well-educated and extremely shy man . . . too polite, too diffident to ask personal questions of these humble folk or even draw them out."[1]

Wolfe was here adhering too closely to his own preference for a style of nonfiction in which the writer stays behind the scenes, doing his work out of sight. He could not seem to reconcile directly personal nonfiction like Agee's or like Mailer's ("Even Mailer's work shows the same odd defect, the same reluctance to take out the notebook and cross the genteel line and head through the doors marked Keep Out") with a kind of all-out reporting that left no stone unturned.[2] But if Agee's account of three sharecropper families in the South during the Depression is anything, it is a monumental piece of detailed reporting. It was intended, in Agee's words, to be an "exhaustive" record and analysis, "with no detail, however trivial it may seem, left untouched, no relevancy avoided, which lies within the power of remembrance to maintain, of the intelligence to perceive , and of the spirit to persist in."[3] Indeed, one of the common complaints voiced against the book is that it is too exhaustive, that Agee was unable to be selective, with the result that the work is a blur of detail.

But in one sense Wolfe was right about Agee. He *was* diffident. But that diffidence was as much a matter of the writing of the book as the reporting that went into it. In a sense diffidence is the major aesthetic principle at work in the book, a stance that Agee adopts toward his material from which the narrative voice, structure, and emotional force of the book flow. And in a sense, too, the question of a proper aesthetic principle becomes one of the major subjects of the book; the reader is asked to grapple, with Agee, over the question of how a work like this is to be written. The "nominal subject" of the book, Agee says, is cotton tenantry as seen in the lives of three tenant families. But he goes on to note another and more central subject: "Actually, the effort is to recognize the stature of a portion of unimagined existence, and to contrive techniques proper to its recording, communication, analysis, and defense" (p. viii). There were two instruments at his disposal, Walker Evans's photographs and his own prose; and these in turn were in the service of a spirit that occupies the center of the book: "individual, anti-authoritative human consciousness" (p. viii).

The anti-authoritative human consciousness springs from Agee's awed awareness of the reality of the lives of his subjects. He is continually overwhelmed by the fact that all the details he gathers about them simply *are*; they exist. He speaks of the effort to "perceive simply the cruel radiance of what is" (p. 11). He says the "one deeply exciting thing to me about [George] Gudger is that he is actual, he is living, at this instant" (p. 240). And he also says about George Gudger:

> I could invent incidents, appearances, additions to his character, background, surroundings, future, which might well point up and indicate and clinch things relevant to him which in fact I am sure are true, and important, and which George Gudger unchanged and undecorated would not indicate and perhaps could not even suggest. The result, if I was lucky, could be a work of art. But somehow a much more important, and dignified, and true fact about him than I could conceivably invent, though I were an illimitably better artist than I am, is the fact that he is exactly, down to the last inch and instant, who, what, where, when and why he is. He is in those terms living, right now, in flesh and blood and breathing, in an actual part of a world in which also, quite as irrelevant to imagination, you and I are living. (pp. 232-233)

The immense reality of Gudger and the other tenant families is so forceful and authoritative for Agee that, in the recall of writing, he must adopt a diffident, anti-authoritative role. He must write them up as little as possible; he must not allow "art" or "imagination" into his account of their lives for this would violate their reality by implying that it was not in itself sufficient, that it needed to be worked on, shaped, heightened. Neither must he allow journalism into the account. Just as literature is a "pretty lie," the "very blood and semen of journalism . . . is a broad and successful form of lying" (p. 235). What he instead seeks to enact is "not a work of art or of entertainment," literature or journalism, but a "human effort which must require human co-operation," a human effort to perceive the actual and find a language to correspond to it. (p. 111)

Agee takes upon himself what he conceives as the sacred duty of allowing the tenant families their own reality, their own truth, and not intruding his own upon them. If indeed "Everything that is is holy," then the writer who seeks such truth must avoid journalism's simplifications and literature's inventions; he must allow that which is its holy and independent life. (p. 459) But if this is Agee's aim, it is not always his practice. In the "A Country Letter" section of the book, he crosses over into the lives of the families, projects his consciousness into theirs, portrays them from within. He writes: "I become not my own shape and weight and self, but that of each of them . . . so that I know almost the dreams they will not remember" (p. 58). Such projections into consciousness, even when acknowledged as such, are at odds with the practice of most of the book. Walker Evans said the material here made him "squirm a little; I think it is a wrong note."[4] Agee himself seems to have sensed the intrusions of the section for he begins the following section by saying:

> But there must be an end to this . . . a new and more succinct beginning: Herein I must screen off all mysteries of our comminglings . . . and must here set in such regard as I can the sorry and brutal infuriate yet beautiful structures of the living which is upon each of you daily: and this in the cleanest terms I can learn to specify.

From this fresh beginning Agee turns back to recording the actuality of the tenants' lives that so "freezes and abashes" his "ambitious heart" (p. 99).

The method that Agee believed followed from reverence for the reality of his material can seem paradoxical. Rather than submerge his own presence and allow the material seemingly to speak for itself, he intrudes himself upon the account, insists upon his own presence, speaks openly about his interaction with the tenant families. His explanation of the method is encapsulated in one of the book's best-known passages:

> George Gudger is a man, et cetera. But obviously, in the effort to tell of him (by example) as truthfully as I can, I am limited. I know him only so far as I know him, and only in those terms in which I know him; and all of that depends as fully on who I am as on who he is. (p. 239)

Agee must tell about himself so that he can truthfully tell about the tenant families; only by revealing himself and revealing his relationship with the families can he allow them their separate reality. To "simplify or eliminate myself from this picture" he is piecing together would be as bad as to give in to the simplifications of journalism or the inventions of literature because he in fact was in the picture. A "chain of truth did actually weave itself and run through" the experience that involved him, and to be true to the experience, he must relate that involvement. (p. 240)

By openly insisting on his presence, Agee emphasizes that he and the material are not one. The separation is made clear not only by revealing his interaction with the tenant families but also through the admission that he is *writing* about them—and writing through recall after the experience. Agee appropriately talks about technical matters throughout the book if only to keep in the forefront of the reader's mind that the work is a written account and not the experience itself. His reprinting of a *Partisan Review* questionnaire on "Some Questions Which Face American Writers Today" is not, as he implies, "digressing from the subject of this volume" (p. 350). It is equally important that the reader should be alerted to the distance between the experience and the writing. Agee often directly addresses the material and the tenant figures from the vantage point of memory: "Down in front of the courthouse Walker had picked up talk with you, Fred . . . I can remember it so clearly, as if it were five minutes ago" (p. 361-362). And he breaks a narrative section of past experience to indicate his present difficulty with the writing: "But somehow I have lost hold of the reality of all this, I scarcely can understand how . . . I have not managed to give their truth in words" (p. 414).

The effect is the reader's strong sense that the account is written, written at a later time through the effort of memory, and written by James Agee who was a participant in the experience but through whose separate eyes and spirit the experience is alone known to us. We have an account of the experience through Agee's prose—and Evans's photographs—but not the experience itself. That is meant to retain its independent identity, its own "cruel radiance" wholly beyond the writer's capacity to chronicle it. All that Agee can do, and the reader through him, is *praise* famous men, honor them from without and from the vantage point of *now*, no matter how intense his portrayal of his involvement or how exhaustive his detail.

Yet if this is an "honest" technique, given Agee's reverent attitude toward the material, it is also a technique certain to fail. Failure is inherent in Agee's method and the final mark of honesty. The experience cannot be captured; the truth that Agee can tell, however rigorously honest his methods, can only be a "relative truth" (p. 239). "I feel sure in advance," he says, "that any efforts, in what follows, along the lines I have been speaking of, will be failures." And he adds: "Failure, indeed, is almost as strongly an obligation as an inevitability, in such work" (p. 238). To fail is to leave the reality of the tenant families' lives intact, unadorned and unsimplified by the writer—and consequently to fail is not only an "inevitability," given the fact, as Agee says, that words can only describe experience and not embody it, but a fundamental "obligation."

Part of the deep tension of the book stems from Agee's straining against his awareness of the impossibility of the task he has set himself. He, in effect, paints himself into a technical corner and then struggles mightily against the barrier. "If I could do it," he says in a famous passage, "I'd do no writing at all here. It would be photographs; the rest would be fragments of cloth, bits of cotton, lumps of earth, records of speech, pieces of wood and iron, phials of odors, plates of food and excrement" (p. 13). He asks the reader to "so far as possible forget that this is a book" (p. 246). But of course it is a book, it is writing, and so "I'll do what little I can in writing" (p. 13). The work will be done not through the familiar forms of art or journalism but through what he calls "open terms" (p. 12). Yet it will tell only a relative truth, the truth of language and not of life.

William Stott has shown that Agee's straining against his own conception of the separation of language and experience provides the book with its basic structure. The book has the form of a series of beginnings punctuated by the sense of failure—an effort to overcome the limits of language, the awareness of failure, then a new attempt to overcome. The book's structure derives from the constant awareness, as Agee says, that "I must make a new beginning" (p. 321). Stott suggests that the book's symbol might be the title of one of the chapters: the colon (in that chapter, Agee breaks off the narrative at one point and writes: "This is all one colon:"). There is a sense, Stott concludes, in which the entire book is one colon that "prefaces and points the reader to reality; a colon to a text that cannot be given."[5] Appropriately, the book ends not with an ending but with a new beginning, another colon. In the last line Agee gathers himself up for yet more description "which I shall now try to give you" (p. 471).

*

Explaining his disappointment with *Let Us Now Praise Famous Men*, Wolfe pointed out that the book was "very short on dialogue."[6] It is; but by dwelling on this point, the main features of Agee's method can be summarized. For Wolfe the extensive use of dialogue is part of literary nonfiction's general drive toward scenic telling; what the reporter is always looking for is the unfolding scene, a scene that is then reconstructed in the writing so that it unfolds again for the reader. But it is exactly this kind of re-creation that Agee resisted, this putting of the elements of an experience back together again in a way that draws the reader into the experience. That attempt was the "pretty lie" of art. With the actual rather than invented experience he was dealing with, the only honest approach was to tell about it himself, and tell about it in a way that conveyed it as past experience rather than present event. This was Agee's diffidence: his insistence on keeping the experience as intact and unchanged as possible.

An illustration is Agee's portrayal of the night he spent with the Gudgers after getting his car stuck. In presenting this material, Agee comes as close as he ever does in the book to creating an extended scene, but it is a scene that bears little relation to Wolfe's understanding of how fictional scene construction can be adapted to nonfiction writing. There is a good deal of dialogue in the account, but it is all given indirectly, without quotation marks. Agee is not dramatizing the account but attempting to tell about it, and tell about it through his present memory of it. The dominant tone of the passage is recall.

The Gudgers are roused from bed, but they insist on providing supper for Agee before putting him up for the night. He does not want them to bother and gives this description of the give-and-take with George Gudger:

> I'm making you enough bother already; but no; Can't go to bed without no supper; you just hold on a second or two.

And this with Annie Mae Gudger:

> . . . with so many words I say, Hello, Mrs. Gudger: say I want to tell you I'm *aw*ful sorry to give you all this bother: you just, honest I don't need much of anything, if you'd just tell me where a piece of bread is, it'll be *plenty*, I'd hate for you to bother to cook anything up for me: but she answers me while passing, looking at me, trying to get me into focus from between her sticky eyelashes, that 'tain't no bother at all, and for me not to worry over that. (p. 413)

But Agee makes clear that even this indirect dialogue is only an approximation of the actuality of the experience. He abruptly breaks off the account to say, from the position of the present writing, "But somehow I have lost hold of the reality of all this, I scarcely can understand how." The recollection overpowers his ability to capture it in language; it is more overwhelmingly real in memory than in his account:

> I have not managed to give their truth in words, which are a soft, plain-featured, and noble music, each part in the experience of it and in the memory so cleanly and so simply defined in its own terms, striking so many chords and relationships at once, which I can but have blurred in the telling at all. (p. 414)

But despite the sense of failure, Agee launches forth again, trying to capture the experience of the late-night meal with a catalogue of precise details. During the meal he and the Gudgers are "talking some," but he cannot record it either exactly as it happened or in its deeper sense. The recording is "beyond my memory," and the deeper level of meaning and implication—which is "somewhat more beautiful and more valuable, I feel, than, say, the sonnet form"—seems to elude all language. But however futile, Agee picks up the task and begins anew, straining to do in language what little he can. "Let me try," he says, "just a few of the surfaces instead" (p. 417). Yet with the meal over and while preparing for bed, he must confront again the sense of impossibility: "and there followed a simple set of transitions which are beautiful in my rememberance and which I can scarcely set down," transitions between eating and sleeping that he finally sets down in a moving passage of indirect dialogue:

> Gudger and I exchange our lamps, speaking a few words in nearly inaudible voices . . . All right in year hain't you?—Ah, sure, fine. Sure am.—Annie Mae told me to say, she's sorry she ain't got no clean sheet, but just have to (*oh, no!*)

make out best way you can.—Oh, no. No. You tell her I certainly do thank her,
but, no. I'll be fine like this, *fine* like this—She just don't got none tell she does a
warshin.—Sure; sure; I wouldn't want to dirty up a clean sheet for you, one
night. Thanks a lot. Door, right head a yer bed, if you want to git out. I look, and
nod:
Yeah; thanks.
Night:
Night:
The door draws shut. (pp. 419-420)

The scene is deeply marked by what Robert Fitzgerald has said marked
all of Agee's best work: a religious sense of life. Fittingly, the "last words" of
the book that come shortly after the scene—although characteristic of
Agee's stop-and-start method, they are not really the last words—are the
words of familiar prayer, the Lord's Prayer. The religious sense of life not
only describes Agee's sensibility but his overall approach to *Let Us Now
Praise Famous Men* as well. As a writer Agee believes he must stand back
from a sacred experience in reverent awe, recording it as he himself took
part in it and remembers it but in no way heightening or distorting it, or
even reconstructing it. He insists that the experience is not a story or a
subject for drama, neither is it material for the journalist or the novelist. It
is simply what it is—and the book about it is what it is, a literary worship
service, in the present and for us, in which past mysteries are recalled as
truly, and finally as impossibly, as they can be.

II

To describe Agee's personal manner in *Let Us Now Praise Famous Men*,
Dwight Macdonald drew a contrast with the "recording angel" methods
associated with *The New Yorker* magazine:

> . . . one of the virtues of the book, both as literature and as reportage, is that
> the author puts himself into it on every page. This allows him a freedom of
> expression and stylistic invention . . . that the Just-Give-The-News-Please or
> *New Yorker*-Objective mode denied, for example, to Truman Capote, whose *In
> Cold Blood* is so deliberately, artfully bare of personal style or comment. The
> idea seems to be to achieve the impersonality of the Recording Angel—though it
> reads more like a blotter entry by one of his less imaginative desk sergeants. As
> for truth, it is odd that by pushing himself with both elbows and feet into the
> foreground, Agee gives if not a more accurate picture than Capote, a more
> truthful one (which is the point, after all) because the reader can allow for Agee's
> personality as a distortion of the picture. . . . But no such allowance is possible
> with a writer who calculatingly keeps himself out of the picture and insists he is
> telling not his truth but The Truth. It is possible, though sometimes difficult, to
> believe in the existence of a man named James Agee, but it is not possible to
> believe in a recording angel named Truman Capote. One meets so few angels.[7]

The passage is interesting for a number of reasons, and I shall refer to it
again. It energetically points up the polar difference between Agee and a
coolly impersonal mode of nonfiction that inevitably brings *The New
Yorker* to mind. *In Cold Blood* first appeared in that magazine. The work

Capote found closest to his own in technique and intention, Lillian Ross's *Picture*, also appeared there. But the pioneering example of the form was John Hersey's *Hiroshima*, published in *The New Yorker* in 1946.

Capote, commenting on predecessors for *In Cold Blood*, found Hersey's work quite different, just a "classical journalistic piece."[8] Wolfe, on the other hand, thought the book "very novelistic" and admitted it into the group of direct ancestors of the New Journalism.[9] The difference of opinion is hard to reconcile, though it probably hinges on Capote's feeling that Hersey did not draw sufficiently on novelistic techniques, especially the use of dialogue. Most observers, however, have found *Hiroshima* a notable early example of literary nonfiction—and also found it, as Macdonald suggested by reference to *The New Yorker* mode of Capote, poles apart in method from Agee's celebrated work.

In noting the differences between *Famous Men* and *Hiroshima*, the first thing to remark is that Agee took part in the experience he wrote about and Hersey did not. Like Capote with the Kansas murders, Hersey had to reconstruct most of the events of the atomic bombing of Hiroshima as those events were later related to him. This difference does not in itself lead to the sharply opposed manner of the two books, but it does point up an altogether different relationship with the material—intense personal interaction as against a more typical journalistic situation in which a story is pieced together largely through what the writer is told. And this in turn suggests a natural distancing of the writer from the material, but the distancing of impersonality and careful ordering rather than that which stems from an immense reverence for the material. Hersey clearly felt his material deeply—the tone of *Hiroshima* is at times as reverent as *Famous Men*, though never as passionately or personally so—but his involvement with it was never such that he could not cast over it the net of literary and journalistic techniques. *Hiroshima* is not a work that struggles against the familiar modes of literature and journalism but rather it draws on them with skill and confidence, deliberately turning the material into a distinguished example of literary nonfiction.

Hersey distances himself from his material through impersonal dominance of it. He subjects the material to absolute control, ordering it into an artfully shaped whole, a work that is not a series of fresh beginnings but a carefully orchestrated development leading to a resonant ending. Hersey's entire method is rooted in dominance rather than in diffidence—the dominance of the recording angel, detached from the material, knowing all and shaping all for calculated effect. Hersey's personality is never dramatically present, and the "I" is absent entirely; the recording angel always keeps its distance and its mask. But Hersey's sensibility and compassion are deeply felt and the work is finally not only an extraordinary feat of detached reporting but also an experience of great emotional effect.

Macdonald once observed that the facts, contrary to popular belief, never speak for themselves but rather are like "Swift's Laputans who have to be roused to practical discourse by attendants touching their lips with inflated bladders. Here, the bladders are one's assumptions."[10] Hersey's facts about Hiroshima do not speak for themselves either; rather they are ordered around a governing idea, an interpretation of the first atom bomb dropped in anger as beyond understanding, a vast and inexplicable human tragedy, an event that brought great suffering yet an event that is not to be subsumed under easy accusations of blame but left instead simply as stark tragedy. Hersey's "assumption" is that explanation is not possible. The bombing is not to be explained away but must be left as a sad mystery amid the sadness of human history.

At one point, one of the bombing victims, Reverend Mr. Tanimoto, reads the Ninetieth Psalm to a dying man: "For a thousand years in Thy sight are but as yesterday when it is past, and as a watch in the night. . . . For all our days are passed away in Thy wrath: we spend our years as a tale that is told."[11] Hersey's interpretation of Hiroshima is precisely—in Macbeth's concluding lines—that it is a tale told by an idiot, full of sound and fury signifying nothing, but characteristically he does not insist on such a view but leaves it unstated, an underlying assumption of the work and not an explanatory pigeonhole into which Hiroshima can be conveniently lodged.

Hersey is careful to deal with one typical response to Hiroshima, the assigning of blame, in an even-handed manner that leads to no conclusion. The Japanese were "the objects of the first great experiment in the use of atomic power, which . . . no country except the United States . . . could possibly have developed" (p. 66). Yet there is evidence, as American authorities insisted, that "the Japanese apparently intended to resist invasion, hill by hill, life for life" (p. 9). Finally, the issue of blame is summed up in a report by a Jesuit priest to Rome:

> Some of us consider the bomb in the same category as poison gas and were against its use on a civilian population. Others were of the opinion that in total war, as carried on in Japan, there was no difference between civilians and soldiers, and that the bomb itself was an effective force tending to end the bloodshed, warning Japan to surrender and thus to avoid total destruction. It seems logical that he who supports total war in principle cannot complain of a war against civilians. The crux of the matter is whether total war in its present form is justifiable, even when it serves a just purpose. Does it not have material and spiritual evil as its consequences which far exceed whatever good might result? When will our moralists give us a clear answer to this question? (pp. 117-118)

The Jesuit's question is left a question. The implication is that there is no answer, at least none apparent to Hersey, and the question of blame is left in the air, a matter of secondary importance to the sheer horror of the bombing.

Hersey follows the letter, with its plea for rational explanation, with a school essay written by a child shortly before the first anniversary of the bombing. The essay, as Hersey points out, is matter of fact and even, on the surface, an account of an almost exhilarating adventure. Yet its undertone is one of immense sadness:

> The day before the bomb, I went for a swim. In the morning, I was eating peanuts. I saw a light. I was knocked to little sister's sleeping place. When we were saved, I could only see as far as the tram. My mother and I started to pack our things. The neighbors were walking around burned and bleeding. Hataya-*san* told me to run away with her. I said I wanted to wait for my mother. We went to the park. A whirlwind came. At night a gas tank burned and I saw the reflection in the river. We stayed in the park one night. Next day I went to Taiko Bridge and met my girl friends Kikuki and Murakami. They were looking for their mothers. But Kikuki's mother was wounded and Murakami's mother, alas, was dead. (p. 118)

The book ends with the child's uncomprehending essay, with the full weight of Hersey's interpretation of the bombing hanging on the final "alas." The word expresses both the tragedy and inexplicability of Hiroshima, an experience of terror beyond rational explanation or adult meaning, an experience that can finally only be alluded to through the flat yet moving language of a child.

The essay sums up as well the general method of the book, which is wholly cast through character and written with restrained, understated prose that always suggests more than it states. The bombing is reconstructed through the experience of six survivors of diverse background—a clerk, a middle-aged doctor, a tailor's widow, a German priest, a young surgeon, a Methodist minister. Through carefully detailed vignettes, the first chapter, "A Noiseless Flash," describes what each was doing moments before the bomb exploded on the morning of August 6, 1945, and their immediate reactions. The second chapter, "The Fire," picks up each of the characters in turn and follows their actions in a series of small, sharply etched scenes through the apocalyptic events of the first day—one escaping to the river to avoid the vast fire storm, another brutally pinned in the wreckage of a factory, the surgeon numbly treating the injured in a city of 245,000 in which nearly 100,000 were killed and another 100,000 hurt.

The third chapter, "Details Are Being Investigated," carefully continues the method, staying close to the details of survival yet extending the time to the first few days after the explosion and introducing into the account some dim comprehension of the nature of the bomb and the extent of the devastation. The fourth and concluding chapter, "Panic Grass and Feverfew," expands the account at a pace with the expanding effects of the bomb, moving from the onset of radiation sickness some days after the explosion to a summary of the characters' lives one year after the bomb was dropped—one crippled, another destitute, others either hospitalized or strangely lacking in energy. Here Hersey adds further details about the bomb and the statistics of devastation but keeps the account closely pinned to the activities and reflections of his six survivors.

Hersey's language is always kept under rigid control—a plain, direct language that rarely reaches for rhetorical effect and remains subordinate to character and event. Occasionally Hersey allows the prose to develop a calculated irony, as when he writes of one of the characters, struck by falling books in the explosion, that "There, in the tin factory, in the first moment of the atomic age, a human being was crushed by books" (p. 23). But mostly the tone of the book is one of artful understatement— appropriate for the muted, uncomprehending suffering of the survivors, and appropriate for the reader; the tone allows him to experience, through a matter-of-fact language pitched carefully below the inherent level of the event, what otherwise might have been unendurable, overwhelming consciousness rather than heightening it.

For example, Hersey describes in these muted terms the suffering in a park into which the wounded have jammed themselves:

> To Father Kleinsorge, an Occidental, the silence in the grove by the river, where hundreds of gruesomely wounded suffered together, was one of the most dreadful and awesome phenomena of his whole experience. The hurt ones were quiet; no one wept, much less screamed in pain; no one complained; none of the many who died did so noisily; not even the children cried; very few people even spoke. And when Father Kleinsorge gave water to some whose faces had been almost blotted out by flash burns, they took their share and then raised themselves a little and bowed to him, in thanks. (pp. 48-49)

The language here is reserved in the same reserved way the Japanese lived through the horror of Hiroshima. Hersey reenacts the sense of resignation of the Japanese yet in no way lessens the horror. The last lines of the work in the schoolbook tones of a child—"They were looking for their mothers. But Kikuki's mother was wounded and Murakami's mother, alas, was dead"—conclude the work characteristically: close to the details of character and deeply understated, yet profoundly saddening.

*

The recording angel method of *Hiroshima* can be underscored by contrast with another example of Hersey's literary nonfiction, *The Algiers Motel Incident* (1968). In this work Hersey operates differently, appearing directly in the work and permitting the reader, as Macdonald said of Agee, to allow for the writer's personality and involvement in the account as a distortion of the picture. And for such a dramatic reversal of method Hersey offers an explanation not unlike Agee's: the material was too "dangerous" for authorial invisibility and the traditional methods of literature and journalism.

The book recounts one of the darker moments in the Detroit rioting of 1967 that followed the assassination of Martin Luther King—the execution by police officers of three young black men in a black-operated motel. When police (accompanied at one time or another by national guardsmen, state police, and private guards) broke into the motel on the third night of rioting, they were searching for snipers. They found a group of black men and two white girls but no snipers. What followed, as Hersey reconstructs it, was a period of incredible brutality during which the men and the girls were systematically and savagely beaten. Before what one of the policemen described as the "game" was over, three of the men had been shot to death.

From this point Hersey follows out the slow disclosure of the murders, suggests official efforts to suppress the incident once the explanation that the men had been killed in an open firefight had been discredited, and relates the frustration and bitterness of the black community over the reluctant machinery of white justice. The story is brought through the death of Robert Kennedy and a federal conspiracy charge against three suspended Detroit policemen pending before the courts.

Such a summary suggests a narrative coherence that the book does not have. Hersey tells the story largely in the participants' words, presumably caught on tape and set down with little editing. To these direct statements, he adds pieces of official documents, reports of hearings and investigations, and his own very cautious speculations—all given not in chronological sequence but in a shifting, back-and-forth, patchwork account. The end product, as Hersey intends, is a fragmented book, a book "not so much written as listened to, in bits and pieces."[12]

Hersey explains the decision to "listen" to his material rather than "write" about it in a chapter on methods. The decision arose, he says, from a sense of the urgency of the material which forced him to appear directly in the account rather than through the indirect artifices of fiction or the conventions of journalism. In his earlier nonfiction he had scrupulously kept himself out of the work, choosing to "come through" to the reader only through the writing—that is, through selection and tone. "But this account," he explains, "is too urgent, too complex, too dangerous to too many people to be told in a way that might leave doubts strewn along its path; I cannot afford, this time, the luxury of invisibility" (p. 30).

In writing the book Hersey felt the need for "total conviction," and he describes the altered method this required:

> This meant that the events could not be described as if witnessed from above by an all-seeing eye opening on an all-knowing novelistic mind; the merest suspicion that anything had been altered, or made up, for art's sake, or for the sake of effect, would be absolutely disastrous. There could be no "creative reconstruction." (p. 33)

Doubts and contradictions had to be left as such. Quotation marks could be used only when verbatim material was at hand. No names could be changed. The story was to be told as much as possible in the actual words of the participants; and when Hersey entered the account with opinion or conjecture, he and it had to be labeled as such. And all of this scrupulous care for the material was not, however, in the "fraudulent tradition of American journalism," to be understood as objectivity. "There is no such thing as objective reportage. Human life is far too trembling-swift to be reported in whole; the moment the recorder chooses nine facts out of ten he colors the information with his views" (p. 34). Hersey's "listening" rather than "writing" approach to his material was simply a recognition of the impossibility of objectivity and an unwillingness, because of the "dangerous" nature of the material, to set up this time as an all-knowing, all-controlling recording angel. Likewise, the chapter on methods was intended to reveal "some of my bias for discount," allowing the reader, at least in theory, to participate actively in evaluating the material and to come to his own conclusion. (p. 34).

Overall, the method of the book is strongly reminiscent of *Let Us Now Praise Famous Men*, with the large exception that save in the chapter on methods, Hersey rarely enters the narrative in his own person. The characters in *The Algiers Motel Incident* have their reality in their own language as set down by Hersey rather than, as in Agee's work, in the writer's exhaustive telling about them through personal recollection. The weight of Agee's book ultimately falls, through him, on the reader, on the frustrated effort to praise famous men adequately; the reader remains separate from the sharecropper families, in his own realms of reality, yet tries to reach across the chasm of separation to establish an intellectual and above all emotional relationship with them. Hersey, who with Agee eschewed literary and journalistic devices for bridging the gap between writer-reader and subject, keeps the focus on untangling the "incident" and following the legal aftermath. We witness the material with a clear sense of separation from it, but the weight of the book remains with the material, on what happened and why.

Hersey radically alters the method of *Hiroshima* not through a reverence for the material that forces distance from it but because of its dangerous ingredient of racism. He says the hope of the book is not so much to secure justice for the murdered men, but to open a "door-crack glimmer of illumination" on the essence of racism; and as a white writer, he is painfully careful to avoid any suggestion of racism in the construction of the book (or from its results: he says in the methods chapter that he will accept no money from the work). Above all, Hersey seems to feel that as a white writer, he cannot presume to deal with the material in the manner of *Hiroshima*—invisible, controlling, shaping for effect—but must take a stenographic role, tracking down the material but shaping and ordering it as little as possible and clarifying his own presence.

The decision to make himself visible and refrain from "writing" is therefore a way of removing all doubt about his own role as a white writer. It is a way of admitting the gap between his own life and the black lives he is confronted with. At one point, describing black-family life, he writes: "This will be but a substitute for the reality that a black writer could give you at this point; I am what I am" (p. 167). It is one way, in other words, of freeing himself from any tincture of racism in a book about racism.

Notes

1. Wolfe, *The New Journalism*, p. 44.

2. Wolfe, *The New Journalism*, p. 44.

3. James Agee, *Let Us Now Praise Famous Men* (Boston: Houghton Mifflin, 1941), p. ix. Hereafter, page references appear in the text.

4. Quoted in *Documentary Expression and Thirties America*, by William Stott (New York: Oxford University Press, 1973), p. 304.

5. Stott, *Documentary Expression and Thirties America*, p. 311.

6. Wolfe, *The New Journalism*, p. 44.

7. Dwight Macdonald, *Dwight Macdonald on Movies* (New York: Prentice-Hall, 1969), p. 12.

8. Plimpton, "Truman Capote: An Interview," p. 190.

9. Wolfe, *The New Journalism*, p. 46.

10. Dwight Macdonald, "The Triumph of the Fact," *Against the American Grain* (New York: Random House, 1962), p. 424.

11. John Hersey, *Hiroshima* (New York: Knopf, 1946), p. 80. Hereafter, page references appear in the text.

12. John Hersey, *The Algiers Motel Incident* (New York: Knopf, 1968), p. 264. Hereafter, page references appear in the text.

8

Recording Angel and Amateur Philosopher

I

If Truman Capote's *In Cold Blood* (1965) has a single distinguishing feature, it is that it is "written" in exactly the way *Hiroshima* is "written" and *The Algiers Motel Incident* is not. Throughout, Capote dominates the material, cutting, shaping, arranging for literary effect. Although the general method is that of the recording angel, the book is not simply a record; although the subtitle says it is "The True Account of a Multiple Murder and Its Consequences," its aim is far more ambitious. The truth Capote seeks, while remaining true to documentary fact, is literature's truth, that sense of being drawn into a world of meaning and inner coherence. This is what Alfred Kazin was referring to when he said the book "has a palpable design on our emotions. It works on us as a merely factual account never had to."[1]

In Cold Blood works on us the way novels do—or used to. It is that old-fashioned spellbinding kind of "novel" that draws us out of ourselves and into the shaped world of the storyteller. Capote's intention, as he made clear in a flood of interviews following publication, was to write a work that was formally a documentary, a work of record, yet that was also a piece of "creative writing" in that it was made as interesting as fiction and done as artistically. And it would have the traditional novel's gradually unfolding sense of meaning. Instead of presenting the reader with a full plant, Capote said, with all the foliage, a seed is planted in the soil of the mind, and the seed, skillfully cultivated by the writer, flowers into a design that unifies the work and informs us what we are to feel and understand about the experience.

Capote christened the work a nonfiction novel, and it remains the purest example in recent literary nonfiction of the effort to apply the techniques of fiction to the materials of reporting in order to create the effects of the traditional realistic novel. No other work of literary nonfiction is so resolutely literary in its intentions. Kazin remarked that one of the most notable things about Capote's statements about the book was his honoring of the profession of the novelist. Although the book stands at the beginning of the recent literary interest in nonfiction, it does indeed pay homage to the novel through its aim of wringing a work of novel-like art from a truthful account.

Capote dismissed most earlier efforts at combining fact and fiction as either lacking in fictional techniques or employing those techniques with less than full skill. His work was different—a "serious new art form"—in that it employed a full range of fictional methods and employed them well. The form, Capote said, "demands that the writer be completely in control of fictional techniques—which means that, to be a good creative reporter, you have to be a very good fiction writer."[2] For Capote, the skills of the novelist were essential ingredients in the nonfiction novel, just as the effect of the novel was the essential aim of the work.

At the same time the book is impressive as a journalistic record. It is a staggering job of reporting; and according to Capote, most of the material he gathered was never used. What *is* used is wholly persuasive and often authenticated by a skillful use of internal reference that makes clear, if the reader pauses to think about it, that the material was available to Capote through official records, interviews with principals in the account, or his own footwork. (There is an irony here. Although the work is so strongly literary, it probably has more documentary apparatus in it than any other example of recent nonfiction: letters, diary accounts, statements, direct quotation from interviews, etc.) The accuracy of the book, however, was questioned by Phillip K. Tompkins in an *Esquire* article that appeared shortly after its publication. Tompkins's point was that the artistic intentions of the book caused Capote to shape the account unconsciously in a way that called into question its factual authority. He faulted Capote on several details, including some crucial details of the murder scene, but the weight of his criticism came down on Capote's sympathetic portrayal of Perry Smith as against Tompkins's conclusion that Perry was an "obscene, semiliterate and cold-blooded killer."[3]

Such inaccuracy, if it exists, is of course devastating. If Capote has distorted Perry's character, the book is fatally weakened as a "true account." But most readers know nothing of the Clutter murders beyond what Capote relates and so are in no position to measure the book as Tompkins does. Even if they could, such detective work might seem of small importance for the book patently reaches beyond its factual grounding to grasp the reader in the manner of the novel. It seeks to be, finally, a work of the literary imagination, and it is on this level that the reader can best measure it.

*

The technical device in the book that has drawn most notice is Capote's skilled use of parallel narratives juxtaposed through quick cinemalike crosscutting. Throughout the work two stories are always being told: first the stories of the killers, Dick Hickock and Perry Smith, set against those of the murdered Clutters, later Dick and Perry set against the forces of law and order. Structurally the book is divided into four sections of nearly equal length; each section is in turn divided into a series of detailed vignettes, most of them fairly brief, that switch back and forth between the main narratives and build strong feelings of suspense.

The opening section, "The Last to See Them Alive," develops a tension between the two killers on the road moving toward their "score" and the unsuspecting Clutter family going about their settled daily routine. Capote moves deftly back and forth between the killers and their victims; the reader, knowing full well what will happen (the opening paragraphs tell of the "four shotgun blasts that, all told, ended six human lives," Dick's and Perry's lives as well as those of the four Clutters), watches helplessly as this settled fate is worked out and wonders how the violence will take place.[4] But although the first section leads up to the murders of the Clutters, Capote does not provide the scene. Instead he ends the crosscutting between the Clutters and the killers with Nancy Clutter writing in her diary before going to bed and Dick and Perry driving up the lane to the Clutter house; then he turns abruptly to the discovery of the bodies the following morning.

The second section, "Persons Unknown," moves from the discovery of the killings to the beginning detective work—and begins the dramatic shift away from the first meaning of the book's title, the cold-blooded murders of the Clutters, to the second meaning, the cold-blooded murders of Dick and Perry by the state. It moves the story, in other words, in the direction of the "consequences" referred to in the subtitle, consequences that clearly draw far more deeply on Capote's literary ambitions in the book than on the deaths of the Clutters. In this section the parallel narratives continue, but now the movement is back and forth between the killers at loose on the road and the developing machinery of justice that Capote centers in the person of Al Dewey of the Kansas Bureau of Investigation, the figure who will eventually restore the distance between the alien worlds that came violently together on the night of the murders.

In this section Capote individuates the killers further by exploring their backgrounds and differences in personality—and he settles on Perry as the more sympathetic of the two. At one point he repeats, from both Dick's and Perry's points of view, a scene in which Dick runs down a dog alongside the road. He also introduces into the account three documents that deepen the reader's insight into Perry, though Capote provides them without comment—a long account of Perry's life written by his father, a letter from his sister, and an analysis of the sister's letter written by Perry's pretentious but insightful prison friend, Willie-Jay. The section ends with a final piece of dramatic juxtaposition that draws the reader's attention back to the murdered Clutters. Al Dewey, walking through the Clutter house, recalls a dream his wife had in which Bonnie Clutter said to her, "To be murdered. To be murdered. No. No. There's nothing worse. Nothing worse than that. Nothing" (p. 154). From that scene Capote switches to Dick and Perry hitchhiking in the Mojave Desert and gaily singing as "marching music" the "Battle Hymn of the Republic" (p. 155).

The passage points up Capote's effective use of detail. In the scene in which Dewey recalls his wife's dream, Capote writes about the Clutter house that "the atmosphere of a house still humanly inhabited had not . . . been diminished":

> In the parlor, a sheet of music, "Comin' Thro' the Rye," stood open on the piano rack. In the hall, a sweat-stained gray Stetson hat—Herb's—hung on a hat peg. Upstairs in Kenyon's room, on a shelf above his bed, the lenses of the dead boy's spectacles gleamed with reflected light. (p. 152)

Dick and Perry, walking in the desert, carry a straw suitcase, the contents carefully specified:

> Perry's souvenirs, plus three shirts, five pairs of white socks, a box of aspirin, a bottle of tequila, scissors, a safety razor, and a fingernail file; all their other belongings had either been pawned or been left with the Mexican bartender or been shipped to Las Vegas. (p. 154)

Throughout, the book is concretely grounded in just this manner. Wolfe argues that such careful recording of detail is one of the major devices of literary realism borrowed by recent nonfiction, perhaps even the central device in that it is the source of the absorbing quality of realism, that is, of realism's power to draw the reader inside a narrative. Surely much of the mesmerizing quality of *In Cold Blood* is located in Capote's use of specific detail in building up a rich texture for the work, together with the suspense created by the alternating parallel narratives.

The third section, "The Answer," brings the story through the arrest and confessions of Dick and Perry. The climax of the section comes with Perry's account of what happened at the Clutter house on the night of the murders, the material up to which Capote had built at the end of the first section but had not provided. The material is not dramatized but given as a monologue by Perry with prompting questions from Dewey and a second detective. The suggestion has been made that Capote's decision to hold back the account of what happened on the night of the murders to some two-thirds of the way through the book and then leave it undramatized shifts the book away from a sensational account in the vein of a *Police Gazette* story toward more of a psychological concern with why the murders were committed and who committed them, Dick or Perry or both together. Whatever Capote's intention, the details of the murder are decidedly played down, sublimated into the broader emotional aim of the work to evoke the reader's feeling for Dick and Perry as well as for the Clutters, to view them all as victims. Perhaps this could not be done if the reader were allowed to become preoccupied with the grisly details of the killings. When jurors are shown photographs of the bodies of the Clutters, whatever feeling they have had for the killers seems to vanish:

> Altogether, there were seventeen prints, and as they were passed from hand to hand, the jurors' expressions reflected the impact the pictures made: one man's cheeks reddened, as if he had been slapped, and a few, after the first distressing glance, obviously had no heart for the task; it was as though the photographs had prised open their mind's eye, and then forced them to at last really *see* the true and pitiful thing that had happened to a neighbor and his wife and children. It amazed them, it made them angry, and several of them . . . stared at the defendants with total contempt. (p. 281)

The last section, "The Corner," treats the trial, offers the final psychological explanation for the killings ("when Smith attacked Mr. Clutter he was under a mental eclipse, deep inside a schizophrenic darkness, for it was not entirely a flesh-and-blood man he 'suddenly discovered' himself destroying, but 'a key figure in some past traumatic configuration' "; or as Perry phrases the same view: "They [the Clutters] never hurt me. Like other people. Like people have all my life. Maybe it's just that the Clutters were the ones who had to pay for it"), telescopes into a few scenes the some 2,000 days Dick and Perry spend on death row, and concludes with their executions by hanging. (p. 302) But just as Capote does not end the first section of the book with an account of the deaths of the Clutters, he does not end the last section with an account of the deaths of Dick and Perry.

The executions are described but without dwelling on details. During Perry's execution, Capote focuses on the reaction of Dewey, who keeps his eyes shut until he "heard the thud-snap that announces a rope-broken neck" and who, rather than feel a sense of completion, finds himself recalling a meeting with Nancy Clutter's friend, Sue Kidwell, in the Garden City cemetery nearly a year before. (p. 340) That experience, Capote says, had somehow ended the Clutter case for the detective. Over the grave of the Clutters he talks with the girl, a college junior, "just such a young woman," Dewey realizes, "as Nancy might have been." The meeting over, Dewey leaves the cemetery and Capote concludes the book: "Then, starting home, he walked toward the trees, and under them, leaving behind him the big sky, the whisper of wind voices in the wind-bent wheat" (p. 343).

The manner of ending the book suggests its basic aim and why Capote insisted it was like a novel and not merely a documentary record. The point of the book is not to inform us about what happened to the victims, both the Clutters and Dick and Perry, so much as to draw out our feelings for them, and indeed make us respond with feeling to the entire account. The epigraph clearly announces this intention with a poem from Francois Villon, roughly translated as follows:

O Brother men who after us shall thrive,
Let not your hearts against us hardened be,
For all the pity upon us ye give,
God will return in mercy unto ye.

And the book's ending confirms it, drawing us out of the account on waves of feeling for both the Clutters and the killers, for lives unrealized and cut short, and leaving us with an evocation of the serene order of the landscape, an order that has been violated yet persists, somehow larger and more enduring than man's evil acts.

The openly emotional ambitions of the work point to an important distinction between Capote's use of the "*New Yorker*-Objective mode" and Hersey's use of the same method in *Hiroshima*. *In Cold Blood* has a palpable design on our emotions, as Kazin said, because of Capote's tendency to draw very close to his characters, to establish a "certain intimacy" between the characters and himself, to make them *his* characters. "Through his feeling for the Clutter family *and* its murderers," Kazin added, "Capote was able to relate them—a thought that would have occurred to no one else."[5] While Hersey, though obviously sympathetic with his characters and detailed in his treatment of them, keeps an even distance, Capote establishes an intimacy of varying intensity with all his figures—with Nancy Clutter, with Dewey, most notably with Perry; the effect is to draw us inside the experience, to bring us uniquely close to a multiple murder and its consequences in that we come to feel it from all angles: the victims', the killers', the law enforcement officers'. This is the "thought that would have occurred to no one else"—an intimacy and feeling for all the subjects that brings the reader inside the "case" to a degree quite unprecedented in fact writing and tangles the emotions in complex ways.

The book is shaped from the beginning to cause the reader to experience such emotional complexity. From the first and obvious meaning of the title we move to a second—the eye-for-an-eye vengeance of the state that results, in Capote's view, from an inadequate understanding of criminal responsibility. Al Dewey, mirroring the reader's response, cannot put the death of Nancy Clutter out of mind yet he responds with compassion to Perry Smith. At the execution Dewey feels nothing for Dick, a "small-time chiseler." "But Smith, though he was the true murderer, aroused another response, for Perry possessed a quality, the aura of an exiled animal, a creature walking wounded, that the detective could not disregard" (pp. 340-341). Dewey manages to separate the two worlds that came together on a Kansas farm on the night of November 14, 1959—the tidy, rooted world of the Clutters and the alienated, on-the-road world of the killers; Dewey rescues order from chaos. But the order of the book's ending is suffused with emotional complexity that embraces Nancy, who had all the world provides and was murdered, Perry, who had nothing and was murdered too, and Dewey, the stoical detective who, like the reader, must contend with both.

*

In Cold Blood, Capote said, was an experiment to see if the novel's emotional reach could be built on the foundation of a wholly factual account. In this sense the book is a brilliant success. It demonstrates as well the novelist's capacity to draw out and universalize the implications of a specific event while remaining true to the historical truth of the event; it touches that "something beyond the evidence," in Forster's phrase, that is literature's truth while remaining an extraordinary documentary record. In an early and perceptive article on the book, William Wiegand referred to a remark of Hemingway's (as recalled by A. E. Hotchner) suggesting Capote's accomplishment: the difference between journalism and literature, Hemingway said, is that the latter has about it a "magnification" which will endure.[6] *In Cold Blood* powerfully magnifies the experience it so carefully reconstructs. For all its documentary apparatus, it finally bears slight resemblance to documentary journalism; it is simply, as Capote said it was meant to be, a work of literary art.

But if the book is a success in Capote's terms, it also marks out the limits of his ambition. The very documentary materials that give the book its air of authenticity limit the emotional effects that can be wrung from the account. If the novel's strange "echo that's meaningless"—in Capote's reference to Forster mentioned earlier—is distinctly present in the book, it is not present to the extent it is in the richest fiction, including Capote's own. Capote can go only so far as the facts allow in his recreation of the principal characters—Nancy and Perry and Dewey—and his interpretation of events; and measured against the novel at its best, this does not seem far enough. He cannot invent "facts" in order to penetrate his characters all the more or enrich the implications of the account. He is restrained, finally, by what can be known and implied from the evidence. To feel more and perceive more, the reader needs to know more, more than the nonfiction novelist can finally provide.

In a review of the book Diana Trilling brusquely dismissed Capote's claim to have invented a new art form. She wrote:

> One can dispose quickly enough of the issue Truman Capote has himself made salient in discussion of his book—*In Cold Blood* is not a novel, as Mr. Capote would have us think; it is "only" a book, a work of journalism of an exceptionally compelling kind. Whatever else it may or may not be, the novel is a literary form in which the writer is free to make any use he wishes of material drawn from real life. It was Mr. Capote's decision to stay wholly with the facts of the Clutter murders; in their presentation he employs various strategies learned in his practice of fiction. This does not mean he has discovered a new fiction form nor—for that matter—a new form of nonfiction.[7]

This understanding of *In Cold Blood* seems to me broadly correct. But too quick a placing of the work as just "journalism of an exceptionally compelling kind" obscures its considerable novelistic power and the extent to which Capote has turned a documentary account into a piece of creative writing that is surely as interesting as fiction and crafted as artfully. Capote did not invent a serious new art form, but *In Cold Blood* remains one of the most novellike of all works of recent literary nonfiction. If it points up the limits of nonfiction's capacity to fulfill the reader's desire to touch that something beyond the evidence, it also reveals the distance the writer can move in that direction while remaining strictly within the historical record.

II

If Capote paid homage to the novel by insisting that *In Cold Blood* was a nonfiction novel, Norman Mailer did the same by subtitling *The Armies of the Night* (1968) "History as a Novel/The Novel as History." His work, like Capote's, was not to be confused with ordinary journalism or documentary; it sought a more elevated level suggested by the polar terms "history" and "novel." The opening chapter begins with a lengthy quotation from *Time* magazine describing Mailer's antic activities during the Pentagon demonstration in the fall of 1967 and ends with Mailer commenting: "Now we may leave *Time* in order to find out what happened."[8] But the book is not meant simply as a corrective of mass media inaccuracy. It is also the demonstration of a form of journalistic writing that in Mailer's view is appropriate to the time in that it reaches beyond journalism's superficiality for fiction's interior truth.

"Journalism is chores," Mailer said at the beginning of his report on New York graffiti. "Journalism is bondage unless you can see yourself as a private eye inquiring into the mysteries of a new phenomenon."[9] To inquire into mysteries was the function of the novelist, or at least Mailer's kind of novelist, and what he tried to bring to all his journalism. He established himself as a novelistic private eye—or as he put it in *Of a Fire on the Moon*, a "detective of sorts"—turned to factual materials that are conceived as the mysteries of a new phenomenon.[10] If the world could be divided, as Mailer liked to divide it, into the provinces of "measure" and "metaphor," he came down on the side of metaphor; his task, the novelist's task, was always to deliver the metaphorical meaning, the philosophical answer. In Richard Poirier's phrase, Mailer always portrayed himself as the "savior of the imagination"; and this role was always set in contrast with the chores and bondage of ordinary journalism.[11]

Describing in *Advertisements for Myself* the column he wrote in the *Village Voice* in the mid-1950s, Mailer said: "What they [the owners of the newspaper] did not know was that the column began as the declaration of my private war on American journalism, mass communications, and the totalitarianism of totally pleasant personality."[12] *The Armies of the Night* can be understood as a continuation of that private war on journalism in that such imagined conflict helps Mailer define a form of journalism with distinct literary aspirations. Early in *Armies* Mailer quotes a conversation with the poet Robert Lowell:

> Lowell: "Yes, Norman, I really think you are the best journalist in America."
> Mailer: "Well, Cal, there are days when I think of myself as being the best writer in America." (p. 22)

The passage suggests Mailer's ambition in all his journalistic work to carry out the high aims of the imaginative writer, to transcend the limits of journalism by taking for himself the role of the private eye inquiring into the mysteries of a new phenomenon.

*

Like Agee's book, *Armies* is aggressively personal and confessional, and partly for the same reason. When Mailer returned to his experience at the Pentagon peace march to write about it (originally for *Harper's* magazine), he discovered that it "insisted on becoming a history of himself over four days, and therefore was history in the costume of the novel" (p. 215). The focus on the self—or, in Mailer's lexicon, a novelistic approach—was necessary not only because he was an active participant in the event but also because the reader was to learn about the march through his eyes, and so had to be in a position to evaluate that vision. As with Agee, we know the experience in and through Mailer, and that knowledge depends as much upon who he is as upon what the experience was. But whereas Agee's focus on the self grows out of deference toward the material, Mailer's stems from a surface concern with media inaccuracy.

The media had created a "forest of inaccuracy" in the reporting of the event, and all in the name of objective journalism. Mailer's frankly personal account may not be more accurate but it is meant to allow the reader, through knowledge of the writer, to make adjustments for bias, laziness, or whatever. If the reader is to glimpse the "horizon from a forest," the writer "must build a tower"—the tower of the self. Mailer goes on:

> Of course, the tower is crooked, and the telescopes warped, but the instruments of all sciences—history so much as physics—are always constructed in small or

large error; what supports the use of them now is that our intimacy with the
master builder of the tower, and the lens grinder of the telescopes . . . has
given some advantage for correcting the error of the instruments and the
imbalance of his tower. (p. 219)

In other words, since we know something of the reporter in this instance—
his person revealed rather than, as is usually the case, hidden—we have
some means for correcting the errors inherent in all human work.

Given such a view, all personal disclosure is theoretically relevant to the
account. Such disclosure creates our "intimacy" with the writer and hence
with his history. So Mailer confesses his distaste for demonstrations ("idiot
mass manifestations") like the Pentagon march and his unease with the
liberal mind, describes in detail a scatological performance at a rally on the
night before the march, candidly probes his feelings for Dwight
Macdonald, Paul Goodman, Robert Lowell and other fellow
demonstrators, and tells about his wife. (p. 18) The lengthy job of building
the tower takes up the first three-quarters of the book, the part Mailer calls
"History as a Novel." This done, he turns to a "most concise Short
History"—that is, a quick view of the horizon from the vantage point of the
tower to discover now "what the March on the Pentagon had finally
meant" (p. 216).

But the Short History lasts only a few pages, and Mailer soon informs us
that "the conceit one is writing a history must be relinquished" (p. 254).
Both parts of the book are to be understood as novelistic because, Mailer
now says, "an explanation of the mystery of the events at the Pentagon
cannot be developed by the methods of history—only by the instincts of the
novelist." The personal, novelistic methods of the first part of the book
must continue—and continue because the meaning of the march is
"interior" and only the novel can sufficiently cope with interior truth. The
novel, Mailer writes, "must replace history at precisely that point where
experience is sufficiently emotional, spiritual, psychical, moral, existential,
or supernatural to expose the fact that the historian in pursuing the
experience would be obliged to quit the clearly demarcated limits of
historic inquiry" (p. 255).

And so, history abandoned, Mailer plunges on novelistically to a
methaphorical ending, emphatically marked for the reader in a section
called "The Metaphor Delivered." What the confrontation at the Pentagon
between the forces of law and order and the tide of demonstrators finally
meant is offered in a wildly rhetorical metaphor of America as a pregnant
woman about to give birth either to "the most fearsome totalitarianism the
world has ever known" or to a "babe of a new world brave and tender,
artful and wild" (p. 288).

Commentators on the book have been divided in their response to the
ending, some find it nonsense, others wholly fitting and earned. To me it

has, in its strong inflations, an air of self-mockery. Veteran Mailer readers will find his speculations on totalitarian America not unfamiliar, but the mockery seems not so much directed to an overworked line of thought as to the very notion of delivering a metaphor that finally yields the meaning of the Pentagon march. In Mailer's nonfiction the "instincts" of the novelist are what matter; the novelist subjects the material to an imaginative scrutiny rather than to the delivery of the historian's statement of meaning or even to the novelist's all-embracing metaphor. To read Mailer for his conclusions, as one suspects he well knows, is to miss what is most interesting in his work.

Mailer's directly personal style of nonfiction is more than simply tower building to allow the reader to adjust the account for bias or quirks of personality. For one thing, the book draws its overall narrative movement from a broad dialectic between Mailer's reluctance to get involved in the march—because of the risks, his irritation with the liberal mentality, his dislike for some of the leading participants, and his sense of himself as what he calls a Left Conservative—and his awareness of the nation poised at a point of crisis. As Warner Berthoff has said, the book establishes a tension between Mailer's "private and public motives, self-regard and national crisis," moving from his reluctant answering of the telephone with the invitation to take part in the march to the release of his instinctive sympathy for the demonstrators and resistance to the war and his final arrest and brief stay in jail.[13]

But the personal focus of the book reaches beyond this broad narrative motion. Early in the account Mailer undertakes to explain why he focuses the work on his own activities and speculations rather than on more central figures like David Dellinger or Jerry Rubin, the real architects of the march. The reason is that the march "was an ambiguous event whose essential value or absurdity may not be established for ten or twenty years, or indeed ever" (p. 53). To focus on the central figures would therefore be misleading and would suggest more clarity about the event than it possessed. So Mailer centers the account on himself, an eyewitness and a participant but also an ambiguous figure and so an appropriate figure for probing an ambiguous event.

Yet the argument for the concentration on the self is put in even larger terms. Here a lengthy quotation is needed:

> Either the century was entrenching itself more deeply into the absurd, or the absurd was delivering evidence that it was possessed of some of the nutritive mysteries of a marrow which would yet feed the armies of the absurd. So if the event took place in one of the crazy mansions, or indeed *the* crazy house of history, it is fitting that any ambiguous comic hero of such history should be not only off very much to the side of the history, but that he should be an egotist of the most startling misproportions, outrageously and often unhappily self-

assertive, yet in command of a detachment classic in severity. . . . Such egotism being two-headed, thrusting itself forward the better to study itself, finds itself therefore at home in a house of mirrors, since it has habits, even the talent, to regard itself. Once History inhabits a crazy house, egotism may be the last tool left to History. (p. 54)

The problem facing the historian of the Pentagon march is not just the forest of media inaccuracy but the question of how to deal with an "absurd" period in human history, a period in which history has entered into a "crazy house." The familiar detached methods of history will no longer do; they must now be coupled with a self-assertive and self-mocking egotism "of the most startling misproportions" that may enable the writer to cut through the cant, hypocrisy, and baffling contradictions of the time. If the history of the time is to be seen as entering a "crazy house," then, Mailer concludes, the "last tool" left to the serious writer may be a concentration on the self.

In part what is implied in Mailer's view is the bringing to bear, through a form of personal journalism, of what Berthoff has called the "saving counterforce of personality" in an increasingly flattened and impersonal world.[14] But Mailer seems to have more in mind, an ambiguously dual way of seeing that is at once detached and aggressively personal, comic and serious, egotistical and reflective—a way of writing contemporary history that combines observation and reporting with a guiding preoccupation with the self.

*

But finally a concentration on Mailer's "egotism" seems to me no more effective a way of getting at the heart of *Armies* than a concentration on his use of the terms "history" and "novel." Mailer's personal journalism is not really very personal; it omits or obscures far more autobiographical material than it includes. Poirier has remarked that Mailer's self-revelations are mostly anecdotes about his public performances and tell us little about his private life; they are not confessions so much as "presentations of a self he makes up for his own as much as for the reader's inspection."[15] Of more use is Mailer's conception of a kind of journalism redeemed by seeing oneself as a private eye inquiring into the mysteries of a new phenomenon. In *Armies* this view takes the form of Mailer's description of himself as a "good working amateur philosopher" (p. 91)— or as he puts it in *Of a Fire on the Moon*, one always poised for a "philosophical launch."[16] The question to ask, then, is what the amateur philosopher comes up with, what the philosophical launch amounts to.

Early in the account, Mailer offers quick character portraits of the other celebrities in the march, especially Macdonald and Lowell, who together with himself make up the book's triumverate of Novelist, Critic, and Poet. Of the two, Macdonald is treated with an uncharacteristic gentleness because, Mailer says, the critic had greatly influenced him. It was

Macdonald who had "given him an essential clue which was: look to the feel of the phenomenon. If it feels bad, it *is* bad." Mailer adds that he could have learned the same lesson from Hemingway; nevertheless, "Macdonald's method had worked like Zen for him—at the least it had helped to get his guns loose. Macdonald had given the hint that the clue to discovery was not in the substance of one's idea, but in what was learned from the style of one's attack" (p. 25). Later Mailer returns to the point, though "now he locates the influence elsewhere: "Hemingway after all had put the key on the table. *If it made you feel good, it was good.* That, and Saint Thomas Aquinas's 'Trust the authority of your senses,' were enough to enable a man to become a good working amateur philosopher." Mailer adds here that it is this philosophical "vocation" that sets apart the "ambitious novelist" from the mere entertainer or storyteller, "a John O'Hara!" (pp. 90-91)

Mailer's philosophical method is to try on ideas, to work them around in language, in order to gauge his intuitive reaction. But as important as the ideas themselves is the method of dealing with them, the intuitive, gut-reaction style of one's attack, the process of locating the feel of the phenomenon through which one is constantly trying to imagine one's way to the truth of events. For Mailer this search becomes a continuing trial-and-error process in which various details and personalities of the Pentagon demonstration are subjected to the inquiring eye to see what if anything they can be made to reveal.

At times, the feeling apparently good, Mailer drives on at philosophical length, pushing his reflections as far as they will go. And at other times, bad vibrations apparently returning, he abruptly drops a line of thought to return to the events of the march. The book moves back and forth between descriptive passages (though rarely *just* descriptive) and flights of philosophical reflection, the one spinning out from the other as Mailer looks to the feel of the experience, trying to become the working philosopher or inquiring eye that separates him both from journeyman journalist and journeyman novelist.

And since it is apparently true for reader as well as writer that the clue to discovery is in the style of one's attacks, the trial-and-error process is not eliminated from the final version of the work. It is left in as part, perhaps the chief part, of the tower building that provides the reader with some intimacy with the writer and thus some means for correcting the imbalances of his account; it becomes as central to Mailer's approach as his self-mocking account of his performance as master of ceremonies at a rally on the night before the march. It allows the reader to glimpse the amateur philosopher actually at his work, sometimes hitting his mark, sometimes not, yet always operating with an "unprotective haste" (p. 216).

Some of Mailer's lines of thought come to nothing—as, for example, when in pursuit of the meaning of the Vietnam war, he concludes that "the

good Christian Americans needed the war or they would lose their Christ."
The point is so bizarrely reasoned that Mailer ends the section with an
appropriate bit of self-mockery: "Mailer slept. Given this portrait of his
thoughts who would make book he did not snore?" (p. 189) Equally
fruitless, to my mind, is Mailer's meditation on small-town America and
the war:

> So he was reminded of a probability he had encountered before: that, nuclear
> bombs all at hand, the true war party of America was in all the small towns, even
> as the peace parties had to collect in the cities and the suburbs. Nuclear warfare
> was dividing the nation. The day of power for the small-town mind was
> approaching—who else would be left when atomic war was done would reason
> the small-town mind, and in measure to the depth of their personal failure,
> would love Vietnam, for Vietnam was the secret hope of a bigger war, and that
> bigger war might yet clear the air of races, faces, in fact—technologies—all that
> alienation they could not try to comprehend. (p. 154)

But at times thought leads to speculations that are memorable. An
example is Mailer's extended reflection on a scene in which the
demonstrators and the military, both groups young, confront each other
across "six inches of no-man's-land" near the Pentagon. (p. 255) "They
looked across the gulf of the classes," he writes, "the middle classes and the
working classes," and he proceeds to consider the scene in light of sharp
class differences. The middle-class young are instinctively the most critical
of America for "neither do they work with their hands nor wield real power,
so it is never their lathe nor their sixty acres" that is threatened. Likewise,
the middle class is the most alienated from America, "forever alienated in
childhood from all the good simple funky nitty-gritty American joys of the
working class." Mailer concludes:

> The working class is loyal to friends, not ideas. No wonder the Army bothered
> them not a bit. But the working class bothered the sons of the middle class with
> their easy confident virility and that physical courage with which they seemed to
> be born—there was a fear and a profound respect in every middle class son for
> his idea of that most virile ruthless indifferent working class which would
> eventually exterminate them as easily as they exterminated gooks. (pp. 257, 258)

But at last neither Mailer's various ruminations on method nor his hit-
and-miss amateur working philosophy makes *Armies* a work of great
vitality. The best parts of the book are those in which Mailer keeps his nose
close to his reporting, to the chores of journalism, yet invests those
moments with novelistic weight and resonance. He does not any more than
the despised news accounts deliver a grand "discovery of what the March
on the Pentagon had finally meant, and what had been won, and what had
been lost"; neither does he broadly "elucidate the mysterious character of
that quintessentially American event" (p. 216). But he does allow us to
ponder the event at a deeper level than journalism ordinarily permits by
making its mysterious character all the more mysterious, by giving greater
complexity to what was already complex. And this he accomplishes in a

variety of small ways that combine detailed reporting with revealing reflection.

Describing a short speech by Robert Lowell before a group turning in draft cards, Mailer says the poet's voice was carried "on a current of intense indignation":

> Each word seemed to come on a separate journey from the poet's mind to his voice, along a winding route or through an exorbitant gate. Each word cost him much—Lowell's fine grace was in the value words had for him, he seemed to emit a horror at the possibility of squandering them or leaving them abused, and political speeches had never seemed more difficult for him, and on the consequence, more necessary for statement. (p. 74)

The same scene fills Mailer with a kind of gloom in that he is overtaken by a sense of "modesty"—and he "hated this because modesty was an old family relative, he had been born to a modest family, had been a modest boy, a modest young man, and he hated that, he loved the pride and the arrogance and the confidence and the egocentricity he had acquired over the years." The modesty sweeps over him when he sees men his own age turn in draft cards and suddenly fears for himself because of the "consequences of this weekend in Washington, for he had known from the beginning it could disrupt his life for a season or more, and in some way the danger was there it could change him forever." At age forty-four he admits to divided feelings about the demonstration; it was "obviously no time to embark on ventures which could eventually give one more than a few years in jail." Yet he cannot escape the consequences, and at last he confronts the decisiveness of the moment in a sentence of striking power: "As if some final cherished rare innocence of childhood still preserved intact in him was brought finally to the surface and there expired, so he lost at that instant the last secret delight he retained in life as a game where finally you never got hurt if you played the game well enough" (pp. 77, 78).

The finest parts of *The Armies of the Night*, like this passage, grow out of Mailer's reporting and his participation in events but also reach beyond— in turns of phrase and vividly rendered moments and flights of amateur philosophizing—toward those places no history can reach. In Mailer's literary nonfiction, this is always the aim and occasionally the achievement: to penetrate the ordinary realms of journalism and history for the novelist's world of feeling and mystery. For as he says elsewhere, "there is no history without nuance."[17]

Notes

1. Kazin, *Bright Book of Life*, p. 210.

2. Plimpton, "Truman Capote: An Interview," p. 191.

3. Quoted in *The Worlds of Truman Capote*, by William L. Nance (New York: Stein and Day, 1970), p. 213.

4. Truman Capote, *In Cold Blood* (New York: Random House, 1965), p. 5. Hereafter, page references appear in the text.

5. Kazin, *Bright Book of Life*, p. 211.

6. William Wiegand, "The 'Non-fiction' Novel," *New Mexico Quarterly*, 37 (Autumn 1967), 251.

7. Diana Trilling, "Capote's Crime and Punishment," *Partisan Review*, 33 (Spring 1966), 252.

8. Mailer, *The Armies of the Night*, p. 4. Hereafter, page references appear in the text.

9. Norman Mailer, "The Faith of Graffiti," *Esquire*, May 1974, p. 77.

10. Norman Mailer, *Of a Fire on the Moon* (Boston: Little, Brown, 1970), p. 14.

11. Richard Poirier, *Norman Mailer* (New York: Viking, 1972), p. 91.

12. Norman Mailer, *Advertisements for Myself* (New York: Putnam's, 1959), p. 278.

13. Berthoff, *Fiction and Events*, p. 304.

14. Berthoff, *Fiction and Events*, p. 308.

15. Poirier, *Norman Mailer*, p. 155.

16. Mailer, *Of a Fire on the Moon*, p. 14.

17. Norman Mailer, *Miami and the Siege of Chicago* (New York: World, 1968), p. 56.

9

Subjective Reality and Saturation Reporting

I

In his essay "Art and Fortune," written some thirty years ago, Lionel Trilling found it questionable whether any American novel since *Babbitt* had told us anything new about our social life. It seems doubtful that the intervening years would have caused Trilling to alter his judgment, for if anything the American novel has paid even less attention to the social world. Such, at any rate, was Tom Wolfe's view of the matter. He repeatedly took the contemporary novel to task for its failure to examine social life, let alone say anything new about it, and celebrated the new literary nonfiction as taking up the abandoned task. He offered his own work as a case in point, and especially *The Electric Kool-Aid Acid Test* (1968), a study of California in the 1960s as "the very incubator of new styles of living." [1]

The book tells of the beginnings of the drug culture in California in the early sixties as it centered on the activities of the novelist Ken Kesey and a group of followers known as the Merry Pranksters. The description is unusually full and rendered in rich detail. In addition, Wolfe also provides an interpretation of what he describes, and in so doing comes to view Kesey and the Pranksters as mythic American adventurers, engaged in a journey that is both a literal tour through the fragmented American landscape of the sixties and an inward journey in search of the full possession of consciousness.

This dual journey takes on in Wolfe's treatment, as do similar journeys recounted in American literature, strong religious implications. Kesey emerges as a prophetic figure, calling the Pranksters and the whole psychedelic movement to a renewed search for a fuller experience of life. In this role, he recalls to mind an Emersonian strain in American life, the sense of the archetypal American as an adventurer searching out the furthermost reaches of life. Emerson called himself an endless seeker with no past at his back. Kesey too becomes that classic American figure, plunging recklessly into the future toward some long-sought "Edge City" of the American imagination.

Paradoxically, in trying to reveal something new about our social life, Wolfe recalls something very old. He casts Kesey in the mold of the American adventurer continually lighting out for the territory ahead of the rest and reenacting in a new time and place what Daniel Boorstin has called our national "love affair with the unknown."[2] He thus links the amazing drug world of the sixties with the venerable American cultural myth of continuous exploration—a myth that celebrates search more than discovery, going more than arriving.

If Wolfe tries in *Acid Test* to tell us something new about our social life, he also tries to tell about it in a new way. In the author's note to the book, he says, "I have tried not only to tell what the Pranksters did but to re-create the mental atmosphere or subjective reality of it. I don't think their adventure can be understood without that."[3] Elsewhere he said that what most interested him about literary nonfiction was the "use of techniques to enable the writer to get inside the subjective reality—*not* his own, but of the characters he's writing about." And he went on:

> In other words, to use stream of consciousness so that I can present the mind of Ken Kesey—as I try to do in a number of chapters of *The Electric Kool-Aid Acid Test*—to get completely inside Kesey's mind, based on interviews, tapes that he made, or letters that he wrote, diaries, and so on. It's still a controversial thing to use, but I was not at all interested in presenting *my* subjective state when confronted with the Pranksters or whatever they had done. It was rather to try to get Kesey's completely.[4]

In Cold Blood, in Wolfe's view, was not as sophisticated as Capote's fiction because it did not try to get inside the minds of the characters. Capote "probably had sufficient information to use point of view in a more complex fashion," Wolfe remarked, "but was not yet ready to let himself go in nonfiction." Wolfe likewise found Mailer's use of point of view limited. Mailer utilized a third-person autobiographical approach that could create an "altogether pleasant mood," as it did in *The Armies of the Night*, but this obviously limited his ability to take the reader "inside the points of view or central nervous systems" of characters other than himself. Generally, Wolfe admired nonfiction that resisted both the omniscient and the autobiographical and attempted "the far more difficult feat of penetrating the psyches, the points of view," of characters, that attempted to give "the reader the feeling of being inside the character's mind and experiencing the emotional reality of the scene as he experienced it."[5]

All of this, a concern with new social developments and a sophisticated use of an interior point of view, was meant to be amply demonstrated in *Acid Test*. It was literary nonfiction that explored neglected subject matter and turned upon it the most complex and experimental—and from a journalistic standpoint, the most questionable—of literary methods.

*

Wolfe begins by telling how he stumbled on the drug subculture in California. All he knew in the beginning was that Kesey was a respected novelist who had gotten in trouble over drugs and had fled to Mexico to avoid a stiff sentence for possession of marijuana. Wolfe got the idea of going to Mexico to do a story on him. But while he was trying to discover Kesey's whereabouts, the novelist sneaked back into California and was arrested by the FBI. Wolfe hurried to California and was allowed a brief interview in which Kesey spoke cryptically about the need to move beyond LSD, to "graduate from what has been going on, to something else." There was no longer any "creativity" in the drug movement, and Kesey saw his own role as helping to "create the next step. I don't think there will be any movement off the drug scene until there is something else to move to" (p. 10).

The meeting with Kesey and the days Wolfe spent in San Francisco afterwards began to enlarge the possibilities of the story. He found that the Beat world of the 1950s that Jack Kerouac had chronicled in *On The Road*, the "whole old-style hip life," was dying and being replaced by a drug world in which Kesey was the acknowledged charismatic leader, the "drug apostle," and that his group, the Merry Pranksters, was the very center of the new activity. He also discovered that Kesey's return from Mexico and his acid graduation ideas were causing the drug world's "first big political crisis." The article had turned into a book, a book that would focus on the acid graduation and the divided response to it but also piece together the events that led up to the creation of "The Life" and Kesey's central role in it. (pp. 12, 13).

Shortly after his arrival at Stanford in 1958 on a writing fellowship, Kesey began taking part in drug experiments at a veterans hospital as a $75-a-day volunteer. His successful novel, *One Flew Over the Cuckoo's Nest*, followed; but as Wolfe reconstructs events, the flow of Kesey's life was now in the direction of the acid life rather than the writing life. People began gathering around him: Neal Cassady, the Dean Moriarty of *On the Road*; the drug experimenter Richard Alpert; writers like Larry McMurtry and Robert Stone; rock musicians and artists and assorted others. In 1963 Kesey moved to an isolated area near La Honda and again a group assembled around him; the Merry Pranksters were born.

In the spring of 1964 Kesey bought a used school bus that the Pranksters crammed with broadcast and recording equipment, painted in brilliant colors, and christened with a sign in front that read "Furthur"—neatly capturing the complex sense of Prankster life, both its serious searching quality and, in the misspelling, its mockery of traditional solemnities—and one in back that read, also appropriately, "Caution: Weird Load." The bus began a madcap voyage to the East, with the Pranksters shooting a movie as they went, blaring rock music from the bus, and generally outraging both citizens and the police—and all the while taking large quantities of drugs.

The trip was wild but not without a purpose—a purpose Wolfe continually alludes to but does not try to explain fully. The trip was a "risk-all balls-out plunge into the unknown," he says, the unknown of group experience and new drug-induced states of consciousness: Edge City. (p. 88). There were risks and bad movements and not all was harmonious on the bus, but the inner journey everyone was on seemed to be leading somewhere. In July the bus reached New York where there was a gathering of Cassady's old pals, Kerouac and Allen Ginsberg, and the Pranksters. In Wolfe's description the meeting is alive with significance, great figures of the counterculture-past brought together with the new prophet and his band, though exactly what significance is left unclear:

> Kesey and Kerouac didn't say much to each other. Here was Kerouac and here was Kesey and here was Cassady in between them, once the mercury for Kerouac and the whole Beat Generation and now the mercury for Kesey and the whole— what?—something wilder and weirder out on the road. It was like hail and farewell. Kerouac was the old star. Kesey was the wild new comet from the West heading Christ knew where. (p. 103)

The closest Wolfe comes to pinning down the meaning of the "Christ knew where" adventure the Pranksters were on is to say that it was somehow religious in nature. He devotes a chapter a third of the way into the book, "The Unspoken Thing," to developing this view:

> How to tell it! . . . the current fantasy . . . I never heard any of the Pranksters use the word religious to describe the mental atmosphere they shared after the bus trip. . . . In fact, they avoided putting it into words. And yet—(p. 125)

If the Prankster experience was essentially religious, it certainly was not so in any of the usual ways. The Pranksters avoided speaking in religious terms and there was no sense of any theology or religious philosophy in the group, no notions of improving the world or of salvation or a life hereafter. Still, Wolfe says, "there was something so . . . *religious* in the air, in the very atmosphere of the Prankster life, and yet one couldn't put one's finger on it. On the face of it there was just a group of people who had shared an unusual psychological state, the LSD experience" (pp. 127-8).

Finally it is this, the emphasis on new experience, that leads Wolfe to consider the meaning of the Prankster adventure in religious terms. All the great religions, he says, "began with an overwhelming *new experience*. . . 'the experience of the holy'. . . 'possession of the deity,' the sense of being a vessel of the divine, of the All-one" (p. 128). In all religious groups there is a feeling of unity because of the new experience; the groups invent special vocabularies, symbols, and life styles; rites are developed— all of which seems strange and incomprehensible to those beyond the charmed circle who have not had the new experience. "Gradually," Wolfe writes, "the Prankster attitude began to involve the main things religious mystics have always felt. . . . Namely, the *experiencing* of an Other World, a higher level of reality" (p. 143).

The religious Other World of the Pranksters was notable for its vividly *present* character, its reversal of any concern with future existence in favor of a search for full participation in the present moment. Wolfe gives detailed accounts of acid trips through the recollections of individual Pranksters, but he leaves to Kesey the interpretation of what was being sought. Kesey speaks about the lag system built into human beings, and especially the lag between sense experience and mental reaction. "One-thirtieth of a second is the time it takes," he claims, "if you're the most alert person alive, and most people are a lot slower than that." The result is a mental life doomed to remembrances of things past. The means for overcoming the lag is of course LSD, the extraordinary means by which one can be moved "out of deadass snug harbor" toward Edge City and the full experience of the moment. When the breakthrough is made and one is at last totally in possession of one's present world, the feeling, Kesey says, is fantastic:

> It'll be like you had a player piano, and it is playing a mile a minute, with all the keys sinking in front of you in fantastic chords, and you never heard of the song before, but you are so far into the thing, your hands start going along with it exactly. When you make that breakthrough, then you'll start controlling the piano. (p. 149)

Once one has been touched by an overwhelming new religious experience, there is a need to extend the new message to others, and in Wolfe's account this explains the direction the Pranksters took after the bus trip. They got the idea of staging "Trips Festivals" and "Acid Tests" as ways of turning on crowds of people to the new sacrament, LSD (this still in the days before California laws against the drug). The Pranksters would throw large parties and through the use of lights and music, as well as LSD, they would try to open the minds of everyone present. According to such an eminent figure in the drug world as Timothy Leary, LSD was to be taken in a carefully controlled and serene environment, but for the Pranksters the setting was as "unserene and lurid" as possible. The idea was that "Everybody would take acid, any time they wanted, six hours before the

Test began or the moment they got there, at whatever point in the trip they wanted to enter the new planet" (p. 234).

The Trips Festivals and Acid Tests were conducted up and down the West Coast and reached a climax in Watts in February of 1966, shortly after Kesey had fled to Mexico to escape the marijuana conviction. Here the LSD was served up in a plastic trash can of Kool-Aid and everyone was invited to help himself, some—like Clair Brush, a young newswoman who gave Wolfe a lengthy account of the experience—unaware of the prank until the effects of the drug set in. The Trips Festivals and Acid Tests staged by the Pranksters and their aftermaths brought the psychedelic movement out of the California bohemian underground and to the attention of the mass media.

But with Kesey in Mexico, the Pranksters lacked a cohesive force and soon split up. Some of the Pranksters regrouped around Kesey in Mexico and there were a few more Acid Tests, but after brushes with the Mexican authorities and growing paranoia about being caught, Kesey decided it was "time to bring the future back to the U.S.A., back to San Francisco, and brazen it out with the cops and whatever else there," and so he came back across the border in elaborate disguise to become the "Prankster Fugitive Extraordinaire in the Baskin-Robbins bosom of the U.S.A." (p. 345) The West Coast drug scene was now in full swing, with Haight-Ashbury in San Francisco the new mecca for young hippies and old bohemians. But rather than try to take control of the broadened movement, Kesey suddenly began to talk about the need to move beyond acid, saying "there's no use opening the door and going through it and then always going back out again. We've got to move on to the next step." When he is told by those quite content in The Life that it is drugs alone that have caused everything, that nothing would have been possible without them, Kesey insists: "No, it's not the drugs. In fact, I'm going to tell everyone to start doing it without the drugs" (p. 364).

And this is what he does, to the consternation of contented acid heads and those profiting from them. When he is finally picked up by the FBI after several hide-and-seek encounters, Kesey announces the Acid Test Graduation. He explains to a TV interviewer:

> It's time to move on the next step in the psychedelic revolution. I don't know what this is going to be in any way I could just spell out, but I know we've reached a certain point but we're not moving any more, we're not creating any more, and that's why we've got to move on to the next step. (p. 380)

At this juncture Wolfe is back to the point at which he entered the story with the Pranksters reassembling in San Francisco around Kesey, now free on bail and preparing for the graduation ceremony in an old warehouse. Invitations are sent out and hundreds show up, including some celebrities and visiting journalists like Wolfe. The heart of the evening turns out to be a rambling talk by Kesey, attired for the event in white leotards. "For a year we've been in the Garden of Eden," he begins. "Acid opened the door to it. It was the Garden of Eden and Innocence and a ball. Acid opens the door and you enter and you stay awhile . . ." (p. 395-6).

At this stage of the evening, the police arrive at the warehouse; and though they leave after merely looking the strange meeting over, Kesey has difficulty pulling the situation back together. "We've been going through that door and staying awhile and then going back out through that same door," he goes on. "But until we start going that far . . . and then going beyond . . . we're not going to get anywhere, we're not going to experience anything new" (p. 397). But Kesey can go no further in his vision, and the graduation soon breaks up into a weird party in which the Pranksters gather together and, in caps and gowns, receive diplomas handed out by Neal Cassady. They graduate, Wolfe asks, "into what on the horizon?"—Kesey's vision of the next step left unspecified. (p. 403)

In the book's final scene Kesey and the Pranksters are shown in a psychedelic nightclub known as The Barn, operating as a Prankster-style musical group. The music they play is, to put it mildly, strange. The Pranksters wear headsets wired to a variable-lag system, so they hear not what they are playing now but a moment ago. "They harmonize off themselves," Wolfe writes, "break up all learned progressions, and only they can hear the full . . . orchestration, a symphony in their cortices, the music of the Prankster . . . ah umm . . . Only the kids in The Barn, can't figure out what's going on . . . It's, like, *weird*" (p. 409). Everyone leaves, and even most of the Pranksters drift off. "It's like a wake," one of them says. Kesey and one other Prankster remain, playing electric guitars and singing a strange dialogue that contains the refrain "We blew it!" (430)

*

The Prankster adventure ends in confusion and failure. But the failure, Wolfe implies, is only temporary, a failure of present vision and direction rather than a repudiation of aims and ambitions. What is "blown" at the end is the Acid Test Graduation; Kesey and the Pranksters cannot bring it off because they themselves seem confused about the next step in the psychedelic movement. Kesey is able to articulate the feeling of stalled movement; the bus is no longer going "Furthur" but simply repeating its journeys. But he is unable to chart new directions. At the end he fails as the prophetic leader because his vision of the future dims.

But again, Wolfe appears to find this failure only temporary. In a brief epilogue, he explains that Kesey got a six-month sentence on a county work farm, that the Pranksters scattered, and that Cassady died in Mexico of apparent heart failure—all part and parcel of the book's dismal ending. But after his sentence, Kesey returned to his Oregon home and began writing again. And the Pranksters began to regroup again. Wolfe concludes the epilogue: "In the spring, various Pranksters . . . began finding their way to Oregon from time to time. Kesey was writing again, working on a novel. The bus was there, parked beside the Space Heater House" (p. 413). The effect of the closing is to reinforce Wolfe's overall interpretation of the Prankster adventure: although the means the Pranksters turned to, LSD, may be problematic, the end they had in view was laudatory.

The book provides moving evidence of the hazards involved in the LSD experience. On the eastward bus trip, a young girl with the Prankster name of Stark Naked goes "stark raving mad," at the final moment shrieking over and over the name of the son she is separated from. The losses here are clear as they are elsewhere in the book. Even Kesey himself is not immune. At one point Wolfe describes him as looking as if he had aged ten years in three months. But Wolfe seems to accept the costs as a necessary part of an otherwise praiseworthy adventure. After describing Kesey's deteriorating physical condition, he shrugs it off by emphasizing Kesey's attitude toward the all-out quest: "No turning back, man! We're on the space ship now . . . going with the flow and we can't duck the weird shit, no matter how weird it is" (p. 194). Likewise, after describing Stark Naked's breakdown, Wolfe tries to place it in the Prankster perspective:

> Stark Naked; Stark Naked; silence; but well . . . That this or a couple of other crackups in the experience of the Pranksters had anything to do with the goofy baboon, Dope, was something that didn't cross the minds of the Pranksters at that point. *Craziness* was not an absolute. They had all voluntarily embarked upon a trip and a state of consciousness that was "crazy" by ordinary standards. The trip, in fact the whole deal, was a risk-all balls-out plunge into the unknown, and it was assumed merely that more and more of what was already inside a person would come out and expand, gloriously or otherwise. Stark Naked had done her thing. (p. 88)

The passage is a key one. Wolfe is re-creating the Prankster response to Stark Naked, but there is nothing to indicate that his own view is any different. The inward trip Kesey and the Pranksters were on was dangerous and exacted its price; there is also the possibility, not dismissed, that it was pointless, an exercise in group delusion. At the end of the Acid Test Graduation, while the Pranksters are gathered together in one of their silent sessions, trying to summon psychic energy, one of Kesey's children begins to cry. A girl's voice from the edge of the onlooking crowd calls out: "See—a-bout—the—child—A—Child—is—crying—That's all—that's—happening—A—child—is—crying—and—no—one—is—do-ing—any-thing—a-bout—it—" (p. 402). The girl represents the voice of "ordinary standards," and there is no certainty that she is not correct; but although Wolfe acknowledges the possibility, he gives it no emphasis. He seems to side instead with the Pranksters' own interpretation of the trip they were on—that it was a risk-all adventure into human consciousness. In the brief author's note that ends the book, he says flatly and with apparent conviction: "For all the Pranksters, as I have tried to show, the events described in this book were both a group adventure and a personal exploration. Many achieved great insights on both levels" (p. 416). And the final image of the bus parked by Kesey's house in Oregon suggests that the strange travels in search of great insights may well begin again.

Indeed, the emphasis on great insights and Kesey's compulsion to keep moving, to keep going through new doors of the mind, locates the adventure within the larger context of a historic search for expanded consciousness and a more complete realization of life. Wolfe seems to view Kesey and the Pranksters as only the latest and most bizarre figures in a long and honorable procession of American experimenters heading out toward the Edge City of human experience, fleeing from the limitations of history in search of the totally experienced present. But whereas in the American past the means to the end of heightened consciousness was usually physical nature—the trackless forest or fenced farm, the village pond or the great river or the flowing trout stream—for Kesey it is nature turned on its head, LSD, the synthetic laboratory product, together with all manner of electronic equipment.

But the drugs and the electronic equipment and all the Prankster antics are the means to inner movement and not an end in themselves. The attempt to move beyond acid comes when Kesey realizes "we're not moving any more, we're not creating any more." "Furthur" is the exactly right Prankster motto, an expression of continual movement without destination. The endless seeking implied in the term may never be rewarded—in one form or another "we blew it" may well characterize all such journeys— but the real point is to be found in the seeking itself, in the reaching out beyond ordinary experience for that which cannot quite be named.

*

At the beginning of the book Wolfe frankly acknowledges his own presence as a reporter. He tells about his original idea to write about Kesey as a fugitive novelist in Mexico, how he interviewed Kesey in San Francisco after he was picked up by the FBI, and how the possibilities of the story began to enlarge for him once he realized Kesey was a leading figure in a drug culture in California that had replaced the hip world of the Beat Generation. He admits to being puzzled by Kesey's strange talk about the need to move beyond acid—and even more puzzled by the strange goings on in the warehouse as the Pranksters prepared for the Acid Test Graduation. He even gives some indication of how the Pranksters responded to his presence:

> The Pranksters took me pretty much for granted. One of the Flag People, a blonde who looked like Doris Day but was known as Doris Delay, told me I ought to put some more . . . well, *color* . . . into my appearance. That hurt, Doris Delay, but I know you meant it as a kindly suggestion. . . . So I kept my necktie on to show that I had pride. But nobody gave a damn about that. I just hung around . . . and I only left to sleep for a few hours or go to the bathroom. (p. 18)

As he hung around the Pranksters, wearing his necktie, Wolfe was drawn into their life. In the constant flow of talk among the Pranksters, "Everybody's life becomes more fabulous, every minute, than the most fabulous book. It's phony, goddam it . . . but *mysto* . . . and after a while it starts to infect you" (p. 21). Gradually in the warehouse he began to see life in the Prankster way and, despite himself, to sense an odd magnificence in it. "Despite the skepticism I brought here, *I* am suddenly experiencing *their* feeling. I am sure of it. I feel like I am in on something the outside world, the world I came from, could not possibly comprehend" (p. 29). But when Kesey joins the Pranksters in the warehouse, Wolfe turns from his own developing feelings to chart the long development that led Kesey to the place and the plans for the Acid Test Graduation.

The turn in the narrative comes when Kesey explains to another reporter the reason he is abandoning the drug movement. Someone has to keep "plunging into the forest," he says, "somebody has to be the pioneer and leave the marks for others to follow" (p. 32). But the price of pioneering is that followers without sufficient faith get left behind. This is what happens to Kesey with his call to move beyond acid; some who previously took him as a prophet drop off the bandwagon, even forming a stop-Kesey movement. In Kesey's lexicon, people without sufficient faith are with him as long as their fantasy coincides with his, but, as Wolfe puts it, "every time he pushed on further—and he always pushed on further—they became confused and resentful" (p. 35).

In a sense this pattern is the story of Kesey's life. It happened when he first appeared on the Stanford campus and was accepted by the local bohemians as a diamond-in-the-rough literary type. That was their fantasy; from the beginning his fantasy was different, and it became increasingly different as he began the volunteer drug experiments. Soon Kesey had left Stanford behind and was on his way to the communal circus at La Honda; those who could not accept his new fantasy shook their heads and said he had gone off the deep end. For Wolfe, Kesey's constantly plunging further while those who could not accept his pioneering role dropped behind becomes a structural device for piecing together the various steps in the odyssey bringing Kesey to his current fantasy, the Acid Test Graduation. From the warehouse fantasy, Wolfe turns back in the narrative to the Stanford fantasy and so on through Kesey's involvement with the Pranksters and his fugitive days until the story is returned to the present and Wolfe's own developing feeling for the Prankster life.

The result is a structure in which two pieces of present action, the planning for the Acid Test Graduation and then its execution and strange aftermath, are separated by a long sustained flashback retracing Kesey's steps. In the lengthy central part of the book, Wolfe for the most part absents himself as a direct presence, and appropriately so, since he was not present during these events and had to reconstruct them from interviews, tapes, films, and written accounts. When he does appear, he is trying to understand the Prankster experience rather than recount it, as in "The Unspoken Thing" chapter when he links what was taking place among the Pranksters after the bus trip to the origins of all new religious groups. When Wolfe finally returns to the present scene, some 250 pages after leaving it to fill in the past, he again clearly establishes his presence: "And the Pranksters . . . by and by . . . I find them in the Calliope garage on Harriet Street. . . . I kept peeking around in the crazy gloom of the place . . . and I couldn't figure out what they had to be so exultant about. It beat me" (p. 378).

But if Wolfe is a direct presence in at least a portion of the account, it is not *his* subjective reality that is meant to be offered to the reader. The "I" provides only a degree of reportorial authenticity for the book, an explanation within the narrative of how Wolfe became involved with Kesey and the Pranksters and began taking them seriously; the focus is meant to be on the characters being written about, on *their* subjective reality. The main device Wolfe uses to get inside his material is, as he said, a kind of stream of consciousness that attempts to re-create from within the mental atmosphere of people and events. In doing this he draws on an uninhibited repertoire of punctuation marks and sentence structures and an expressive vocabulary that ranges from pop-culture vernacular to high academic—a pyrotechnic display intended to get the reader inside the Prankster world rather than simply permit him to view it from without.

The level of stream of consciousness varies considerably throughout the book. Often it involves nothing more than slipping into the idiom of the Pranksters or the acid world. The section Wolfe apparently sees as the most fully realized example of the method—he reprints it in *The New Journalism* to show how stream of consciousness can be used in nonfiction—is called "The Fugitive" and recreates Kesey's growing paranoia in Mexico about the police closing in on him. It opens with a burst of typographical effects:

> Haul ass, Kesey. Move. *Scram. Split flee high vanish disintegrate.* Like *run.*
> Rrrrrrrrrrrrrrrrrrrrrrrev revrevrevrevrevrevrevrevrev or are we gonna have just a late Mexican re-run of the scene on the rooftop in San Francisco and sit here with the motor spinning and watch with fascination while the cops climb up once again to *come git you*—
> THEY JUST OPENED THE DOOR DOWN BELOW, ROTOR ROOTER, SO YOU HAVE MAYBE 45 SECONDS ASSUMING THEY BE SLOW AND SNEAKY AND SURE ABOUT IT (p. 287)

Wolfe follows this opening with a reporter's paragraph that establishes the situation: Kesey, high on drugs, is in the upper-room of a beach house in Puerto Vallarta, just on the edge of the jungle, and believes that a car passing outside contains Mexican police hunting for him.

The chapter moves ahead with Wolfe trying to re-create Kesey's enflamed consciousness on several levels, with the capitalized sections most completely inside him, and at the same time locating the scene with pieces of external information—and all the while Kesey is counting down the seconds before the police will break into the room and arrest him. When time finally runs out, Kesey rouses himself to action and dashes into the jungle: "THIS IS TRULY IT . . . . ZERO : : : : : : : : 000000000 : : : : : : : : RUN!" (pp. 298-9) The chapter ends with Kesey safely hidden in the jungle, his paranoia subsiding as he smokes grass, with Wolfe once again after his subjective reality, this time Kesey's feeling that, totally inside the present moment, he is free from the jungle insects and all other terrors:

> . . . if he sits very still, the rush lowers in his ears, he can concentrate, pay total attention, an even, even, even world, flowing into *now*, no past terrors, no anticipation of the future horror, only *now*, *this* movie, the vibrating parallel rods, and he can *feel* them drawn into the flow, his, every verruga fly, velvet ant, murine fleas and crabs, every chinch and tick, every lizard, cat, palm, the very power of the most ancient palm, held in his will, and he is immune— (p. 305)

But does it work? Do we really get the subjective reality of Kesey and the Pranksters? Do we get inside their mental atmosphere?

Wilfrid Sheed scoffed, engagingly, at Wolfe's claims to evoke his subjects as they really are. He argued that Wolfe was far more a novelist than a journalist, in the sense that he drew everything—whatever the accuracy of his reporting—into his imagination and what came out was a Wolfian version of events and people, what Sheed called "Wolfe-truths." His real subject was his imagination as affected by the subjects he wrote about. Sheed pointed out that Wolfe's language, supposedly attuned each time to the subject at hand, was strikingly the same whether he was writing about stock car racing, Leonard Bernstein, or the Merry Pranksters. His language was the language of literature, a "distorting mechanism," a language that "obliterates uniqueness and drags everything back to Wolfe's cave." And this, Sheed concluded, was "what artists do, and it's strange that he [Wolfe] refuses to recognize it. In his frenzied assault on the Novel, he allies himself with some quite talented but prosy journalists who don't do any of this, in order to beat up on a form much closer to his own."[6]

Wolfe said he was able to delve deeply into Kesey's mind in "The Fugitive" chapter because he had unusually rich records to work with—lengthy letters Kesey had written at the time, tapes made while he was in the jungle, and material developed in interviews with Kesey and others. Much of the direct interior monologue, Wolfe said, was taken from Kesey's letters. For my part, I am persuaded that the chapter as well as the entire book is adequately based on Wolfe's research; I can believe, as Wolfe insisted, that interior material—including Kesey's paranoia—is available to the persistent reporter. Nonetheless, I have only scant feeling of actually being inside Kesey's mental process; here as elsewhere in the book I have little sense of Kesey's subjective reality. Indeed, one of the odd features of the book is that despite Wolfe's strenuous efforts to bring Kesey to life, whether in terms of his mental atmosphere or simply of his physical presence, he remains a dim figure, neither very clearly seen nor understood.

To say this is not to imply that the book is not a substantial piece of reporting, but instead to suggest that Sheed is essentially correct: *Acid Test* is more Wolfe than Kesey, more Wolfe's imaginative reconstruction of the origins of the drug culture in the 1960s than a report on the thing itself. In "The Fugitive" chapter, the reader is more instructed in the varieties of Wolfe's style than in the actual workings of Kesey's paranoid psyche; or perhaps more accurately, even if the reader *is* drawn inside Kesey's mind, this journey pales before the fireworks display of Wolfe's *writing* about Kesey's mind. No one reads Wolfe just for his reporting, Sheed said; likewise, I suspect no one is principally engaged in *Acid Test* by Wolfe's portrayal of the subjective reality of Kesey and the Pranksters, however accurate the portrayal may be. It is Wolfe's frantic imagination as affected by Kesey and Pranksters that is the book's most attractive feature.

It may well be, as Sheed speculated, that Wolfe's insistence on his role as a reporter has the effect of keeping his nose "down near the details where it works best." But upon the materials of reporting, Wolfe "imposes his own consciousness, his own selections and rhetoric" and consequently he is "halfway over the border into the hated Novel." Sheed said the book "may well be the best literary work to come out of the Beat Movement, yet the material is quite inaccessible to anyone else." He went on:

> I pity the poor writer following Wolfe to the Coast hoping to find what he found. It is all in Wolfe's skull. The Beats probably weren't like that at all, as far as anyone else could see. In fact, rumor has it that all they wanted to do was splash his white suit.[7]

But even if Kesey and the Pranksters were exactly as Wolfe says they were, it is still Wolfe's highly personal rendering of them and the interpretation he draws of the meaning of their experience that makes the book a satisfying literary experience and one of the best works to come out of the renewal of interest in literary nonfiction. Like all recent examples of the form, the writer imposes upon the materials of reporting his own consciousness, selections, and language and so moves the work in the direction of the novel. That is the whole point of the form. Wolfe's "halfway" just leans more in the direction of the novel than the work of some others who also made excursions into literary nonfiction.

II

In Wolfe's talk about the New Journalism he allied himself, Sheed said, with some "quite talented but prosy journalists" whose work had little in common with his. Despite their intensive reporting and use of fictional devices, these prosy journalists remained just that; Wolfe, on the other hand, belonged in the literary camp—or there, at least, more than with the journalists. The effect of all Wolfe's talk about being a journalist among journalists, Sheed concluded, was simply to "give literary glamour to some good journeyman reporters . . . and provide some company for himself."[8]

The writer Wolfe most often allied himself with was Gay Talese. Wolfe credited Talese with one of the earliest examples of the New Journalism, a 1962 *Esquire* article on Joe Louis, and with major contributions to the development of the form. Talese returned the favor, frequently citing Wolfe as a fellow traveler in the effort to turn reporting into art. But in fact Wolfe and Talese, as Sheed suggested, were on quite different sides in their interest in literary nonfiction. Partly the difference was one of subject matter; Talese noted that Wolfe was attracted to the new, the current, while he was more interested in the enduring and the impact of the past on the present. But the larger difference between the two was one of writing method and a consequent difference of effect.

In interviews Talese referred to himself as an artist, and like Wolfe he saw himself in competition with novelists. "I think I can write as well as any novelist going today," he said. "I don't have great respect for the novel. I don't want to write the novel." And he went on: "[P]eople who really care about reporting are artists, can be artists as much as a novelist can be an artist." But in his public statements Talese emphasized that he was a *reporter*-as-artist: "I'm dealing with facts, I'm reporting; but I am *not* unambitious, and I am pushing this as much as I can in my own way to fulfilling an ambition I have to be an artist."[9] The distinction was important, for however ambitious Talese was in pursuit of a form of nonfiction that read like fiction, his work remained notably journalistic. If Wolfe could be placed on the literary end of the new nonfiction spectrum, Talese belonged on the journalistic end. If Talese was a reporter reaching for the levels of art, Wolfe was an artist who also happened to be a reporter.

By such a rough distinction I do not mean to suggest that Talese ranks a cut below Wolfe in some nonfiction pecking order. Talese is a solid reporter and a careful writer, and he chooses to allow these admirable qualities to be the most distinctive features of his work. He does not dramatize his own role as reporter, as Mailer does, nor is he a virtuoso stylist like Wolfe or an elaborate mannerist like Capote; only in the effort to reveal interior states does he have any technical concern in common with Wolfe, and even this similar concern is realized quite differently. Since he has taken a more familiar reportorial stance toward his work, Talese has been subjected to less criticism than Wolfe, Mailer, and Capote. The accuracy of his reporting has aroused little suspicion, and his avoidance of a highly visible use of literary devices has lessened charges of imaginative re-creation. From a traditional journalistic standpoint at least, Talese has seemed the least troublesome of the new nonfiction writers.

*

Honor Thy Father (1971) tells of the relationship of a Mafia father and son, Joseph Bonanno and his son Bill. The father is a gangster in the old style, Sicilian born, bold, dramatic, elegant—a movie-version Mafia chieftan. The college-educated son is not his equal, though he struggles to be, nor are the times the same; he honors his father by trying to follow his footsteps, but finally he cannot emulate him. "It's a book about failure, really," Talese said, "—a book about how the second generation failed to match the sum of the strengths of the older generation."[10]

The book opens with a gangland kidnapping of Joseph Bonanno on a New York street in the fall of 1964 that catapults the son into leadership of the Bonanno organization. The leadership cannot be exercised, however, with the father's fate still in doubt; and after several weeks of hiding in fear of his own life, Bill drives to Arizona, where his father has a home and Bill had gone to school. After his college days and his marriage, Bill had settled down to a seemingly normal family life in Arizona, joining the Kiwanis Club, working for the March of Dimes, and having infrequent contact with his father, then living in semi-retirement in Tucson. But when the Apalachin meeting of 1957 brought the Mafia to renewed public attention, Joseph Bonanno fled to California and Bill was left in charge of his father's interests.

Bill's secure life was suddenly changed, though the change was not without appeal. He took a more active role in his father's affairs, Talese writes, "because he had to and because, in a strange way, he wanted to":

> It was an interesting discovery, his awareness that he wanted to do it, wanted to become deeply involved in what he knew was precarious. It meant giving up the life in Flagstaff, the respectable conventional life that most Americans led and that he thought he could lead, wanted to lead. But now he was not so sure, doubting that he truly belonged even though he gave the appearance of belonging. He probably did not belong anywhere except at his father's side or in his father's shadow because, in spite of his education, he was not really qualified to do anything important in the so-called legitimate world.[11]

The real reason for coming to the aid of his father, an uncertain identity and lack of jobs skills aside, was that he loved the man and could not separate himself from him. He could do nothing less than honor his father.

Bill had moved to New York and was deeply involved with the father's business, as well as with the crosscurrents of Mafia feuds, when his father was kidnapped just prior to an appearance before a grand jury. From an anonymous telephone caller, Bill learned his father was all right and that he should do nothing, but he unwisely discloses this to a lawyer and the lawyer announces it to the press. As a result Bill is summoned to testify about his father's whereabouts; and when he refuses, he spends three months in jail for contempt of court.

Through the winter of 1965, while his father is still missing, Bill directs the Bonanno organization's affairs, which in addition to various illegal activities included a feud with a faction of the group led by Gaspar De Gregorio. On January 28, 1966, a truce meeting, set up in an Italian neighborhood in Brooklyn, turns out to be an ambush by the De Gregorio faction, and Bill narrowly escapes death. The result is a Mafia war that came to be known in the press as the Banana War. Joseph Bonanno, now back in public after the mysterious kidnapping, moves into his son's Long Island home and, constantly surrounded by bodyguards, takes control of the household (much to the discomfort of Bill's wife Rosalie), as well as the gang's activities.

One result of the sporadic killings of the Banana War was a shortage of money among organization members. The war was costly to finance; and with members off the streets and in hiding, regular revenue-producing activities were reduced, causing some gang members to resort to hijacking trucks to gain needed cash. When Bill in February of 1968 takes a trip to Arizona to defend himself in a government tax case, he uses a credit card belonging to one Don A. Torrillo, a man on the fringe of the organization, and signs Torrillo's name to the charge-account slips; this careless mistake was one he presumably would not have made under normal circumstances. Bill is eventually charged with fraudulent use of the credit card, convicted, and sentenced to four years in prison, a term he begins serving at the book's end.

The credit-card case illustrates one of Talese's main themes: that Mafia life is not the glamorous thing popularly pictured but a life of tedium, suspicion, and small details magnified out of all proportion. Bill is finally brought down not by a gangland slaying or a major criminal activity, but for unthinking use of a credit card in a time of stress. Talese says directly:

> When the average American citizen thought about the Mafia, he usually contemplated scenes of action and violence, of dramatic intrigue and million-dollar schemes, of big black limousines screeching around corners with machine gun bullets spraying the sidewalk—this was the Hollywood version and while much of it was based on reality it also wildly exaggerated that reality, totally ignoring the dominant mood of Mafia existence; a routine of endless waiting, tedium, hiding, excessive smoking, overeating, lack of physical exercise, reclining in rooms behind drawn shades being bored to death while trying to stay alive. (pp. 354-355)

But if Mafia life is less romantic than popular imagination has it, many Mafia leaders try to live up to the romantic image. Talese repeatedly stresses Bill Bonanno's considerable ego, his compulsion to travel first class on airplanes and rent Cadillacs and display a manicured, sun-tanned appearance in courtroom sessions when in reality he is flat broke and living in cheap hideaways. Such display, Talese adds, not only fed Bill's conception of himself as a gangland leader but was an essential duplicity in a secret society where appearances of power and prosperity were everything.

The final part of the book gives a full account of Bill's trial in New York on the fraudulent use of the credit card. The owner of the card testifies that the card was extorted from him through fear and that he did not freely give permission for its use. Torrillo's testimony, Talese implies, is the result of pressure placed upon him by government agents in exchange for special treatment in another case. Bill's lawyer is able to discredit the story by showing that Torrillo reported the loss of the card some two months after the man he originally gave it to (who in turn gave it to Bill) was killed in the Banana War. But the fraudulent use of the card is beyond dispute, and Bill is convicted after short deliberation by the jury.

The four-year sentence is lighter than expected, and Bill feels a strong sense of release when the case is concluded. Free on bond, he returns to San Jose, California, where his wife and children are now living, to await the start of his prison sentence. During this period, which stretches through the spring, summer, and fall of 1970, he tries, unsuccessfully, to explain to himself and his children why he is going to jail while others, though they committed what Bill takes to be far greater crimes, are free. He unwisely used the credit card, he reasons with himself, because of his preoccupation with the gangland war and the cash shortage it caused.

But he realizes this explanation is part of a larger issue, the forces that turned his life into that of a Mafia leader. And these forces are also those that had shaped his father's life, forces that the son inherits because of his need to honor his father. His father's story is that of a man who fled the Sicily of Mussolini and came to America during the glamorous and lawless era of Prohibition and chose a Mafia life rather than an immigrant existence of digging ditches or driving trucks. Joseph Bonanno had in fact been offered a job as a barber when he arrived in America and had politely refused. Talese writes:

> If he had accepted it, the recent history of the Bonannos would doubtless be quite different today—Bill almost certainly would not now be going to jail; but if his father had accepted the job, he would not have been Joseph Bonanno, the vain, proud, unusual man that Bill had tried without success to emulate.

Talese adds that Bill saw his father as "a misplaced masterpiece of a man who had been forged in a feudalistic tradition but had been flexible enough to survive and prosper in midtwentieth-century America" (p. 490).

Bill admires and loves his father, and can do nothing other than honor him by following in his footsteps despite the clear knowledge that he is not the same man his father is. He even has the suspicion that his father went into hiding and turned the organization over to him at the worst possible time in order to save his own reputation. He knows, at any rate, that his relationship with his father has been destructive for himself—and that this destruction is his chosen fate. At his sentencing, the judge had lectured him: "There is hardly any excuse for the type of conduct of which you were found guilty. . . . You are not the product of a ghetto. . . . I don't see that because of family relationships you were under any great handicap. . . . You could have gotten a job" (p. 483). But Bill is certain he could not have gotten much of a job with the Bonanno name. To do so would have meant changing his name and disowning his father, and if he had done that "he would not have been Bill Bonanno, a son who deeply loved his father although recognizing that the relationship had been destructive; curiously, more destructive to him than it had been to his father, who had not spent time in jail, who had fewer legal problems than Bill, and was no doubt more cunning, more careful, stronger, more selfish perhaps, and less loving" (p. 491).

Bill concludes his reflections on his relationship with his father—and Talese his interpretation of that relationship—with the realization that he had been lured into his father's world of feudally organized crime just when that world was rapidly passing away. In the fall of 1970 Joseph Bonanno was one of the last remaining Mafia dons. Most of the others who had come to the country in the 1920s were dead or old and, Talese notes, "their Americanized sons were too smart, or not smart enough, to replace them. Bill Bonanno was among the last of his generation to make the attempt, and he would not have tried had his father not been so successful and awesome, offering to Bill what appeared to be great opportunities and advantages, a status at birth that had seemed almost regal" (p. 491).

Bill at length is told to report to prison on January 18, 1971. The book's last chapter recounts his emotional leave-taking of his father and his wife and four children. He is not deeply distraught at the prospect of prison; he will be forty-one when released, and he looks forward to starting something new, though he has no idea what. But the separation from his family is a harsh experience, and Talese ends the book with a grim and depressed Bill flying alone to Los Angeles and unceremoniously turning himself in to a federal marshal.

*

The reader turning to *Honor Thy Father* for inside information about the workings of the Mafia is disappointed. Talese has little more such information than a good crime reporter might, and in fact several times he quotes newspaper stories speculating on Mafia activities. The picture of the Mafia one does get in the book is of a tired and out-dated organization, harrassed by law-enforcement agencies and with its power and affluence greatly inflated in the press. Talese devotes little attention to the precise illegal activities of such Mafia organizations as that of the Bonannos. Joe Bonanno is said to have refused to traffic in drugs, but beyond this bit of information Talese is vague about the organization's dealings, which has the effect of making Bill and his father seem unfairly persecuted by the police and the federal authorities.

Talese's real concern is elsewhere, with the domestic relations of one Mafia family. In an author's note he says that what drew his attention to the Bonannos was an interest in how Mafia men "passed the idle hours that no doubt dominated their days, about the roles of their wives, about their relationships with their children," and this is the material his book concentrates on. (p. 512) The book is filled with long and engrossing scenes in which Talese details various domestic activities that usually involve Bill's interaction with his father or his wife: a family dinner in which Bill cooks chicken on an outdoor barbecue; the marriage of Rosalie's sister at the Stanford University chapel that Bill refuses to attend because a cousin of his was not invited; Rosalie's leaving Bill while his father is using their home as a refuge and taking the children along with her in a brief fling at freedom in a rented beach house.

A typical scene occurs late in the book when Bill, living with his family in San Jose, and under indictment in the credit-card case, is shown driving his two sons and his wife to a music school at which the boys will be examined after spending weeks taking guitar lessons. During the examination the boys are awarded trophies for their competence on the guitar, but it soon becomes clear that the whole thing is really intended as a sales pitch for expensive electric guitars. Talese reproduces the scene in careful detail, showing Rosalie's embarrassment when she finally realizes what is taking place and Bill's desire to keep up appearances, which forces him to brave the situation through to the point of agreeing to pay $1,000 for two guitars even though he is impossibly in debt at the time. On the way home Bill insists that he will somehow come up with the money despite Rosalie's insistence that they cannot afford it. The resolution comes the following day when Rosalie tells the salesman on the phone that the guitars must be returned because she cannot arrange for transportation to the lessons that come with them; Bill overhears the conversation but now says nothing.

The scene helps establish Talese's characterization of Bill and Rosalie— Bill impulsive, a victim of his ego, and ever the optimist; Rosalie cautious, sensible, wanting only a normal existence within the mainstream of American life. And the scene furthermore helps make Talese's overall point that the life of a Mafia leader is filled with the same domestic crises that afflict everyone else, the need to maintain working relations with wife, children, relatives, and community and the need to be concerned with where the money is coming from. A life in the Mafia only adds to life's ordinary dilemmas.

The scene also illustrates Talese's explanation of how he was able to get close enough to the Bonannos to get at the intimate details of domestic life. The scene is replete with extended dialogue, indicating that Talese must have been present (in the author's note he says he spent considerable time with the family in San Jose), and he was allowed to be present in such circumstances, he suggests, because of the Bonanno family's need to communicate with each other. Both in his personal relations with them and as the writer of the book, he served as a go-between, saying things for them that they could not say themselves. He was able to get close to Bill, he says, because Bill felt misunderstood; likewise, Rosalie confided in him as a way of communicating both with Bill and her father-in-law. "I had become a source of communication," Talese concludes his author's note, "within a family that had long been repressed by a tradition of silence" (p. 517).

The explanation provides a justification for the broad method of the book, which is to concentrate on the father-son and husband-wife relations within the Bonanno family through a cautious reproduction of internal states of mind. Talese gives us Bill's mind and Rosalie's, though in the manner of the traditional psychological novelist and never to the stream-of-consciousness depths that Wolfe attempts. A typical rendering of Bill's mind comes near the end of the book when he is trying to assess for himself the reasons he is going to jail:

> He thought of how radically things had changed in his own lifetime with reference to social mores and customs, marriage and sex, literature, films. He remembered that once he has been expelled from boarding school because he led a group of students into *Forever Amber*, a film that now, in a period of permissiveness and nudity, was mild indeed. He had been born near the end of Prohibition when moralists were still condemning the vices of alcohol, yet now liquor was not only legal and acceptable but was a substantial source of income to the government that prior to 1933 had opposed it. . . . They were changing the laws with regard to acts that thousands of men long dead had been arrested for doing—it was all a matter of timing, Bill thought morosely, sitting behind lowered shades in his living room, it was a matter of being at the right place, the right time, and being on the winning side of wars, and having enough money to avoid using a credit card offered by Perrone, and having enough sense to not sign the name "Don A. Torrillo." (p. 506)

Such modest and balanced internal rendering raises few if any of the questions that have troubled critics of literary nonfiction. One can easily believe that the material was available to Talese, and in the writing his cautious treatment of it raises few cries of fabrication.

A small exception is Talese's treatment of Joe Bonanno. In the author's note he indicates that the father maintained a skeptical attitude toward the book project, and elsewhere he said that he could not have established the intimacy with Joe Bonanno that he did with his son. Nevertheless, the reader is occasionally given a glimpse of Joe Bonanno's thoughts—being told, for example, that the father was "comforted by his son's presence in New York," that he was "apprehensive, and yet strangely proud" when Bill is elected to a high-ranking position in the organization. (p. 224) At the beginning of the book, describing Joe Bonanno's abduction in New York, Talese says he was "seeming enraged and stunned," but then goes on to say, without the qualification, that he "tried to regain his composure, to think clearly as the men forced him along the sidewalk, his arms numb from their grip" (p. 4). But with the meticulous care given the rest of the book, one wants to assume these small details were also made available to Talese, if not by Joe Bonanno himself then by Bill or someone else close to him.

Likewise, Talese's stern avoidance of any hint of personal journalism removes another strain of criticism directed to recent nonfiction. Only once in the book does he come even close to revealing his presence in the reporting, and that occurs when he relates that Bill contacted "One of the more persistent" reporters who had covered his New York court experiences to inform him of the attempted Brooklyn ambush. (p. 162) In the author's note Talese reveals that he was the reporter Bill contacted. Talese takes a formal third-person omniscient approach to the writing; he is, like Capote, a recording angel, though unlike Capote he avoids even a slightly mannered style or a manipulation of chronology to intensify the drama of his story. He explained, as did Capote, that the problem with first-person reporting is that you have to stay with the first person and consequently you yourself become the focal point and thereby limit your capacity to deal with other characters. He found *The Armies of the Night* a strong book but added that with Mailer's personal methods "we do not get depth, we do not get a sense of other people in great depth." For Talese, depth came from switching from one character to another and being able to portray them both inside and outside. The work of a film director was a rough analogy:

> I'm like a director, and I shift my own particular focus, my own cameras, from one to the other to the other; eventually I have a whole gallery of people I'm writing about. And you can only do this with the third person. I find that I can then get into the people that I am writing about and I just shift. That's where my own subjectivity, or creativity, as you will, comes into play.[12]

Talese's shifting camera in *Honor Thy Father* carries no personal stamp. His prose style is direct, fairly formal, wordy, a serviceable if unremarkable style. He does not try to capture the tone or subjective reality of his characters in his prose; instead he maintains his own control over language, even to the extent of eschewing lengthy reported dialogue because of the writer's tendency, as he said, in effect to stop writing when he turns to such material and consequently to lose contact with the reader. Nor does he reach for literary effects with his prose. It remains throughout the book a functional journalistic medium. Just as the photos that accompany the book aim only at useful illustration, the prose aims only to carry the story along and is not offered as an object of authorial performance.

In all, *Honor Thy Father* rests firmly on the journalistic end of the literary nonfiction spectrum despite its use of fictional techniques, and especially its use of varied interior points of view. Talese's most notable contribution to the form is its most journalistic element, a close-to-the-skin style of saturation reporting. He said that what made nonfiction an exciting form for him was that "You can do all the novelist can do—you just have to do a *hell* of a lot of research." *Honor Thy Father* displays only a few of the novelist's skills but illustrates the engrossing power of extensive reporting handled in fairly straightforward narrative ways. Talese added about the demands of saturation reporting:

> You have to know your people very, very well. And you have to be able to work within their words, and work within the framework of their lives. But if you dig deeply enough into their lives, you come up with so much that it gives a lot to work with, and you can still be creative and selective in what you choose to work with.[13]

Within these terms Talese seems creative enough, even the artist of reporting he aspires to be. His book simply rests, within the confines of literary nonfiction, at a considerable distance from Tom Wolfe's. That it even carries an index is a final measure of the distance.

Notes

1. Wolfe, *The New Journalism*, p. 30.

2. Daniel J. Boorstin, *Democracy and Its Discontents* (New York: Random House, 1974), p. 84.

3. Tom Wolfe, *The Electric Kool-Aid Acid Test* (New York: Farrar, Straus and Giroux, 1968), p. 415. Hereafter, page references appear in the text.

4. Bellamy, *The New Fiction*, p. 85.

5. Wolfe, *The New Journalism*, pp. 32, 85, 116, 188.

6. Sheed, "A Fun-House Mirror," p. 295.

7. Sheed, "A Fun-House Mirror," pp. 295, 296.

8. Sheed, "A Fun-House Mirror," p. 296.

9. Brady, "Gay Talese: An Interview," p. 110.

10. Brady, "Gay Talese: An Interview," p. 89.

11. Gay Talese, *Honor Thy Father* (New York: World, 1971), pp. 75-76. Hereafter, page references appear in the text.

12. Brady, "Gay Talese: An Interview," p. 97.

13. Brady, "Gay Talese: An Interview," p. 97.

Letting Subjects Grow

A good many works of literary nonfiction have their origins in magazine assignments, and some entire book-length works first appeared within magazines. Surely the most influential magazine in the development of recent literary nonfiction has been *The New Yorker*, despite similar claims for *Esquire* and *Harper's*, and here I want to look at two books that were published in complete form within its slender columns, Jane Kramer's *The Last Cowboy* (1977) and John McPhee's *Coming into the Country* (1977).

Jane Kramer acknowledges in the introduction to her book the aid of William Shawn, Harold Ross's successor as editor of *The New Yorker*; and the copyright page of John McPhee's book says that the work was developed with the "editorial counsel" of Shawn and another of the magazine's editors. Numerous other writers for *The New Yorker* have portrayed Shawn as a major figure in shaping the union of fact writing with literary form and intention in recent years. In his memoir of the magazine, Brendan Gill recalled Shawn's work with Capote on *In Cold Blood*—a model, Gill said, of "how to combine diligent reporting with an appropriate literary form." "This is an art," he went on to explain, "that Shawn has helped many writers to master. . . . Few writers are as clever at organizing their information as they are at amassing it; Shawn's exceptional lucidity of mind finds a structure for the most intractably diverse materials."[1]

There have been two overarching structures into which nonfiction has been cast by *The New Yorker* under Shawn's guidance: narrative reportage (in which some or many devices of fiction are used to re-create factual events in the form of fiction) and the extended journalistic report. Within these broad confines there remain, of course, numerous and complex structural questions for the writer and editor to determine. *The Last Cowboy* is a work of narrative reportage, nonfiction in the manner of fiction, though it contains many journalistic or essaylike elements as well. *Coming into the Country* is more journalistic in manner; it is a report from a distant place by a sensitive traveler, though employing many fictional elements and creating fictional effects. The book's roots lie not so much in the effort to emulate the novel as in the attempt to extend the range of journalism while remaining within journalistic forms. This second kind of fact writing has received less attention than the nonfiction novel or Wolfe's brand of New Journalism but, at least in McPhee's hands, it belongs as a sturdy part of the recent interest in the literary possibilities of nonfiction.

There is another sense in which *The New Yorker* has encouraged nonfiction writers beyond helping them find effective literary structures for the materials of reporting. McPhee located the source of his work in the magazine's tradition of encouraging fact writers to "let their subjects grow."[2] In the introduction to her book, Kramer thanks Shawn for "letting me go [to the Texas Panhandle, the locale of her book] and trusting me to stay until I knew what it was I wanted."[3] Especially during the sixties and seventies, *The New Yorker*, together with *Esquire* and *Harper's* and other magazines, allowed nonfiction writers both the reporting time to develop their subjects in depth and the editorial space to shape them in fresh and inventive ways. They gave fact writers, in other words, some of the artistic freedom of fiction writers to concentrate their attention on the requirements of the material rather than insisting on strict editorial formulas.

I

Kramer begins *The Last Cowboy* with an introductory chapter that is a model of the kind of information on methods the writer of literary nonfiction in the form of fiction owes the reader. She tells how she went to the Texas Panhandle looking for a cowboy to write about because she wanted a subject that seemed uniquely American after a period of writing about Europe for *The New Yorker*. The cowboy she finally settled on, Henry Blanton, was an accidental choice, a figure who captured her imagination because he seemed different from the other cowboys she met, one who had "settled into his life, but he could not seem to settle for it" (p. viii). There was something troubling about him because he exemplified both the myth of the heroic West and its sadly anachronistic quality. Henry Blanton's story, as she came to write it, became "a kind of parable of failed promise" in America, of grand hopes impossible of fulfillment. (p. ix).

Kramer does not go into detail about her reporting methods but simply thanks Henry and his wife Betsy for their cooperation. They never, she says, "flinched or reconsidered at the sight of a stack of notebooks, getting bigger every day, on the bench by the kitchen door at the Willow Ranch headquarters" (p. x). The brief comment is enough; it indicates that the Blantons knew what the writer was up to and that she was able to spend considerable time in their presence. Nothing that later comes out in the story causes one to doubt that the material was available to the writer, though the normally laconic cowboys were apparently unusually expansive in her presence. The introduction, in other words, eases the reader into the story, effortlessly removing questions about the role of the reporter and the cooperation of sources.

With the opening section, Kramer carefully removes herself from the account, turning the focus on Henry Blanton on an April day when he turned forty, an event that provides the narrative spine of the story. We quickly learn of Henry's still-firm dedication to the cowboy myth as displayed in the Western movies of John Wayne, Gary Cooper, and Glenn Ford and his real-life enactment of the myth as the skilled foreman of a ninety-thousand-acre ranch. At the same time, we learn of his tangled emotions, the classic cowboy composure that eludes him and the vague discontent that sends him, to the concern of wife and neighbors, on drunken escapades. And finally we glimpse the source of Henry's unrest in the changed landscape of the Western myth, a modern West of fences and feedyards and future brokers and ranch owners, like Henry's, who live on Eaton Square in London.

With the second chapter, Kramer turns away from the opening scene on Henry's birthday to sketch the development of the cowboy myth, then she devotes a subsequent chapter to a vivid description of Willow Ranch and the routine of the Blantons. With the book's fourth chapter, the narrative line resumes on the evening of Henry's fortieth birthday where in the town of Pampa Henry and his brother Tom celebrate with a drunken brawl. Further chapters continue the alternation of background material—on the history of Panhandle ranching, the nature of the meat industry, Henry's early years—with narrative sections showing Henry at work on the ranch, Henry and Betsy visiting neighbors, and one section concentrating on Betsy and her efforts to cope with Henry's despondency and her own growing isolation and loneliness as her daughters grow up and leave the ranch. In the narrative sections, Kramer employs both specific scenes with extended dialogue and generalized time sequences in which Henry and Betsy speak only to the hidden writer.

On his fortieth birthday Henry, aware that "Here I'm getting a certain age, and I find I ain't accumulated nothing," had made a resolve to change his fortunes. (p. 24) His chance comes some days later when Lester Hill, the college-trained manager of Willow Ranch, makes one of his rare appearances on the range land and Henry tells him he is thinking of quitting. Hill counters with an offer of a partnership on some cattle he will buy to be grazed on the ranch for a season under Henry's care, the profits to be split when the cattle are sold. The deal is a chance for Henry to accumulate some of the capital he needs to go into the ranching business himself, and his spirits soar. But true to the code of the West, the deal is only a handshake. Neither Henry nor his acquaintances like or trust Hill, but Henry cannot separate himself from the myth of how business dealings are properly conducted, despite his knowledge of a similar deal with an old rancher that had fallen through when Henry was a young man.

It is apparent to the reader that the deal with Hill is fated to fail, and in the book's final chapter, set on a June day some two months after Henry's birthday, it does. Hill calls Henry on a two-way radio and informs him he is selling the cattle because a summer drought makes the deal too risky. There will be no profit from the sale. Hill does not mention his agreement with Henry, and Henry does not bring it up. He responds instead by getting drunk and spending the night in his pickup parked by a cowpath, unable to face his wife. With the dawn, three bulls from a neighboring ranch appear in the pasture, stalking his heifers. He awakens one of the ranch hands and they round up the bulls; and then in a startling last scene, Henry emasculates the bulls with his knife, knowing full well his act of revenge is improper for a cowboy but unable to help himself.

Kramer prepares for the emasculation scene as carefully as a novelist prepares for the ending of any novel. In an earlier scene Henry and his men had spent a normal workday castrating calves; consequently the final scene seems, in retrospect, as inevitable as it is surprising. At the same time, it illustrates through dramatic action the author's view of Henry as a man seething with pent-up frustration because he is wedded to a mythical vision of the cowboy that no longer fits—if it ever did—the realities of the cattle business. Henry is aware of the changed situation. "It's what's on them ticker tapes that counts," he says about the cattle situation. "It's high finance, and if a man's out working with his hands, there's no telling how much he's going to be losing" (pp. 50-51). Yet he continues to wear black outfits like Gary Cooper in "High Noon" and to consummate business deals with a handshake and to dream of having his own ranch and cattle. Although Henry tries to live out the cowboy ideal of dignity and integrity in a natural environment, he is tormented by his adherence to another and contradictory myth of wealth and power, that of the cattle baron rather than the cow puncher. The people he admires are not only cowboys who maintain the old ways but well-to-do ranchers like George and Emily Smith who drive a Continental and shop in Paris.

In its revelation of character, its strong thematic quality, its tight focus on the time surrounding Henry's birthday, and its careful movement to a powerful ending that continues to linger in the mind, *The Last Cowboy* is an extremely novellike work of nonfiction.[4] At the same time the book has in it a good deal of information on the Texas Panhandle and cattle ranching that, though proper background for understanding Henry and his life, Kramer does not try to disseminate in a novelistic manner. A background chapter midway through the book begins:

> Last year, Americans ate twenty-seven billion pounds of beef—a hundred and twenty-nine pounds per capita—and "the new ranching," as it is practiced today in the Texas Panhandle and across a good part of the Western plains, supports and speculates on their enormous appetite. (p. 62)

The chapter goes on to explain the development of the new ranching that transformed the Panhandle from a grazing kingdom into a vast feed yard. The information, once again, is important for the reader's sense of Henry as the "last cowboy" of the title; but it is treated simply as information, and the author allows it to break the narrative flow of the book.

The Last Cowboy is at once novelistic and journalistic in its treatment of fact, the two forms held together by Kramer's overriding concern with the character of Henry Blanton as affected by his environment. One leaves the book remembering Henry, yet also recalling a remark in the introduction about an editorial worker who checked the facts in the book so thoroughly he "started dreaming about the grain sorghum price index and differentials in the Ogalalla water table" (p. ix). Of course novels, including nonfiction novels, often convey large amounts of detailed information, but in Kramer's book the information is, for the most part, structurally separated from the narrative line of the work, the two strains moving together in a back-and-forth manner toward the dominant novelistic conclusion.

II

John McPhee's study of Alaska bears little formal resemblance to *The Last Cowboy*. It is long and comfortably repetitious rather than lean and taut, loosely formed rather than narrowly focused, richly lyric in its prose rather than understated, and often personal rather than rigorously impersonal. Although it too examines both an exotic part of the American environment having strong mythical elements and the effects of that environment on character, the cast of characters is large and their responses to the environment are sharply diverse.

In twelve earlier books McPhee has amply demonstrated his skill as a journalist of an eccentric sort, one who has turned unlikely subjects—oranges, bark canoes, the Pine Barrens of New Jersey—into slim accounts engrossing in their detail and graced with subtle prose. This work seems to me to illustrate the higher journalism in contrast to the art-journalism or literary nonfiction that is my subject. I assume Capote had some such distinction in mind when he insisted *In Cold Blood* was not, as he put it, a strictly classical journalistic piece but a fully realized work of art. McPhee's work is surely an example of creative reportage—another of Capote's terms to describe his book—yet it belongs more to the category of the journalistic report, developed to book length, than to the category of nonfiction either in the form of the novel or with some of the novel's effects.

The distinction may be unduly fussy, and I mention it simply to suggest that *Coming into the Country* seems to me to stand apart from McPhee's earlier work as far more ambitious and artful; it is a distinguished work of literary nonfiction which nevertheless retains the broad form of the journalistic report. Thomas R. Kendrick's distinction, mentioned earlier—between using "art forms to extend journalism" and using "facts to make art"—is a useful way of remarking two different strains in recent nonfiction writing. In this book I am concerned with what Kendrick calls using facts to make art, with a kind of nonfiction that self-consciously seeks the level of art. Writers of this kind of nonfiction have tended to talk about their work in relation to the novel and to draw on various narrative techniques associated with the novel. But literary nonfiction need not emulate the novel in form and method, as the works of Agee and Mailer demonstrate; it is not finally the use of certain techniques that makes nonfiction literary or journalism art, but the capacity to make factual experience meaningful through the process—as Bellow said—of giving weight and significance to the particular, of endowing the particular with resonant meanings. To my mind *Coming into the Country* is nonfiction of just this sort.

The book is divided into three parts. The first, "The Encircled River," recounts a canoe and kayak journey McPhee took with a governmental study team examining water conditions on the Salmon and Kobuk Rivers in the remote Brooks Range country above the Arctic Circle. McPhee with four companions (among the very few non-Eskimoes to take such a trip), drifts on the rivers, fishes, makes camp, takes long walking tours and ponders his companions—describing everything in a prose that is both leisurely and minutely exact. Into the account of the journey he also introduces a flow of information about Alaska—about its awesome size and thin population, about the Native Claims Settlement Act of 1971 that provided forty million acres and a billion dollars for sixty thousand natives, about the eighty million acres set aside for future national parks, about the habits of grayling and salmon and grizzly bears.

"My bandanna is rolled on the diagonal and retains water fairly well," McPhee begins the section. "I keep it knotted around my head, and now and again dip it into the river. The water is forty-six degrees."[5] From the specific scene, he turns to supply background information, tell about his companions, pursue miscellaneous facts brought to mind through association, and even to quote from books about Alaska; then he periodically returns to specific scenes and events of the river journey. The structure is loose yet complex, the texture of the section richly varied.

The section ends with the sighting of a grizzly bear fishing along the river edge. The boats drift toward the bear and McPhee notes: "If we were looking at something we had rarely seen before, God help him so was he." At length the bear turns away and enters a copse of willows, and McPhee concludes the section by turning back to the opening image—and, whether intentionally or not, creating an ending that brings to mind the conclusion of Hemingway's story "Indian Camp": "Then we came to another long flat surface, spraying up the light of the sun. My bandanna, around my head, was nearly dry. I took it off, and trailed it in the river" (p. 95).

The return to the opening image echoes the circuitous direction of the river journey. A helicopter had taken McPhee and his companions from the village of Kiana a hundred water miles to the upper Salmon River, from where they had drifted to the juncture with the Kobuk River, and then down to Kiana—"closing a circuit," McPhee notes—from where they will be flown out by plane. (p. 40) The return to Kiana takes place less than midway through the ninety-page section, and from the return McPhee smoothly shifts the account back in time to describe the helicopter journey and the arrival on the headwaters of the Salmon in "the most isolated wilderness I would ever see" (p. 50). From this point the river journey is again recounted until the reader is brought back nearly to where he began, the bandanna being cooled again in the water.

Just before the arrival in Kiana, with the trip ending, McPhee remarks that from the beginning "no one has once mentioned anything that did not have to do with Alaska" (p. 39). The line expresses the controlling theme of the "The Encircled River" as well as the entire book—the way in which the state dominates the attention of those who spend any time in it, McPhee included. The dominance stems first of all from an awareness of the immensity and the beauty and even the forbidding quality of the land, the ultimate wilderness, and McPhee superbly evokes these qualities. The state is so large and unpeopled, he tells us, "that if anyone could figure out how to steal Italy, Alaska would be a place to hide it" (p. 57). In the barren Arctic a grizzly, we learn, needs for forage "at least fifty and perhaps a hundred square miles that are all his own" and that he will do his traveling through it at the pace of eight miles a day, scratching his belly as he goes by walking over trees. (p. 64) And we sense, through McPhee's own moments of fear, a world in which "If I wanted to, I could always see disaster running with the river, dancing like a shadow, moving down the forest from tree to tree" (p. 92). But the dangers of the country, like the river trip itself, have a quality of circularity, a feeling of heightened life springing from the fear for life:

What had struck me most in the isolation of this wilderness was an abiding sense of paradox. In its raw, convincing emphasis on the irrelevance of the visitor, it was forcefully, importantly repellent. It was no less strongly attractive—with a beauty of nowhere else, composed in turning circles. If the wild land was indifferent, it gave a sense of difference. If at moments it was frightening, requiring an effort to put down the conflagrationary imagination, it also augmented the touch of life. This was not a dare with nature. This was nature. (p. 93)

Alaska overwhelms attention in another, more cerebral way as well. Everyone who comes into the country gets caught up in a questioning of what is to become of the state, relentlessly debating the issues "of preservation versus development, of stasis versus economic productivity, of wilderness versus the drill and the bulldozer" (p. 83). McPhee gives voice to the debate by allowing others to talk, and in the opening section the talk comes mostly from those who wish to preserve. One of McPhee's companions maintains that the "most inventive thing to do . . . was nothing. Let the land stand wild, without so much as a man-made trail" (p. 83). In the two other sections of the book, the debate heats up and takes on more complexity, as McPhee continues to provide—as one reviewer noted—a kind of chorale for Alaskan voices and finally offers his own somewhat surprising position.

The book's second part, "What They Were Hunting For," recounts an inspection trip via helicopter taken with a committee charged with selecting a new capital for Alaska. The seat of government is to be moved from Juneau, a remote outpost impossible to reach or even approach by road, but not to either of the rival cities of Fairbanks or Anchorage. Settling on a new site involves passionate political and commercial interests, but the task is narrowed by the very nature of the state. Most of Alaska is still untouched, roadless, and inhospitable to human life. Consequently, as McPhee remarks, "if a group of people had to choose a townsite near a road and a railroad, off permafrost and on fairly low but well-drained ground, and not inordinately far from the main pockets of existing population, nearly all of Alaska would recede from the conversation and by the facts the people would be ushered into the Susitna Valley" (p. 108).

The inspection committee flies over the Susitna River, which flows between the Alaska Range and Anchorage, and the trip gives McPhee the opportunity to turn the book from the wilderness experience and probe more deeply the question of the state's future. He presents various positions through the committee members who argue them, the people carefully delineated and often left to speak in their own words. The most memorable figure is Willie Hensley, the twenty-seven-year-old chairman of the site committee, a native of Arctic Alaska who has become a "Brooks Brothers native" and who represents, in the wake of the Native Claims Settlement

Act, a newly influential class in the state. (p. 149) Hensley is troubled by the cost to the state of a new capital but, since the move has been mandated by voters, he is determined to find an appropriate site. At the end of the section, the committee flown back to Anchorage, McPhee relates that the site finally selected as one of three by the committee and then chosen by voters is near the small Susitna Valley town of Willow.

The third section of the book, "Coming into the Country," introduces another range of Alaskan types, neither simply preservers nor developers, who live in the Upper Yukon area they respectfully refer to as "the country," precariously clinging to life along its rivers with what McPhee calls a clannish sense of place. This is the longest part of the book and concerns the region of Alaska with the deepest claim on McPhee's sensibilities, the area in which he apparently spent most of his time. The human center of the region is the village of Eagle, a bush community near the Canadian border whose population in recent years has expanded to over one hundred, making it the "largest sign of human material progress in twenty thousand square miles of rugged, riverine land" (p. 184).

In and around Eagle, McPhee finds characters of sufficient interest to populate a dozen novels: John Borg, mayor, postmaster, and town entrepreneur; Sarge Waller, a former marine whose cabin yard is littered with "tarps, stove parts, cans, buckets, Swede saws, washtubs, tires, sawhorses, fourteen fifty-five-gallon drums, and five snow machines in different stages of dismantlement" and who explains that "Aesthetics are not compatible with survival"; Michael John David, the educated young chief of Eagle Indian Village, who tries to relearn Indian ways and to prevent white bootleggers in the community from selling liquor to his people. (p. 212) But the Yukon types who intrigue McPhee the most are the river people, those who find even Eagle too constraining and leave it behind to carve out self-sufficient lives on the Yukon River or one of its tributaries.

The "acknowledged high swami of the river people" is Dick Cook, who with his self-effacing wife, Donna, lives the life of the hunter, trapper, farmer, and fisherman fifty miles into the bush from Eagle and some six miles off the Yukon. (p. 404) Cook has mastered the many arts of wilderness survival and is not reluctant to dispense his wisdom to newcomers who arrive in Eagle in the summer months to prepare to enter the country for the great testing time of winter. A stern realist, Cook tells McPhee that the "woods are composed of who's killing whom" and that the word "ecology" really means "who's eating whom, and when." When McPhee asks if he is frightened by anything, Cook says, "There are a lot of things up here that can kill you. You've got to have a healthy respect for the country" (pp. 416, 417).

McPhee himself has abundant respect, but not only for the hard realities of true wilderness. He respects as well the necessary self-reliance of those who come into the country—and stay. At the end of the section, he gives his own response to the question of Alaska's future, coming down on the side of the preservers—but a preserver of the way of life of those who do for themselves, the most endangered species of all, and not simply a preserver of the land from those who would make of it "a crater you could see from the moon" (p. 430). His softly voiced plea for the country as a necessary "frontier outlet" for the larger society, "a pioneer place to go," is echoed in the section's closing scene in which he recalls meeting a young man in Eagle who bore an eagle feather and the dogtooth jaw of a salmon in the band of his hat and planned to head into the country to reinvent his life along the Yukon. (p. 436) "I wished him heartfelt luck," McPhee writes, "and felt in my heart he would need it. I said my name, and shook his hand, and he said his. He said, 'My name is River Wind' " (p. 438).

The ending is as carefully calculated as that of any novel. It has the effect, like the ending of "The Encircled River," of turning the reader back upon the account and recalling to mind all the resolutely independent people McPhee has described, those for whom Alaska is the final place in which to act out the dream of a new life. River Wind's dream is as elusive as his name, a dream about which one can be of two minds, yet a dream, McPhee makes us feel, that we must honor and take seriously just as we must honor and take seriously the last land in which it might be realized.

The ending is also personal in that the "I" is directly, though far from insistently, present. Throughout the book McPhee handles his authorial presence with immense care and shrewdness. His references to himself are usually fleeting and often amused, as when after eating the flesh of a grizzly he remarks: "In strange communion, I had chewed the flag, consumed the symbol of the total wild, and, from that meal forward, if a bear should ever wish to reciprocate, it would only be what I deserve" (p. 421). And when he states his own views on the future of Alaska, he is brief, almost whimsical, and aware of the strong influence of the moment on his thinking. But his revelations of the self are strategically placed in the report, coming at just those points when the reader needs the grounding of McPhee's corporeal presence and exposed consciousness to grasp a land and its inhabitants that are nearly overwhelming. McPhee never becomes a subject himself nor does he insist that the material can exist for us only through him, but the personal tone and point of view of the book and McPhee's carefully arranged appearances help bring his vast subject to concrete and haunting life.

In its structure the section is equally artful. McPhee moves the account along through leisurely association, a fact or incident or person suggesting another, and maintains the broad back-and-forth movement between specific scenes and various kinds of background material that mark the earlier sections. The time frame of the account, as in the other sections, is kept loose, allowing for abrupt shifts that enrich the texture of the material. For example, near the end of the last section, McPhee tells about a walk he must take, alone, from Dick Cook's cabin to a rendezvous with Sarge Waller on the Yukon. Unarmed and fearful of bears, he wishes he were taking the trip in winter when the bears are hibernating. With his thoughts about winter, the account shifts back to recount a similar trip taken in winter with Cook and his dog team, then returns to the present "with the snow off the ground and bears upon it" and McPhee "too abashed to confess my fright" (p. 411).

*

The editor of a special issue of *The Antioch Review* devoted to "essay-fiction" observed that "we are sometimes hard put to it to pin down the quality or the innovation which gives to a particular piece of writing that denomination." He went on: "Yet in some of the less flamboyant reportage of the day there appears an increasingly effective liason of the personal essay with narrative technique. One of the better demonstrations, published recently in *The New Yorker*, was John McPhee's Alaskan 'Coming into the Country.' "[6] The literary qualities of McPhee's book may indeed be hard to pin down, largely because the work comes out of the tradition of the extended journalistic report cultivated by *The New Yorker* rather than from the more overtly literary forms of narrative reportage or the nonfiction novel drawn on by Kramer. But some things can be noted about the work beyond McPhee's evident skill as a reporter: a pleasing complexity of structure, subtle use of point of view, carefully composed and strongly suggestive endings to each of the book's sections, vivid characterization, and a highly personal and evocative prose style. And beyond all such technical matters, and most important of all, there is an overall approach to the subject that clearly seeks beyond the flow of fact— as engrossing as that is in itself—to endow fact with both the coherence and the odd resonance that belong to a work of art.

Both *The Last Cowboy* and *Coming into the Country* are journalistic books that inform about place and character, yet at the same time they are patently more than that. They balance the journalist's search for correspondence with the facts of the world with at least something of the fiction writer's creation of order and meaning, the role of observer with that of maker, and they ask the reader to respond simultaneously to the truth of history and the truth of art. The undertaking is difficult and daring. It is a happy aspect of recent writing that some major magazines, and especially *The New Yorker*, have provided writers like Jane Kramer and John McPhee with the freedom and editorial counsel needed to pursue the complex ambitions of the form.

Notes

1. Brendan Gill, *Here at The New Yorker* (New York: Random House, 1975), p. 318. On the acknowledgments page of *In Cold Blood*, Capote also paid tribute to Shawn, "who encouraged me to undertake this project, and whose judgment stood me in good stead from first to last."

2. Stephen Singular, "Talk with John McPhee," *New York Times Book Review*, 27 November 1977, p. 48.

3. Jane Kramer, *The Last Cowboy* (New York: Harper & Row, 1977), p. ix. Hereafter, page references appear in the text.

4. In a thoughtful review Diane Johnson found *The Last Cowboy* "so like a novel in many ways that it makes you wonder, as people have often wondered before, just why a work is or isn't one." This question states the case exactly, if one keeps in mind the qualification "in many ways"; as I note, there are portions of the book no one would confuse with a novel. Although my focus in this chapter is unlike that of the review, I am indebted to it for linking Kramer's book with *Coming into the Country*. "Ah, Wilderness!" *New York Review of Books*, 23 March 1978, p. 3.

5. John McPhee, *Coming into the Country* (New York: Farrar, Straus and Giroux, 1977), p. 5. Hereafter, page references appear in the text.

6. Paul Bixler, "The Essay-Fiction Complex: A Preface," *The Antioch Review*, 36 (Winter 1978), 8.

11

A Subject That Won't Date

Capote said the first step in writing a nonfiction novel was choosing a subject that would not "date" like the contents of most journalism, a subject that would at least endure through the years it took to research and write the book. For his book he selected the Clutter murders because, he said, the "human heart being what it is, murder was a theme not likely to darken and yellow with time."[1] Numerous nonfiction writers followed Capote into similar reconstructions of the enduring world of crime and punishment; among them, Thomas Thompson in *Blood and Money* (1976), Joseph Wambaugh in *The Onion Field* (1973), and Edward Keyes in *The Michigan Murders* (1976).

The three works, each a best seller, derived from painstaking research into celebrated murder cases, and they carefully utilized Capote's recording angel methods—the writer hidden, working behind the scenes through selection, arrangement, and emphasis to tell and order harrowing stories in the manner of the realistic novel. They also highlighted, by contrast, Capote's great skill with language, narrative pacing, control of emotional effects, and his capacity to draw from his factual materials a coherent structure of meaning. Although the three writers were well versed in reporting methods, none had Capote's sure command of a wide range of fictional techniques or his insistently literary intentions. The result was works of literary nonfiction that, for all their individual achievement, had the effect of illustrating Capote's capacity to unite factual material with literary form and intention at an unusually high level.

I

Thompson provides no mention in *Blood and Money* of his methods or aims. Only the dust jacket claims the book a "true story." But the book indirectly asserts its verifiable accuracy through the use of the usual paraphernalia of documentary: scenes constructed in minute detail, careful attention to dates and times, and the inclusion of legal documents, letters, statements, and courtroom transcripts. A central documentary device that is omitted, photographs, presumably could also have been included since the people Thompson writes about were public figures who frequently drew media attention. The omission probably results—as it probably does in most works of this sort—from Thompson's desire to keep the documentary side of the book from overwhelming his literary intentions: his desire to create character, to bring an environment to life, to wring from the story emotional effects, and especially the desire to cast over the story a net of symbolic meaning.

On the surface the story Thompson reconstructs is one of soap-opera complexity, but it is finally ordered into a tragedy of archetypal simplicity. It begins with the adoption of a baby girl by Ash Robinson, a larger-than-life Texas oil millionaire, and his wife. The child, Joan Robinson, grows up suffused in the father's overpowering love, her every whim accommodated, and becomes a talented equestrienne and a glamourous figure in Houston café society. In 1957, two marriages behind her, Joan marries Dr. John Hill, a handsome plastic surgeon and accomplished musician—a union no more suitable than her others.

After eleven years of marriage, with no interests in common, Dr. Hill and his wife lead separate lives. He takes a mistress and a series of breakups and reconciliations begins; Ash Robinson is always in the background, ordering, manipulating, wanting his daughter for himself. In 1969 Joan Robinson Hill suddenly dies at age thirty-eight under strange circumstances. Ash Robinson immediately thrusts himself into the case, charging that Dr. Hill has murdered his daughter. The bungled autopsy report leaves the exact cause of death unclear—an acute inflamation is all that can be determined—but under constant pressure from Ash Robinson, a grand jury investigation results in an indictment of Dr. Hill for "murder by omission" for failing to give his wife adequate medical attention.[2]

At the trial Dr. Hill's new wife and former mistress is allowed to testify for the prosecution. She blurts out a bitter story in which she claims Dr. Hill told her he murdered his former wife and that he tried to murder her. The testimony, wildly biased and unsupported, turns the trial into chaos and a mistrial is declared. Dr. Hill later marries for a third time and this time enjoys an idyllic marriage to a woman as devoted to music as he is. But suddenly he is shot to death in his house, apparently by a robber; and immediately rumors begin flying that the killing was actually a contract affair arranged by a frustrated Ash Robinson.

Here the story takes a new turn, away from the monied world of Houston doctors, lawyers, and oil men and into a Texas underworld of thieves and prostitutes. Thompson recounts the background of the killer, Bobby Vandiver, his prostitute girl friend, Marcia McKittrick, and a middle-aged woman, Lilla Paulus, who beneath a outwardly ordinary domestic life ran a school for crime and prostitution. Bobby Vandiver is killed by a policeman before he can come to trial; Marcia McKittrick and Lilla Paulus are put on trial as accomplices. The girl gets ten years. A key witness against Mrs. Paulus turns out to be the daughter of the Watergate prosecutor and an old friend of Joan Robinson Hill, Joanie Jaworski Worrell, who testifies to having seen Mrs. Paulus in the presence of Ash Robinson. But the most damning testimony comes from Mrs. Paulus's daughter, who tells the jury that she was trained and managed as a prostitute by her mother. Mrs. Paulus is found guilty and sentenced to thirty-five years.

The book ends on an inconclusive note, and the role of Ash Robinson in the murder of his son-in-law is left unclear. A final scene shows the old man brooding in his palatial home over the trial of Mrs. Paulus with an unnamed friend. Ash admits to knowing Mrs. Paulus, but only to the extent of asking her for incriminating information about Dr. Hill; he insists that he is innocent of any murder plot, acknowledging only his enduring hatred for his daughter's husband. He is left, however, considering one last involvement in the bizarre story. He might remove Joan's body from the place John Hill buried her to the small farm where she kept horses. "In a place like that," Thompson writes, "Ash could ease his heavy body down beside her. And there, with Joan at last able to sleep at the side of the only man who really loved her—and proved it—only then would their story finally, mercifully, be done" (p. 450).

The lines illustrate the straining for language effects that occasionally mar the book and intrude on a story that needs no enhancing. Thompson also at times is swept into a pulp-magazine style in reaching for evocative detail. Joanie Jaworski Worrell, when she testifies against Lilla Paulus, is described as showing "the marks of the years, her hair dyed a not quite believable honey, her eyes set deep in the cobwebs of time and not concealed by expensive potions" (p. 424). When she speaks, her voice is said to be "raw with the groove marks of cigarettes before coffee" (p. 425). But for the most part Thompson re-creates the story with a professionally competent prose, letting the astonishing plot and the often earthy style and language of the characters engage the reader's feelings.

Except for the opening, the book also unfolds in a straightforward manner. The opening is a dramatically rendered scene that takes place on the March morning in 1969 when Dr. Hill comes to tell Ash Robinson that his daughter is dead. The old man is asleep and his wife begs Hill to wait for him to wake up. At this point Thompson turns to an account of Ash Robinson's history, the adoption of Joan, her pampered childhood and success as a horsewoman, and finally her marriage to Dr. Hill; a fourth of the way through the book he returns to the opening scene, with Dr. Hill saying to an awakened Ash Robinson, "We've lost Joan," and continues a chronological narrative. (p. 116) With the killing of Dr. Hill, Thompson breaks into the narrative to give detailed accounts of the seamy backgrounds of Marcia McKittrick and Bobby Vandiver, then continues it with their slapdash flight from Houston after the killing of Dr. Hill, their capture and Vandiver's death, and finally the trials of Marcia and Lilla Paulus that bring the story to a close.

In overall structure *Blood and Money* is divided into three parts: "Joan," "John," and "Pursuit and Trial." For each part Thompson takes as an epigraph a line from Revelation that is appropriate to the section and that suggests the broad interpretation he imposes on the story. The full passage is given as the epigraph of the third part: "Behold a pale horse: and his name that/ sat on him was Death,/ and Hell followed with him."

"Behold a pale horse," the epigraph of the "Joan" section, effectively points to Thompson's portrayal of Joan as the spontaneous, vulnerable, blonde product of wealth and parental affection, in love first with horses and then with John Hill and unable to break free of him long after it is apparent that he has no feeling for her. The epigraph of the "John" section—"and his name that sat on him was Death"—suggests the portrait of the mysterious plastic surgeon who craves money and music and who, if he did not actually kill his wife, seems fully guilty of massive carelessness in treating her strange illness.

The epigraph of the third section—"and Hell followed with him"— evokes the petty thief and his prostitute accomplice who murder Dr. Hill, and beyond them, the dominating figure of Ash Robinson. Ash Robinson's role in the killing of Dr. Hill is as uncertain as that of Hill in the death of his wife, and the last lines of the book are given over to his protestations of innocence. But it is certain that the old man wanted the doctor dead and did all in his power to get the state to convict him. Whether he did more than that remains an open question. But matters of provable guilt aside, the framework of meaning that Thompson casts over the book involves a triangular relation of Joan, John, and Ash in which Joan assumed the symbolic role of the sacrificial pale horse, John that of Death, and Ash the avenging figure of Hell.

"Always," Thompson writes at the beginning of the story, "Ash had drawn nourishment from his money and his blood." But his wealth and patrician Southern background are, "in the winter of his life," turned inside out, becoming the means of what Thompson suggests is Lear-like disaster. (p. 6) "Ash's money," he says at the end, "had bought him nothing but tragedy" (p. 449). What his money had finally nourished, in one way or another, was the blood of his daughter and son-in-law. Thompson wisely places such a thematic structure on his materials with a light touch. Similarly, he does not argue any particular view of who was guilty or of what. He seemingly lets the story unfold through character and event without attempting through direct statement of his own point of view a final clarification. Yet the story is not without strong symbolic overtones that bind together its bizarre elements and carry it beyond the realm of simple documentary.

The story is powerful as a story, but at the same time it is more than a story. It structures the reality it reconstructs, orders it, throws over it the larger design of the archetypal, dimly incestuous triangle of father, daughter, husband. Thompson does not go nearly as far as Capote in the exploration of event as meaning; he remains more observer than maker, more documentary journalist than literary artist. Yet *Blood and Money* clearly seeks out the edges of art in Thompson's capacity to find in a factual event, and suggest in his reconstruction of it, a clarifying tissue of significances.

II

Unlike Thompson, Joseph Wambaugh opens *The Onion Field* with a note to the reader in which he calls the book a "true story" based on the "intimate revelations" of some sixty people. Beyond this his claim to factual authority is modestly phrased. "The re-creation of events," he writes, "was at all times done as accurately as possible," and he adds that courtroom dialogue in the book "was not re-created" but taken from court transcripts, implying that the reverse is presumably true for the rest of the book's dialogue. The note to the reader also acknowledges that some of the book's re-creation could be done in "great detail" only because Wambaugh had access to a "frank, unpublished autobiography" written by one of the principal characters in the story.[3]

The story opens with an account of the developing relationship of two policemen, Ian Campbell and Karl Hettinger, who have become patrol-car partners in the Hollywood district, then turns back to develop in detail the background of each man. With the book's third chapter and the ninth day of the new partnership on March 9, 1963, Wambaugh introduces "two other young men driving toward Hollywood that night in a maroon Ford coupe, who had begun a partnership on exactly the same day as Ian Campbell and Karl Hettinger" (p. 36). The two, Gregory Powell and Jimmy Smith, are well-armed petty thieves.

Wambaugh devotes lengthy sections to the backgrounds of Powell and Smith that parallel similar sections on the two policemen, interspersing this material with brief narrative sections that carry the story forward on the evening when the policemen and the thieves will meet. Also interspersed with the present narrative and the various background accounts are brief italicized sections dealing with a gardener going about his work on a November day in 1969 and thinking about his recent penchant for shoplifting, petty crimes that overshadow in his mind a dark experience one night in an onion field. The book actually begins with such an italicized section, and it is only considerably later that the reader realizes the gardener is Karl Hettinger, now a deeply disturbed personality, and that the day on which he is shown at work as a gardener is the day before the trial of one of the thieves, Jimmy Smith, will be concluded.

The two sets of partners, the patrolling policemen and the thieves looking for a store to rob, come together a quarter of the way into the book. The cars pass and the policemen, finding something strange about the small car with a Nevada registration, decide to stop Smith and Powell on a charge of having no license-plate light. But Powell pulls a gun and the disarmed policemen are forced into the car and taken on a ninety-mile drive that ends near midnight on a dirt road surrounded by farm fields. The policemen do not resist, wanting to believe they will be released in the lonely area; but when they are out of the car and facing their abductors, Powell suddenly fires at Campbell, hitting him in the face. Then one of the two stands over his fallen body and fires four shots into him.

Hettinger immediately runs, zigzagging through fields of growing onions, while Powell fires at him. Hettinger runs until he comes across a man driving a tractor in from the fields and is helped to safety. Meanwhile Powell and Smith have split up in the search for Hettinger, Powell on foot and Smith taking the car and immediately abandoning Powell, who throughout is pictured as the leader, the one who carried out the abduction and the killing.

Powell steals a car but is quickly captured and gives a confession in which he says Smith fired the final shots that killed Campbell. At this point Wambaugh introduces Pierce Brooks, a Los Angeles homicide detective who has been assigned to handle the case and who finds it one of the strangest he has experienced, the kidnapping and execution of a policeman. Wambaugh follows Brooks's careful piecing together of the crime, his questioning of Powell and Hettinger, the autopsy and funeral of Campbell, and finally the arrest of Smith in a rooming house. Smith implicates Powell as the killer. Hettinger believes Smith is the one who fired the four final bullets into Campbell; but since he was running at that moment, he is not certain. This uncertainty becomes a crucial issue in the case. If it cannot be proved that Smith fired the shots, then he will escape the gas chamber since Powell readily admitted firing the first shot.

Another problem is introduced at this juncture, one with serious implications for Hettinger. The Los Angeles police are divided about the conduct of the two policemen on the night of the killing, especially regarding their surrender of weapons without a struggle. A "survival" memorandum is handed down to the force that makes clear that the two officers were unwise in their actions and that the killing was preventable. Wambaugh writes: "Both the dead man and the survivor were implicitly tried by police edict and found wanting" (p. 233). Hettinger is clearly disturbed by the memorandum and other indications that his fellow officers feel he did not handle the situation properly. He even receives crank mail accusing him of cowardice.

The trial of Smith and Powell during the spring, summer, and fall of 1963, re-created by Wambaugh in great detail, results in first-degree murder convictions for both. In handing down death verdicts, the presiding judge says the evidence shows that Powell fired the first shot and Smith the other four. Smith and Powell are taken to San Quentin and for a time are bitter enemies. Then when another convict tells Smith that only Powell's testimony about the final shots fired at Campbell can save his life, the situation changes; Smith makes up to Powell and turns flatterer. Prison records of the time note that he was found guilty of "committing oral copulation" on Powell. (p. 322)

With Smith and Powell on death row, Wambaugh switches attention to Hettinger's deteriorating physical and mental condition. The policeman is afflicted with dreams of the night in the onion field that keep him from sleeping. He loses weight, becomes withdrawn, has long crying spells, turns impotent, and has his first "baffling and inexplicable" experience as a shoplifter, apparently reverting to a minor activity of his childhood. (p. 334) Eventually he is caught taking cigars from a supermarket and summarily forced to resign from the police department.

To get a disability pension from the department, Hettinger is required to see a number of psychiatrists. In their reports—extensively quoted by Wambaugh since they are later entered as courtroom evidence— Hettinger's stealing is connected with unconscious guilt for what he feels was a lack of decisive action on the night of the murder. Also the reports suggest that the police department did not assist him as it should have with psychological treatment after the murder but simply returned him to his work. Hettinger finally receives a 70 percent disability pension and takes a new job as a gardener, but he cannot forget the night in the onion field or his stealing. He thinks repeatedly of the gun he surrendered to Jimmy Smith, the act that ended in the death of Campbell, and yearns to turn the gun on himself.

In 1966 the Supreme Court handed down the Miranda decision that reversed a kidnapping and rape conviction on grounds that police had tricked a confession. Miranda had been arrested the day Ian Campbell was buried. In July of 1967 the California Supreme Court reversed the convictions of Smith and Powell on grounds that Brooks, through establishing an air of trust and friendship while questioning the killers, had coerced them in a manner condemned by the Miranda decision.

The retrial of Smith and Powell, as Wambaugh describes it, becomes one of the most complicated and frustrating in California's history, resulting in a 45,000-page transcript, the longest in the state's history. Smith's lawyer, a tenacious figure who would one day defend Charles Manson, files pretrial motions right and left, hunting out every possible cause for reversal. Hettinger is subpoenaed and the lawyer makes his competency as a witness a prime issue. The courtroom is turned into chaos, until at last Smith and the lawyer have a falling out and the lawyer is dismissed from the case. On November 6, 1969, the retrial actually starts. When Hettinger testifies, he is a radically changed man. He repeatedly says "I don't recall," and almost all specific detail has vanished from his testimony. (p. 394)

Powell is again found guilty, but the jury is hung during the penalty trial and it must be repeated. During the new penalty trial, lasting four and a half months, all of Hettinger's psychiatric reports are read into the record. Finally, a new jury brings in the death verdict and Wambaugh turns to the retrial of Smith. Hettinger again must testify, an exhausted and broken man subject to sudden crying spells. Powell, called as a witness, refuses to testify on the grounds that his answers might incriminate him, and thereby makes good his promise to come to Smith's aid. The jury gives Smith life imprisonment.

In 1972 the California Supreme Court strikes down capital punishment, and Powell also escapes execution. As Wambaugh tells it, Powell's prison life at San Quentin is not unhappy. Prison turns out to provide the kind of controlled environment in which he functions at his best. Smith spends his days at Folsom Prison, more bitter and frustrated than Powell. Hettinger's life takes a gradual upswing. He enrolls in college courses, is less afflicted with dreams, and takes a new job that requires moving away from Los Angeles. But ironically the job, supervising workers in a plant nursery, takes him back to within a few miles of the onion field in which Campbell was killed.

This final irony is but one of many in *The Onion Field.* Indeed, the story Wambaugh reconstructs centers on two large ironies—the courtroom tactics and legal decisions that drag out for years the trials of the killers and that finally permit them to escape execution, and the psychological deterioration of the policeman who escaped execution that night in the field. The laws of the state allow the killers to retain their lives but reduce the surviving victim to a broken man. Hettinger's escape from the onion field was only the beginning of a long agony that rendered him not the victim of Smith and Powell but of an insensitive police department, lawyers for the defendants, and his own self-doubts. The violators get more help from the law than the man sworn to uphold it.

Wambaugh tells this story of ironic reversal with a good deal of narrative power. He employs devices of scenic telling, and especially extended dialogue, much more extensively than Thompson. Likewise, *The Onion Field* is a more self-consciously literary work than *Blood and Money* in both its use of parallel narratives generating reader suspense and the inclusion of italicized passages that interrupt chronology with the portrayal of Hettinger's broken condition long after the killing and before his final trial appearance. The book is an engrossing documentary and at the same time it draws from the documentary record a structure of meaning that reverses the roles of the killers and the victims in a manner that recalls *In Cold Blood*, though the purpose here is not to evoke feeling for the killers as Capote did, but simply to point out the development of a central irony. Like *Blood and Money, The Onion Field* has clear thematic intentions that reach beyond the reconstruction of an actual event, though in neither work are the thematic intentions as broad, or as broadly realized, as in Capote's book.

This last point can be illustrated by reference to the ending of Wambaugh's book as compared with Capote's. The final cemetery scene in *In Cold Blood* has the effect of restoring to uneasy balance the worlds of the murdered Clutters and the murdered killers, returning the reader to the situation that prevailed at the beginning of the account—though now with a knowledge of tragedy that does not permit an easy comfort in the fact of separation. With Alvin Dewey's conversation with Sue Kidwell and the evocation of the landscape in the book's last lines, the reader is back in the world of decency and tranquility with which the work began, only now there is a cemetery as the setting for the final scene and the recent memory of two executions by the state. The emotional crosscurrents of Capote's ending are complex and lingering.

The Onion Field concludes with a scene between Ian Campbell's mother and his two daughters long after the killing. The girls are visiting in Los Angeles, and one of them suddenly tells her grandmother that she is going to learn to play the bagpipes, just as her father did. The innocent comment brings the memory of the lost son rushing back over the grandmother and she is startled by grief, then redirects her attention to the girl and says that learning to play the bagpipes would be a lovely idea. The scene, like Capote's final scene, gives the reader the sense of an ending by returning him to a recollection of Campbell's loss while at the same time merging the death with the fact of continuing life. Campbell's daughters, like Sue Kidwell, draw the reader back to death and also away from it to life, and the reader is meant to be left, like Al Dewey and Campbell's mother, somewhere in the middle, aware now of both.

But Wambaugh's ending is not as forceful in its effect as Capote's. Unlike Dewey and Sue Kidwell, Campbell's mother and his daughters are marginal figures in the story Wambaugh tells. Their appearance at the end does not grow naturally out of the account, as Capote's final scene seems to do; they are simply meant to conclude things in a manner reminiscent of Capote's book but without a similar sense of narrative and thematic rightness. The scene has more the effect of yet another sad irony—the daughter taking up the bagpipes as the slain father once had—in a long line of similar ironies.

III

Unlike the books of Thompson and Wambaugh, *The Michigan Murders* reveals few literary ambitions, and I mention it simply to point up something of the difference between skilled factual reconstruction and what I take as nonfiction writing with a literary purpose. Although Keyes casts his book in the manner of a novel, he makes no attempt to discover in the events he reconstructs a unifying theme or pattern of implication. The book is a telling example, in Donald Pizer's terms, of the exploration of a historical event simply as event rather than as meaning.

In a period from 1967 to 1969 seven women ranging in age from thirteen to twenty-three were brutally killed in the Michigan county in which Eastern Michigan University and the University of Michigan are located. A student, named James Armstrong in the book, is finally arrested for one of the murders and convicted on highly circumstantial evidence. The panties of one of the dead girls bore traces of hair clippings from the basement of the house of Armstrong's aunt and uncle, a house Armstrong had access to while the owners were on vacation. Armstrong's aunt had regularly cut the hair of her children in the basement. Armstrong is given life imprisonment for the crime, the only one of the Michigan murders for which there is enough evidence to indict him.

Keyes tells the story in a straightforward chronological narrative. He gives detailed background material on the murdered girls and on Armstrong, though there is no evidence in the book that he ever interviewed Armstrong himself; most of the material appears to have come from the police, with the result that the book is almost wholly a "whodunit," the mystery solved when Armstrong is at length jailed and convicted. Keyes only slightly probes the killer's possible motives. Armstrong had no criminal record but had been involved in a series of thefts, apparently only for the thrills involved. Keyes hints at a possible psychological explanation for the murders in Armstrong's relations with his mother, an overprotective woman with a lover who paid some of her bills, including some of her son's college expenses.

During the trial Armstrong's lawyer is uncertain whether to put the handsome and self-possessed young man on the witness stand. To test his reactions, he taunts him with a series of mounting accusations: "He was a thief. A cheat. A sadist. . . . He was a pervert, homosexual, bisexual! . . . He'd tried to rape other girls. . . . He'd almost killed his sister once because she was a tramp, a pig! His *mother* was a kept woman, a *whore!*" Armstrong finally breaks under the rhetorical pressure and lashes out at the lawyer, his Jack Armstrong All-American-boy image vanished: "You lousy sonofabitch! I'll break your mouth!"[4]

After the boy's conviction, the mother breaks down in the courtroom and Keyes writes: "Crying loudly, she clutched her son, hugging him, pulling his head to her bosom, patting him, caressing him . . . a pitiful tableau echoing centuries of tragedy and sorrow" (p. 366). But he pursues the mother-son relationship no further, giving it none of the weight that attaches to the father-daughter relationship in *Blood and Money*; it is left only as a suggested motive for the savage slaying, Armstrong's hatred of his mother taken out on his innocent victims. The reader is never brought close to Armstrong in the manner of Capote's treatment of Perry Smith, or close to Armstrong's victims in the manner of Capote's treatment of the Clutter family; Armstrong's actions are not dramatized in the way Wambaugh dramatizes the actions of Jimmy Smith and Gregory Powell. The reader remains wholly outside the material, carried along by the competent fictionlike reconstruction but never drawn inside a fictionlike world of implication and meaning.

The Michigan Murders is a careful and unpretentious book—and Keyes's foreword is a model of cautious statement of aims and accomplishments—but a literary work only in the passing sense that some of its basic techniques are drawn from the practice of fiction.

Notes

1. Plimpton, "Truman Capote: An Interview," pp. 191, 192.

2. Thomas Thompson, *Blood and Money* (Garden City, N.Y.: Doubleday, 1976), p. 203. Hereafter, page references appear in the text.

3. Joseph Wambaugh, *The Onion Field* (New York: Delacorte Press, 1973), "Note to the Reader." Hereafter, page references appear in the text.

4. Edward Keyes, *The Michigan Murders* (New York: Reader's Digest Press, 1976), pp. 359-360. Hereafter, page reference appears in the text.

12

Forms of Involvedese

Although Capote had followers in both subject and method, the stronger influence on recent literary nonfiction was exercised by Mailer. His subjective and participatory approach to nonfiction writing, a variant of autobiography, seemed to many a more appropriate style for a time that proclaimed itself committed to authenticity and involvement. Morris Dickstein, for example, observed that within a national literary and political culture in the 1960s that "cherished immediacy, confrontation, personal witness," Mailer, with his self-assertion, self-display, and willingness to report on his internal responses as well as external events, stood out as "the quintessential New Journalist." [1]

Capote said he avoided the use of the "I" because he thought it would distract the reader from the story he had to tell. Talese felt the "I" would limit his ability to move the focus of his narrative to other people, and especially his ability to reveal the interior states of others. But the attraction of the openly personal for other writers was not a technical issue so much as a widespread feeling that the writer should no longer mask his presence or hide his biases; only the openly personal could be truly authentic because in fact the writer was always involved either with the material itself or with the process of ordering and shaping it. For the writer to hide himself elaborately within his story, selecting and managing for effect as Capote and Talese had done, could seem of a piece with a general exercise of impersonal authority in American life that cultural currents of the sixties and seventies sought to resist.

But if writers were attracted to directly personal nonfiction for largely cultural reasons, there was at least a sense in which the form also could be seen as a way of addressing a critical problem. As suggested earlier, personal nonfiction could seem a more adequate solution to the essential technical issue confronting the writer of literary nonfiction: how to merge the dual roles of maker and observer, and merge them at the highest levels. Through a concentration on the self—whether the self as participant in the story or as writer or both—the writer could seem to meet the historical requirements of his material and at the same time exploit fully his literary ambitions by pursuing directly, rather than indirectly through more detached and impersonal methods, matters of meaning and thematic intention. In this sense *Let Us Now Praise Famous Men* and *The Armies of the Night* could seem richer and more satisfying as works of literature than *Hiroshima* and *In Cold Blood* in that they imposed fewer limitations on the writer's novelistic powers, his capacity to pursue the interior resonance of fiction while remaining true to the external correspondence of history.

At any event, the emphasis on the directly personal in recent nonfiction was so marked that, despite the considerable amount of work in an impersonal vein, critics like Benjamin DeMott could broadly define the work as the "New Involved Journalism" or "Involvedese."[2] Viewed in this light, Mailer, more than Capote, appeared the Pied Piper of literary nonfiction, setting out in a direction of personal involvement and personal writing that many followed—with mixed results.

I

Tom Wicker's *A Time to Die* (1975) tells two stories, one about the uprising of prisoners at the Attica State Correctional Facility in upstate New York in 1971 and the other about Wicker's rather desperate concern to see himself as a worthy figure. The two stories are told in alternating sections of the book—a "shish kebab," Kurt Vonnegut said in a review—the one told in the manner of a journalistic documentary with carefully noted sources and accompanying photographs, the other related through the use of novelistic scene, detail, and characterization. In a sense the method of alternation mingles, or tries to, Wicker's two careers as successful columnist and associate editor of the *New York Times* and unsuccessful (in his own terms; he says in the book that he once told James Baldwin he would trade his white skin for Baldwin's literary ability) author of seven novels. The cohesive force—the "skewer," Vonnegut said—is the figure of Wicker himself, at the center of both stories and referred to throughout as "Wicker."[3]

It would have been difficult to write the documentary portion of the book with any less concentration on himself since Wicker was in fact a central figure in the Attica story. When inmates rebelled against prison conditions, they took fifty hostages and then requested outside observers, Wicker among them, to negotiate with authorities. For four days Wicker and the other observers, at considerable personal risk, met with the prisoners, who were barricaded with their hostages in one of the prison yards, and with prison authorities. The meetings with the latter took place in a hostile atmosphere; the observers were regarded by security men and townspeople as sympathetic to the prisoners and responsible for delaying a quick return to prison order. Wicker worked tirelessly for a negotiated settlement, even pleading with Governor Rockefeller in a last-ditch effort to prevent the bloodshed that would certainly occur during a prison takeover by heavily armed guards and troopers.

But finally the patient talking and appeals for restraint could not stave off disaster. While the prison yard was retaken in a fiery assault, Wicker was huddled in a prison room far away from the action, a wet handkerchief against his face as protection from tear gas. Ten hostages and twenty-nine inmates died in the assault.

Wicker's account of the rise and fall of the Attica uprising is thorough, painfully engrossing, and—almost against his will—ultimately balanced. Although his feelings come down strongly on the side of the prisoners, Wicker also tries to see the situation from the viewpoint of the prison authorities and from that of the villagers who live near the prison. Furthermore, he was aware of the need to examine it in light of the pervasive racism that effectively blinds white jailers and predominantly black inmates from any common ground of shared humanity. Wicker's experience at Attica and subsequent research into prison literature convinced him that "the *idea* of prison was wrong," that caging men inevitably imposed on them the kind of indignities that produced the Attica uprising.[4] He also concluded that prisons were costly institutional failures because they not only fail to reduce crime, they probably increase it. About such matters Wicker is passionate and persuasive. But at the same time he does not lose sight of the other side of the coin, the need of society to deal in some way with criminal behavior. Nor does he lose sight of the simple human failure that renders all social arrangements less than satisfying. The idea of prison may be wrong, but Wicker knows he has nothing better to offer in its place.

Wicker's balance in his treatment of Attica can perhaps best be seen in his inability to ignore the crimes committed *by* the inmates any more than he can those committed against them daily by their jailers. The crucial issue at Attica was the inmates' demand for amnesty for any crimes committed during the uprising. Prison and state officials would not accede to this demand, though they were willing to accept or consider a number of others; nor were the inmates willing to release the hostages without an amnesty guarantee. The stalemate on the issue finally doomed the rebellion to its violent end, an end that Wicker condemns as a failure of courage, intelligence, and the human spirit, but a failure that belongs to both sides. The hard problem with amnesty at Attica, beyond the massive institutional intransigence on the issue, was that a guard had been killed when inmates took over the prison. The circumstances of his death were unclear but its fact remained, an irremovable obstacle to amnesty both for the state and Wicker.

At one point Wicker confronts an inmate with the illogic of the amnesty demand:

> "One thing I don't understand," Wicker said. . . . "I see why you guys did what you did and the changes you want made. What I don't see is the logic of demanding complete amnesty for it. No matter what your justification, people were hurt and crimes were committed, weren't they?" (p. 112)

The inmate responds with a lengthy and passionate account of the prison crimes committed against him by the state that, in his view, cause any crimes committed during the uprising to pale. Amnesty in this situation appears only a justified tradeoff. Wicker indicates that he was impressed by the inmate's response but not convinced. He tells himself that even though violent acts may be necessary and understandable, those who commit them must necessarily accept the consequences. Throughout the book he debates this old-fashioned doctrine of responsibility with himself, trying to cut free of it in an effort to establish his solidarity with the prisoners and roundly condemning it as an institutional defense and at bottom an example of white racist logic. But he is unable to abandon the view wholly. Complete amnesty is unacceptable to the state and, finally, to Wicker himself.

Wicker comes to realize that if the state will not yield on the issue, and perhaps should not, then the prisoners must, if killing is to be avoided. Was this, he wonders, what the observers should be telling the inmates rather than skirt the issue? What would happen if in the prison yard he were to "take the microphone and state the truth as plainly as he could?" (242) Would he be believed if he told the inmates what such popular observers as William Kunstler and Bobby Seale had not told them? Wicker's questioning in the prison yard at Attica is a decisive moment in the book, turning the entire account in upon his own central role:

> . . . the straw lay there to be grasped at, that September afternoon in the fading light of D-yard. Wicker saw it clearly. He did not doubt the imperative to speak that had been placed upon him by the realization. Fear, not least for his own safety, offered its insidious counsel, but he understood that the possibilities were as unclear one way as the other, whether he spoke or did not. He knew what was expected of him, what he expected of himself. . . . But he did not speak . . . it seems. (pp. 242-243)

(The "it seems" at the end of the passage is an odd and inexplicable addition. Perhaps Wicker means it as an ironic underscoring of his inability to act in this confused and frightening situation. It is, at any event, a strange line lacking any clear reference, and in this similar to the book's puzzling last line, a line to be looked at in a moment.)

Wicker does not speak the truth on amnesty, nor does anyone else. It is something the inmates do not want to hear and surely would have ignored had they heard it. Their thinking is as entrenched in its way as the state's. For compelling reasons, they lack, as does the state, Wicker's reluctant balance, his capacity to see the claims of both sides while yet being humanly drawn to the prisoners' plight. In a sense Wicker cannot escape his role as a traditional journalist, weighing all sides of a complex issue. When the killing is at last over and he finally leaves the prison, he responds to reporters' questions with a reporter's attempt at even-handed detachment. When he is asked if he feels the killing was unnecessary, he says:

> I think any event of this kind where 37 people are killed is unnecessary . . . but I'm not saying it's unnecessary by somebody's . . . dereliction. I just don't know. . . . I'm expressing regret, not making an accusation.

And he concludes about his response: "So he was a moderate to the end" (p. 298). He is indeed a moderate in his account of Attica in that he cannot avoid recounting it as a series of conflicting claims between the prisoners and the state. These claims come to be centered on the prisoners' demand for complete amnesty, an eminently understandable demand but one neither the state nor Wicker himself can accept. His story of Attica makes many accusations but finally it is dominated by regret, a moderate emotion perhaps but one that does not seem inappropriate given the hard facts of the situation.

*

If Wicker could hardly help injecting himself into the book's documentary part, he need not have done so in its novelistic part. That part, of course, need not be in the book at all, and some readers have found its inclusion an annoyance. But Wicker seems compelled to include it, and to include it as cast in very personal terms, both because of his desire to succeed as a novelist and because Attica coincided with a crisis in his personal life and offered a way of resolving the crisis or forcing it to a head. *A Time to Die* is not only about the Attica uprising but also about Wicker's attempt to use the event for his own ends—and do so in full public view.

The book opens with Wicker at a posh luncheon in Washington, surrounded by powerful men and enjoying elegant food. This is the high plateau to which his journalistic career has brought him, a small-town boy from the South who has risen to the world of the high and mighty. But all is not well with him. A divorce is coming and his children have not been told; yet Wicker's problems go deeper. When the call comes about Attica he decides to go, he says, first because of the opportunity for an "experience and a story few other writers could have had," but also because the experience and the story "might make him think better of his work, even of his life" (p. 6). Here Wicker lays out the theme of the book's novelistic side. Attica offered the chance to do the kind of book he had so far failed to do, genuinely to "signify" as a serious writer; and it offered the opportunity to lift his life—through its likely risks, its call to some decisive action—to some higher level on which he could finally feel true to his best self. (p. 21)

At age forty-five and despite possessing "what the world called good fortune," Wicker describes himself as a "disappointed man who believed he had fallen short." The indictment goes on:

> . . . he was overweight, affluent beyond his sense of decency, a writer who feared he had written nothing that would last, a political commentator who believed he preached mostly to the converted. He secretly doubted his own character and openly questioned many of the values of the society in which he lived. (p. 11)

Wicker tells about growing up in Hamlet, North Carolina, and of parents who imprinted on him a sense of specialness, a need to live a life that counted. That need stayed with him, unmet by his rapid rise to distinction as a journalist, and reached a crisis point at the time of Attica under the pressure of his coming divorce. When he first entered the prison, the thought came to him that "perhaps the time had arrived for his life to be put to the challenge." He had arrived at the age and time when "neither his profession nor his sense of self yielded him an essential feeling of worth." His sense of self now required that he "go into the pit" (pp. 131, 132). The book is itself offered from the pit—a point to return to. But it also recounts, in its novelistic aspect, Wicker's attempt to take that decisive step during his days at Attica, to signify once and for all as a person and writer.

To "signify" involved, as Wicker dramatizes the story, two main things. One has already been mentioned, the feeling that he must break out of the balanced or moderate response to events that seems the product of his journalistic experience. He recognizes in Kunstler, Seale, and other observers men who had "crossed the line" into decisive, revolutionary action. Wicker strongly admires Kunstler's willingness to "abandon the system's structure of material and professional rewards—to throw his life and career into the struggle rather than to cheer on one side or the other from the sidelines" (pp. 186, 187). Many times he feels a powerful sense of unity with the embittered inmates and the more radical observers; he feels himself off the sidelines and into the pit. At one stage, going into the prison yard under the eyes of the armed troopers, he seems at last living up to himself:

> He felt no fear, no doubt. He was caught up in the euphoria of decision,

leadership, action. He felt bigger, stronger, better than he ever had. He thought he could handle anything, and he was prepared to try. He felt true to himself. (p. 228)

But the feeling does not last. His courage falters, but more than that, he is unable to take decisive action, to adopt a leadership role, because his sense of the situation is too divided. Kunstler's willingness to align himself fully with the prisoners and his general revolutionary zeal is beyond Wicker's capacity, however much he questioned many of the directions and values of the society. At best, he realizes, he "was a dissident, not a revolutionary" (p. 186). He cannot reject the system, any system, because at bottom he feels the real flaw is not to be found in human arrangements but human nature. He cannot help but see both sides and detect elements of truth or necessity in each. He remains moderate to the end.

The other sense in which Wicker approaches the pit is in his effort to break free of his own and the society's racism. The fierce racial tensions at Attica cause him to reflect on a Southern upbringing in which blacks were vague background figures, neither fully real nor fully human. He tells of shaking hands with a black man for the first time in college and of a long troop train ride in a box car with twenty-seven blacks and three whites in which he made the belated discovery that "black people were just that— people, individuals, human as he was" (p. 162). As a journalist Wicker had shown a "professional concern with the race question" but in his personal life had little contact with blacks; at Attica he wonders if he still does not think of blacks as "more nearly a class than individuals." In what ways, he wonders, "did he really recognize them as people?" (p. 163)

A moment comes in the story when Wicker seemingly crosses over the line of racism. Late in the book, with the assault by prison authorities at hand, a young black convict comes up to him and says, "Brother, we got to *win*" (p. 248). Wicker is deeply touched, feeling an instant communion with the man that bridges the gap of color:

> In the prison yard, before the onslaught, for the first time in his life he sensed that nothing racial stood between him and a human being who happened to be black. He felt himself free, for once, of his prideful sense of individuality. He put his arms around the youth and held him fast, held him hard, believing he had overcome the deepest fears his life had given him. In that moment, for at least that moment, he knew himself to be at last an equal part of the great human brotherhood—no more, no less.
>
> When he stepped back, Wicker put his hand on the youth's head, which came barely to his shoulder.
>
> "We gonna win, brother," Wicker said. "We gonna win."
>
> The boy smiled and nodded and Wicker walked on, thinking he was *free at last free at last.* (pp. 248-249)

But he is not. He is no more freed of his racial instincts than of his intellectual moderation. Moments later, as the observers leave the barricaded yard, Wicker is embraced by a convict known as Big Black. Over the man's shoulder he sees armed troopers beyond the gate and suddenly believes they are going to start firing; all he can think to do is keep the black man between himself and the guns. Later he sadly realizes how the experience canceled out the earlier feeling of brotherly communion:

> He thought longingly of the fleeting moment when he had clasped a gentle youth in his arms and imagined himself *free at last free at last thank God thank God* . . . but, within minutes of that moment, he had wanted to hold Big Black between himself and the troopers' guns.

Racial feeling, he concludes, ran so deep that no American could be free of it. The national curse was an "inescapable truth" that those "who had sought to be masters would be forever slaves" (p. 254).

*

In both its documentary and novelistic aspects *A Time to Die* is a story of failure. The work of Wicker and the other observers failed to bring a settlement of the prison uprising; the final assault took a heavy toll of lives, both inmates and hostages, with most of the latter killed by shots fired by the assault troops. Everyone shared in the failure—prison authorities, state leaders, the observers, the prisoners themselves—and Wicker accepts his own share. "He did not know how much of that failure was rightfully his alone to bear," he writes. "But it was enough, he knew, enough for anyone" (p. 295). Likewise, Wicker fails to break free of his sense of an unfulfilled life. He recounts moments when he feels himself at the razor-edge of life— involved in a truly dangerous situation, taking decisive action, experiencing a deep sense of brotherly communion. But these moments pass and Wicker is left a seemingly unchanged man. At the end of the book he shows himself back in his journalistic role, the role that brought him to the elegant luncheon with which the book begins, a role that does not satisfy his deepest needs but that is instinctive and comfortable:

> As the police car pulled out of the [prison] parking lot and wound down the hill, past Mancusi's white Georgian house and the booted and armed men at the road block, through the town of Attica, and on to the bleak road to Buffalo, he was not even angry. He was just tired, but not too tired to be professional again. He calculated that if he could catch a midafternoon plane to LaGuardia, he could make his first edition deadline.

But Wicker does not quite end the book here, with the professional journalist thinking about his column. Instead he adds: "But he knew there would have to be a time for anger" (p. 298). The line seems oddly dangling and with little relation to the feeling of sadness and resignation that fills the book at the end. What it apparently refers to is the book to be written about Attica, a book in which Wicker would be something other than the professional journalist compulsively doing his job. Of his original decision to go to Attica, he had said that it might provide him with a "story few other writers could have had." And this story "might make him think better of his work, even of his life." That story is presumably this book, a book offered from the pit, written in anger, in which Wicker is at last true to his desire to signify as a serious writer and serious human being.

Whether Wicker feels his "time for anger" accomplished those ends is left unsaid, something for the reader to decide. But this aspect of the book evokes only modest interest. The novelistic side to the book is useful in that it draws the reader closer to Wicker and consequently brings him to share at a deeper and more sympathetic level the confounding problems posed by Attica. It adds something to see those problems confronted by a man we come to have some knowledge of and to think well of. But Wicker's "use" of Attica to think better of his work and life is too thinly sketched and too overwhelmed by the facts of the prison revolt to be of more than passing interest. The documentary is what stays in the mind. The novelistic elements mingled with the documentary, with "Wicker" as the subject, seem finally only a bow in the direction of some of the literary currents of the time, a Mailer-like gloss on a book by a real journalist who cannot cease being a journalist.

II

Professional journalists of Tom Wicker's stature were not the only ones drawn toward "involvedese." Personal writing, with the writer revealed and openly participating in his work, penetrated even the world of scholarship where notions of impersonal detachment have generally ruled the day. Martin Duberman's *Black Mountain: An Exploration in Community* (1972) combines some of the features of Wicker's style of personal literary nonfiction with a scholarly history of the experimental college and community in North Carolina that had a precarious twenty-three-year existence yet attracted as students and teachers a large number of innovative poets, painters, musicians, and scholars. First and foremost the work is an academic history of the most ambitious sort. But it also seeks to be more than that—an account or revelation of a historian's involvement with his subject and with the process of writing about it.

Duberman makes no literary claims for his history. Nor does he make use of fictional devices, combining them, as Wicker does, with a journalist's documentary account of an event. His concern is solely with revealing the "I" and showing how that "I" became involved with the material, interacted with it, finally was affected by it. One of Duberman's epigraphs for the book is part of a poem by Charles Olson, one of the major figures in Black Mountain's history: "I would be an historian as Herodotus was, looking for oneself for the evidence of what is said."[5] The historian is always looking himself for the evidence, but that fact is rarely revealed in any direct way nor is the process shown by which the historian goes about his looking. For Duberman this is a crucial issue; his book is meant to oppose the course of traditionally written history by bringing what is usually hidden into the open.

In the book's introduction Duberman says the point is not whether a historian should appear in his books—he always does this through his selection, ordering, and interpretation of materials—but whether he should do so covertly or overtly. Duberman takes the latter course:

> I believe it's time historians put their personalities as well as their names to their books—their personalities are in them anyway, however disguised and diluted by the profession's deceptive anonymities. To my mind the harshest indictment that can be made of academic historical writing is its refusal to acknowledge, other than in the most *pro forma* way, that a person is writing about other people—a person, not an IBM machine or a piece of blotting paper.

But to say that the historian is always in his books regardless and might as well directly acknowledge the fact is not to say how he should go about revealing himself and what benefit this might have for both the history and the reader. Duberman offers his book as a demonstration of one way of doing this, one way of showing the historian's "feelings, fantasies and needs, not merely his skills at information-retrieval, organization and analysis" (p. 13).

The particular means Duberman uses to reveal his presence within the work are varied. He includes diary entries made while he was at work on the book that allow him both to comment directly on his research materials and reveal aspects of his own life. He reproduces minutes of faculty meetings at Black Mountain that include the addition of his own comments as if he had been involved in dialogue with the principal figures of the college. He relates "counterculture" events of the 1960s that help shed light on the general counterculture atmosphere of Black Mountain. He directly addresses the reader to clarify his own views about complex events in the life of Black Mountain, as in this characteristic example: "All this is by way of forewarning that the account which follows is necessarily colored by my own views. But I'd add, too, that the absence of sympathy . . . in any account is itself always a position" (p. 178). And he concludes the book on a frankly personal note that argues once again for the necessary admission of the personal:

> I completed the book a few minutes ago. I'm strangely, idiotically, near tears. . . . Is it really over; do I want it to be over—the place, my writing about it? . . . And all those extraordinary people, their foolishness, their valor, their *trying*—yes, above all, their trying. Have I done that effort justice? Have I done some of the individuals serious injustice? Probably a mixed answer to both. But I've tried, too—that I do know; tried for a personal search to match theirs; taken more risks than I'm used to—how could I not, writing about people for whom risk was so often a way of life? (p. 413)

Whether Duberman's personal history significantly adds to an understanding of Black Mountain is a question for historians to decide. But for me the work is illuminating and engaging in a manner all too rare in conventional academic histories, the risks Duberman refers to indeed appropriate to the subject and well worth the running. Throughout the book he is alert to the major hazard of personal history: "*mere* self-revelation, belaboring the personal to the point where it eclipses the narrative." He knows that, finally, it is the subject that matters, that the method of the book, whether personal or impersonal, is in the end simply a means of communicating the subject. "I believe . . . that although we may not learn from history," he says in the book's introduction, "we might learn from historians—might, that is, if historians put themselves into relationship with their materials whereby each is explored in conjunction with the other" (p. 13). *Black Mountain* is a striking illustration of that position, a way of learning from a revealed historian about a substantial subject.

*

In *John Brown's Journey* (1978) Albert Fried makes no theoretical claims for the self-revelation in his history. He simply chooses to shape the work according to the process by which he first became interested in Brown, then step by step immersed himself in study of the man and the pre-Civil War period, and eventually arrived at what he considered a fresh understanding of Brown's role in American history. This chronological process provides both the outer shape of his book and its essential texture, groping, tentative, marked by the feeling of a historian in the act of grappling with his subject. In the book's foreword, Fried says that he has tried to "chronicle an act of understanding"—to cast in full view, in other words, the slow and complex journey by which he arrived at an interpretation of Brown's journey, "his astonishing leap into history."[6] The book's subtitle appropriately refers both to the revealed authorial participation in the work and its conjectural quality: *Notes and Reflections on His America and Mine.*

Fried's America is that of the political activism and racial conflict of the 1960s. Into the story of Brown, he weaves references to his own time and details of his own life. His intention is not self-revelation, of which there is little, less than in Duberman's book, so much as a counterpointing of the tumultuous time he was living through while researching the book with the tumultuous slavery controversy that marked Brown's 1850s. Fried does not try to link the two periods in detailed ways, but the loose connection provides a basis for his feeling of sympathetic kinship with Brown as a prophetic figure who took extreme action in an extreme cause. Fried concludes that historical actions such as Brown's raid at Harpers Ferry must be placed against the historical dimension of the action—as opposed to being seen in removed psychological terms—and that this was a view brought home to him by the "convulsive moment" he himself was living through, a "moment of extremity, apocalypse, much like the 1850s." Brown himself and his recourse to direct and violent action in the name of conscience or higher laws became "credible" to the historian because he witnessed a similar response to the events of the 1960s. (p. 272)

Fried opens the book at the time when his interest in Brown was first stimulated—by overhearing the remark passed between two black students at Columbia University that Brown had been "the only good white this country's ever had" (p. 4). His curiosity aroused, he launched into preliminary study of the basic facts of Brown's life; then he turned to a systematic reading of the available biographical material, and in the book he takes up each work in turn, adding to his portrait of Brown while probing the strengths and weaknesses of the critical literature. This task done—and occupying the first part of his book—Fried felt he had an adequate hold on the essential materials of Brown's strange career.

In the book's second part he tells of widening his concern, turning especially to the antislavery and abolitionist controversy that dominated Brown's time and, at the end of this stage of his study, arriving at his overriding insight that the raid at Harpers Ferry was not so much meant to incite a slave revolt as provoke sectional warfare that would lead to emancipation. His understanding of Brown thus complete, Fried turned to composing an outline of the book he would write, and that outline—given in several-page summaries of various stages of Brown's career—becomes the substance of the book's third part, concluding once again with the unifying view that Brown had realized that armed conflict between North and South was the necessary condition for freeing the slaves.

In the book's final chapter Fried says he set the study of Brown aside for five years because of developments in his own life together with an inability to settle on the kind of book he wanted to write. He did not want to do yet another study along "conventional lines" (p. 275). When at length he returned to his materials following a debate with a colleague who considered Brown simply a terrorist ideologue, he was aware again of the process by which he had come to his contrary view and also glimpsed the kind of book he might do. It would be a history of his own "encounter with John Brown," the material presented in a manner "pretty much as I'd accumulated it, doing justice to the sense of curiosity and discovery that had drawn me deeper and deeper . . . into his life and times" (p. 276). It would, that is, be a book about an act of understanding in which the act, the process, conducted as much as possible in full view of the reader, would provide the form and substance of the book.

John Brown's Journey is not, like *Black Mountain,* a major effort of original scholarship but a meditation on a familiar historical figure and the critical literature that has grown up about him in light of recently current attitudes. The scholarly merits of the book, and especially Fried's hypothesis about Brown's prophetic role in American history, are again matters for historians to settle. Yet Fried's book has the not insignificant merit of bringing Brown and his time to contemporary life and urgency, of making both his complex subject and the complex crosscurrents of his time concerns that matter for this time.

III

The risk in all forms of personal writing is the tendency of the "I" to replace rather than enhance the subject—"*mere* self-revelation," as Martin Duberman saw. That professional scholars would run the risk seemed to some even more troubling than the similar inclination of journalists—the "ultimate in self-disclosure," a fellow historian said in a review of *John Brown's Journey,* in an age devoted to self-exposure. And he concluded about Fried's book about doing a book: "After the beckoning gesture and the enticing smile, the raincoat is flung open, to reveal—nothing."[7]

I find a more appropriate example of such loss of subject in *Heroes* (1976), an exercise in literary nonfiction in a personal manner by Joe McGinniss. McGinniss was brought to prominence with an earlier and best-selling book on the ad men's reconstruction of Richard Nixon, *The Selling of the President, 1968,* a journalistic account that drew heavily on fictional techniques and found favor with Wolfe as a representative work of New Journalism. *Heroes* also uses fictional techniques, but this time McGinniss is a central participant rather than a hidden observer; and the "I" is insistently present throughout.

As in *A Time to Die,* there are two stories in *Heroes.* One is McGinniss's attempt to understand what a contemporary hero might be and, in a series of interviews with likely candidates, perhaps find one. The other is an impressionistic account of his own floating existence in the wake of the success of his first book and the breakup of his marriage. The two stories are seemingly meant to come together in the sense that the search for heroes and the inability to find any becomes a counterpart—even, in McGinniss's view, a justification perhaps—of McGinniss's own sharply nonheroic conception of himself, and also in the sense that the book on heroes is intended to get McGinniss back in the literary limelight, back to reliving the earlier success he still relishes.

At the end of the book, concluding that heroic lives in the grand manner are no longer possible (the existence of modern heroes is hardly a matter of suspense in the book, however; very near the beginning McGinniss gives his judgment that "we did not have heroes any more because *there were no heroic acts left to be performed*") and that we must get along with "private symbols," McGinniss says he is now at work creating his and finding the effort useful. He is doing this through writing, and even though he is writing about loss—the loss of heroes, the emptiness of his personal life—the writing gives the loss "meaning."[8] Thus his two subjects are brought together and resolved: they have become meaningful through the process of telling about their lack of meaning.

The thinness of the book's conclusion, its reliance on a vague notion that the act of writing somehow adds a meaning to experience that it otherwise lacks, suggests its overall problem: McGinniss has no real subject. He has only himself, and since his talk about himself is merely sketched and not related to or intermingled with a serious subject, it becomes the merest self-revelation, lacking a sufficient claim on the reader's interest. McGinniss of course does have a subject, the modern hero, but his pursuit of the subject is so fragmented and is carried out on such a superficial level that it is hard to believe he has more than passing interest in it.

He had a theory, he says, that America no longer has national heroes because the values and ideals that heroes once personified have dried up, the end coming somewhere in the 1960s. Apparently tied to this—though it is hard to see that it logically follows—is McGinniss's notion that there are no more heroic acts to be performed. He discusses the idea of the hero with brief references to Joseph Campbell and Paul Zweig and sets off for interviews with those he thinks might be present-day heroes or might have something to say on the matter. His list is singularly unpromising, surely designed to reveal that his notions about heroes and heroic acts are correct: George McGovern, Eugene McCarthy, William Styron, Daniel Berrigan, William Westmoreland, John Glenn, Arthur Miller, a former prisoner-of-war in Vietnam, and a Medal of Honor winner.

What McGinniss finds in his interviews is that many of his subjects are public posers or self-serving or as lost and adrift as he portrays himself. Only at the end of the book does he give up his quest for heroes among the well known. He goes out to the test pilot school at Edwards Air Force Base in California and takes a dizzying ride in a jet plane. At one point the pilot turns the controls over to him, and he has command of the plane; but even though the experience is described in exhilarating terms, it does nothing to change his view of the lack of heroic possibility in modern life.

All human possibility seems tarnished because of McGinniss's sense of personal failure. Partly this sense of failure comes from abandoning his marriage and his separation from his children; but though the latter draws out some strong feeling, it does not seem a matter of real regret. The strongest source of his sense of failure seems to be that he has not maintained the literary success that once was his—and more than the literary success itself, the style of life, especially the association with the successful, that went with it. Of being present as a reporter in the hospital where Robert Kennedy dies, he says: "I felt pride. . . . *I had been there, on the inside, as a Kennedy had died.* It seemed the ultimate status symbol of the Sixties" (p. 8).

McGinniss presumably means to mock his earlier delight in being an insider, but the book gives little indication that he now understands the shallowness of this view or, if he does, that he has the capacity to replace it with something better. He goes about asking people like Daniel Berrigan—presumably with a straight face—whether God might be considered the "ultimate hero," to which Berrigan properly responds with laughter. Later Berrigan remarks that McGinniss has an "interesting face" but adds: "I wonder what it will look like in ten years" (pp. 79-80). One does wonder since McGinniss portrays himself, consciously or not, as insistently vacuous, an inner portrait that emerges not only from the feeble search for heroes and the revelation of McGinniss's thin capacity for sustained personal contact but also in the book's clipped, compressed, yet frequently sentimental prose. Of a reunion with his girl friend, McGinniss writes:

> We drove home through thunderstorms and heavy traffic. She touched my cheek, she kissed my neck, I touched her breasts. I told her how I loved her; told her my fantasies, my fears, and my desires.
> We got home. The house was dark. We did not turn on any lights. We left her luggage in the living room and climbed the stairs. We heard the rain falling. Then we touched. And then we heard only our longing and our love. (pp. 60-1)

Throughout the book McGinniss reaches for effects—in the search for heroes, in the revelations of his personal life, in the prose—that finally ring false because they lack effective reference to a compelling subject. This hollowness can be seen as well in the book's structure. It strings together McGinniss's thoughts on heroes and his quests for them, old columns written for the *Philadelphia Inquirer*, remembrances of growing up, dramatized recollections of past experiences with his girl friend, journal entries—but the complex structure ultimately seems purposeless, a vague literary flourish at most. Finally *Heroes* seems a nonbook, lacking a subject seriously pursued or an engaging sensibility. The decision to put the writer at the center of the book, revealed and revealing, makes him seem only all the more empty handed.

Notes

1. Dickstein, *Gates of Eden*, pp. 137, 143.

2. Benjamin DeMott, "In and Out of Universal City," reprinted in Weber, *The Reporter as Artist*, pp. 271, 272. Erica Jong saw all contemporary writing, fiction as well as nonfiction,

in the light of "involvedese." She wrote: "The most characteristic literature of our age—whether it bills itself as fiction, 'faction,' nonfiction or even poetry—consists of a kind of bearing witness: bearing witness to history seen through the prism of personal experience, to personality formed in the crucible of society." "Coming of Age in the Sixties," *New York Times Book Review*, 29 May 1977, p. 7.

3. Kurt Vonnegut, Jr., review of *A Time to Die*, by Tom Wicker, *New York Times Book Review*, 9 March 1975, p. 2.

4. Tom Wicker, *A Time to Die* (New York: Quadrangle, 1975), p. 64. Hereafter, page references appear in the text.

5. Martin Duberman, *Black Mountain: An Exploration in Community* (New York: Dutton, 1972), p. 9. Hereafter, page references appear in the text.

6. Albert Fried, *John Brown's Journey: Notes and Reflections on His America and Mine* (Garden City, N.Y.: Anchor, 1978), Foreword. Hereafter, page references appear in the text.

7. David Herbert Donald, "Mr. Fried's Journey," *New York Times Book Review*, 2 April 1978, pp. 12, 13.

8. Joe McGinniss, *Heroes* (New York: Viking, 1976), pp. 21, 176. The italics in the first quotation are McGinniss's. Hereafter, page references appear in the text.

13

Illuminating Recent History

DeMott observed that in "involvedese" the writer invariably spoke with a "self-deprecatory tic" and that the deepest purpose of such work was to "explore a literary mode of self-suspicion." The involved reporter was not trying to "bring a world into general view" but was instead pursuing the self through the currently chic process of revealing, even reveling in, one's various failings—the writer finding himself out, DeMott said, in order to authenticate himself as a member of a cynical age. Such self-deprecation had little to do with real humility or real conviction of failure and everything to do with the writer's adherence to a "literary mode." Ultimately it was a form of self-indulgence that deflected the writer from a "caring, knowledgeable concern for the life that is not our own."[1]

DeMott found such literary self-absorption endemic to involved journalism, though it surely described as well a tendency in contemporary fiction. What he pointed to was a loss of subject under the weight of the writer's preoccupation with the self. McGinniss's book illustrates the point as a work of personal literary nonfiction that fails to get beyond what DeMott called the "cage of self."[2] Wicker's book is more a borderline case in that the attentions to the self do not overwhelm the subject—and the subject is clearly a matter of real importance whether the writer chooses to involve himself with it openly or not—but neither do they affect it in deep and essential ways.

Yet the possibility does exist for the writer of literary nonfiction to write openly of the self and at the same time care for and illumine a subject independent of himself—indeed, to merge self and subject in such a way that they seem both inextricable and more clearly seen and understood than they otherwise might be. In its best moments *The Armies of the Night* is personal nonfiction of this sort. So too are Jo Durden-Smith's *Who Killed George Jackson?* and C.D.B. Bryan's *Friendly Fire.*

I

Who Killed George Jackson? (1976) is a notably Mailerian performance, with the large exception that it wholly lacks Mailer's self-mocking wit and cunning, metaphorical playfulness. Compared to its ponderous density, *The Armies of the Night* seems light and swift. The parallels with Mailer occur in Durden-Smith's self-conscious musings on the roles of fiction and history in nonfiction writing, his use of those opposed terms as a way of structuring his book, and finally his use of a directly personal approach to convey his deepest understanding of his subject.

The book is an attempt to uncover what happened on the August day in 1971 when the black revolutionary hero George Jackson was shot to death as he ran, gun in hand, across the yard of San Quentin Prison. Durden-Smith, an English journalist, came to the story with preconceived sympathy for Jackson. Jackson's book, *Soledad Brother*, had been for him a moving account that summed up and focused his own feelings as a sometimes participant in the radical politics of the sixties. The book "ensured Jackson's status as an authentic revolutionary hero and guaranteed him continued fame." He was certain, too, that Jackson had been executed by reactionary forces. It was simply an "open-and-shut case, a paradigm of what happens in America to those who know too much and talk too loud."[3]

Durden-Smith had filmed a television documentary inside San Quentin and knew something of its terrors. He also knew people who knew Jackson and considered him, as he did, the "truest voice of his generation." And he was convinced that the official story handed out by prison authorities about Jackson's death was full of contradictions. But what finally moved him to go to California and write a book about Jackson's death was the feeling that, with the radical movement in tatters and its adherents retreating to their own lives, he needed to make a personal effort that would clarify for himself and others the mood of an age, especially the mood of final defeat. Through making an "act of commitment to Jackson" and unraveling what he calls Jackson's "politics of feeling," he hoped to find the "answer to the question of why we had failed, why the smell the sixties still gave off was the smell of defeat" (p. xxv).

The book he eventually wrote is, he says, fully factual, a work of history, but it also goes beyond the facts to treat ideas, feelings, and fantasies, and in this sense is to be considered a work of fiction. The opening section, "History as Fiction," is a narrative account of what took place in San

Quentin on the day Jackson was killed. It is for Durden-Smith a fictional section in that it "distorts and omits; it dodges what is inexplicable and avoids those complicated moments when eyewitnesses radically disagree." He also calls the section fictional because he was unable to talk with the other prisoners who, like Jackson, were kept in the Adjustment Center cells of San Quentin on the day of the killing. His material thus largely came from the guards, and so is "unproven rather than true." The book's second section, "History as Fact," examines in discursive fashion the complications the fictional section glossed over: it deals with Jackson's background and the events leading up to his death; it looks at various scenarios of the killing; it talks at length about the paranoia of the California radical underground; it tells of radical militia forces and double agents and prison killings. It is history, Durden-Smith says, "as seen and reconstructed by the investigative journalist" (p. xxvi). The final section, "History as Feeling," is a personal account of what happened to Durden-Smith in California. It relates his fears and uncertainties during the investigation; and, as candidly as he can, he tells what he learned about the subject and himself. The section concludes with a two-page account that sets down, with a new tone of terse detachment, a simple summary of Jackson's life and death.

The novelist, the journalist, and the autobiographer, Durden-Smith says, ask different questions of history; and his book is shaped to take into account those differences. The answer to the question "Who killed George Jackson?" involves all three approaches—and even then is not wholly, definitively answered.

The narrative section of the book reads smoothly but, as Durden-Smith intends, is unsatisfying. It tells the bloody story of a prison breakout that resulted in the deaths of three guards and three inmates, including Jackson, and the brutal aftermath during which prison authorities restored order. The account is thin on motive and explanation, leaving too many questions unanswered, especially in view of the reader's knowledge of Jackson and his role as a revolutionary hero. The second, journalistic section takes up these questions at great length, filling in background, checking through various explanations of how Jackson came into possession of a gun, what he planned to do with it, and why he made a final, desperate, and futile run for the prison wall. As Durden-Smith digs ever more deeply into the story, the sketchy clarity of the opening section vanishes and is replaced by a numbing complexity of theories, charges, and countercharges.

There is no way of knowing with certainty what took place on the day of Jackson's death, and Durden-Smith admits as much. But at the end of the section, he maintains that a "general truth" emerges. (p. 228) It is here that the questioning title of the book takes on a second meaning. Durden-Smith suggests that Jackson was as much a victim of the fantasies people had about him as he was of a particular chain of events in the prison on the day he died—fantasies that are knowable as a general truth in the way the particular truth of his death is unknowable.

The final section of the book tells about these fantasies as Durden-Smith came to understand them, enlarging the answer of the book's title from the "state" that he assumed in the beginning to be Jackson's killer to "everyone." Everyone had a vision of Jackson, and every vision was equally fantastic. He was not as totally evil or purely revolutionary as the prison guards or California authorities thought, and he was certainly not as warm and affectionate as his supporters maintained. In prison Jackson had done what others had done, and worse: run dope, controlled prison gambling, raped, knifed, and coldly killed a guard. Jackson lived and died, Durden-Smith says, at the crossroads of the various fantasies about him, and each played a role in killing him.

The section turns the focus of the book on Durden-Smith himself because he comes to believe that any explanation of Jackson's death can only be given in personal terms. He soon discovered during his research in California that "facts" were dependent on who was giving them to him. Everyone he talked to was described by someone else as an agent or informer; there was even talk that Durden-Smith himself was in the pay of someone else. As a result he had to collect character studies as well as information, weighing everything told him in light of who said it, what his politics were, and what he had to gain or lose from the disclosure. He felt turned in upon his own responses, having to "pay attention to my own feelings rather than rely . . . on other people's judgments" (p. 235).

Just as his investigation pushed him toward the personal, it pushed him toward the political. It became necessary to evaluate the politics of everyone he came in contact with in order to gauge their credibility. Also he learned that Jackson's death had not been the simple execution he originally thought. The evidence suggested that Jackson was indeed involved in a plan to escape from prison, as the authorities maintained, and that the plan was engineered from outside the prison. So Durden-Smith's investigation shifted away from the prison; and as it did, he was caught up in the crosscurrents of Bay Area radical politics.

This led him toward his general truth, the belief that Jackson was the victim of contradictory fantasies held about him by the Left as well as the Right, admirers as well as enemies. He came to believe that the revolutionary struggle as waged within the prison system was a simple "we-against-them" conflict and had little connection with the more complex politics at work outside the prison, and that the people who visited and supported Jackson in prison had little real aid to give him, nor he them.

There was a tragic lack of connection between Jackson and his admirers, an inability to distinguish between two quite different fields of radical struggle, and Durden-Smith speculates at length about the effects on Jackson's self-understanding of his being kept "in a prison within a prison," cut off both from the realities of his own situation and that of his admirers. (p. 244)

As the same time Durden-Smith was coming to understand Jackson's isolated situation, he was learning that many who knew Jackson from inside prison, guards and fellow prisoners, regarded him as brutal and violent, almost surely the murderer of a new and harmless guard named Mills. One ex-prisoner told Durden-Smith: "He was the meanest mother I ever saw, inside or out. And you want to know why he was what dumbass people on the street call a prison leader? 'Cause everyone was shit-scared of him" (p. 270). Durden-Smith also concludes that *Soledad Brother* was altered for publication, the book bearing little resemblance in style and tone to unpublished letters by Jackson that he saw.

Durden-Smith's attitudes toward his subject repeatedly shift. From believing Jackson a saint, he comes to consider him a monster—and then comes to view him as a victim of both responses to him:

> He was not a particularly good man. He was violent and vindictive; he profited from other men's weakness. But then, he was a prisoner, the kind of man that prisons like San Quentin create. And there was a terrible presumption in asking him to be better than the environment that was forced on him. (pp. 286-7)

The Left wanted Jackson to be a revolutionary hero, and with rhetoric and action pushed him toward that vision. Likewise, the authorities wanted him to be the evil genius of the militant underground, and through manic counterinsurgency tactics pushed him in that direction. Jackson was really killed, Durden-Smith concludes, piece by piece by the contradictory visions wished upon him.

Durden-Smith set out in the book to expose Jackson's killers—and he does, though not in the straightforward historical way he intended. All that he is able to say in that sense is what he knew from the start, that Jackson was killed trying to escape from prison. But he arrives at what he takes as the larger and more important discovery that Jackson was killed "because he was at the crossroads of people's fantasies about him" (p. 289).

He also set out in the book to see in Jackson's death a key to the failure of the radical movement, especially its sense of nagging defeat as it entered the seventies. This was the "politics of feeling" he sought to understand—and he does come to understand it, though again not in the way he intended. He learned that the movement failed because it lost touch with genuine human feeling, living instead in a fantasy world of roles and images, never really grasping the particular feelings of others. The failure of the movement to understand Jackson as an individual human being becomes the key to this general truth. Durden-Smith concludes: "So the movement, in the end, could never make use of the outrage the ordinary men and women of America feel. All it could do was underline their prejudices. And that was its greatest failure" (p. 289).

*

Who Killed George Jackson? is a difficult book to read—repetitive, contradictory, self-indulgent. At the same time, there is a groping honesty about it that is deeply satisfying. Like Agee and Mailer, Durden-Smith offers the process of the book as an inherent part of it, perhaps its most important part. It is really a book about trying to do a book on the death of George Jackson and finding it could not be done, at least not in the way the writer originally meant. Durden-Smith recounts at length his changing attitudes, explains the structure of the book, tells of problems as a reporter, and confesses frequent feelings of failure. Awash in difficulties and contradictions, he is moved to write in one instance: "This was the point at which, perhaps, I should have cut my losses and gone home" (p. 237). The reader is tempted to agree.

There is always something a little too precious in writing about the problems of writing a book, or something arrogant in expecting the reader to struggle through the writer's own struggles. Why should we care? The writer's task, if he is to reveal the process of the book, is to convince us that the method illumines or engages the subject in a way that would otherwise not be possible, that method and subject are so deeply wedded that no other method is possible. This may well not be the case, but it must seem to be.

The strength of Durden-Smith's book is his ability to make the reader believe that the process of his book, openly declared, *is* essential to the subject, the only way in which it could be apprehended. If one considers the areas of reporting that were closed off to him—Jackson himself, key figures of the radical underground—and the conflicting information he received and the dangers involved in even doing the story at all, it is hard to see that Durden-Smith could have approached his task any differently. He convinces us that it could not be a detached novellike narrative or a straightforward documentarylike work of history by showing us the deficiencies of both methods. Like *Let Us Now Praise Famous Men*, the book is a series of new beginnings, each one moving closer to a full realization of the subject; and it seems essential that this development become part of the book if the reader is not to be misled into an overly simple or plainly inaccurate answer to the question posed in the book's title.

But just as with *Famous Men*, the full realization of the subject never comes. The book finally offers only further questions, and Durden-Smith is less able than Agee to face up to this inconclusiveness. He tries too hard for a general truth at the end, for a summary statement of the meaning of Jackson's death in social or cultural terms, for a way of concluding. But the weight of the book cuts against any such statement; it emphasizes more the process of learning about the death of Jackson than final clarity. The question mark in the book's title remains. And the book's final pages—the terse description of what little beyond dispute there is of Jackson's life and death—have the effect of turning away from Durden-Smith's stated conclusions and emphasizing again, and appropriately, all that remains unknown.

At the beginning of the book, Durden-Smith says that "The answer to the question 'Who killed George Jackson?' is not the name of a man or the makeup of a society or the identification of a fantasy"—all theories the book takes up and in one way or another dismisses. "It is all three," he adds, "and much more" (p. xxvi). The book effectively shows that it is indeed much more, and in so doing illumines—through catching some of its political passions and intellectual contradictions—a piece of recent history. The writer convinces us that his open meditations on methods, his false starts, and his concentration on the self—however irritating or demanding—are inseparable from the subject, and that his subject is a real subject, part of the disorder, the actuality, of real life.

II

The directly personal is made to seem just as essential in C.D.B. Bryan's *Friendly Fire* (1976). The book seems to demand, as Bryan says it does, that he enter the story, reveal himself, speak in his own voice. As in *Who Killed George Jackson?*, the story Bryan tells comes eventually to center on his own interaction with the subject; his involvement becomes not just a feature of the reporting, something he can choose to reveal or not, but inextricably part of the book's central theme. Perhaps *Friendly Fire* could have been a rigorously impersonal work and conveyed Bryan's views with the same clarity and emotional weight. But Bryan convinces us that his personal manner is right and inevitable and that it permits him to draw close to his material in ways that otherwise would not be possible.

On the surface *Friendly Fire* is a simple account of what happened to an Iowa farm family that lost a son in the Vietnam war. But in Bryan's telling, the story is given complex depths that extend its implications to a whole society that lost a last remaining core of innocence in a pointless war. It is a book about loss, the loss of life and the loss of faith—faith in neighbors, in country, in the essential decency and honesty of national leaders. At its deepest level it is a book about the greatest casualty of the war—the loss of truth.

Michael Mullen, a graduate student in animal nutrition, was drafted into the Army and sent to Vietnam as a sergeant in September of 1969. Six months later he was dead, the victim of "friendly fire" from U.S. artillery shelling enemy positions. His parents, Peg and Gene Mullen, operators of a small farm near La Porte City, Iowa, became convinced, and for good reason, that there was a cover-up of the exact details of his death, that the Army was protecting itself from an embarrassing case of negligence or worse. The Mullens were given only cursory and impersonal information about Michael's death ("He was at a night defensive position when artillery fire from friendly forces landed in the area") in a bureaucratic language that seemed to conceal more than it revealed.[4] There was confusion and delay in the return of Michael's body to the States; and when it did arrive, the parents were shocked to learn that their son, presumably torn to pieces in an explosion, bore hardly a scratch.

The Mullens responded to Michael's death with sweeping outrage. Their anger was stoked by the proper yet confused handling of the death by military authorities, by the insensitive actions of their parish priest during the funeral arrangements, and by their own temperaments. The Mullens were not people who blindly accepted official statements or suffered injustice lightly. Peg Mullen especially could be impatient and aggressive. The Mullens refused a military funeral for Michael and found it incredible that other families accepted the loss of their own sons without protest. When a letter came from the White House saying President Nixon was sorry for the loss of their son and including a xeroxed collection of his Vietnamization speeches, Peg mailed it back with the notation: "Return to Sender. Not interested" (p. 73).

The day after the funeral the Mullens got a letter from Michael's commanding officer, Lieutenant Colonel Norman Schwarzkopf, giving the first real details of his death. The officer said that the artillery in Michael's unit was "adjusting artillery to provide a predetermined range of fire in the event of enemy contact. During the testing, Michael received a fatal missile wound when an artillery round fell short of its intended target and detonated near his position" (p. 102). But the explanation only raised more questions for the Mullens. From Michael's old letters, they found the names of his friends in the unit and wrote them asking for more information. Return letters left them more certain that the Army was involved in a cover-up because of the circumstances surrounding Michael's death. When his death certificate arrived, the space for explaining the circumstances of death was left blank—lending more fuel to their suspicions.

As the Mullens continued to pursue the facts of their son's death, they became subjects of media attention. In turn the Mullens used the media to promote their opposition to the war. With Michael's Army gratuity pay, they printed a striking full-page ad in the *Des Moines Register* that included 714 crosses, one for each Iowa serviceman dead in Vietnam, and the words: "A Silent message to the fathers and mothers of Iowa" (p. 129).

Likewise, Peg began a wide correspondence with families who had lost sons in the war, bombarded members of Congress and the Army with letters charging that the truth about the war was being hidden from the public, and went to Washington to take part in demonstrations.

The Mullens' lives became consumed by their anti-war activities and their conviction that the full truth about Michael's death was being kept from them. "The Mullens did not believe they were unpatriotic," Bryan says. "The government was unpatriotic" (p. 191). The only way they could show their love of country and their love for their son was to protest—but at the same time that their protest spurred them to more and more activity, it left them lonely, cut off from the rural community, unable to think about anything but the war. A year after Michael's death the Mullens were "disillusioned, angry, suspicious, wounded and confused by all they had suffered and learned." They wanted to "alert their fellow Americans to what might befall them by holding themselves up as examples." They were "horrified that never before in the history of this nation they so loved had its government so rigorously dedicated itself to the accumulation of power at the expense of its citizenry" (p. 231).

This part of the story occupies the first two-thirds of the book. Bryan reconstructs it through a series of dramatically rendered scenes linked with descriptive material on the Mullens' roots on the Iowa land and details of the war. Peg and Gene are vividly characterized and effectively set against a background of a tradition-minded rural Midwest, members of the Silent Majority who suddenly lose their silence and anonymity as they wage war against a war.

In an author's note at the beginning of the book, Bryan carefully reveals his methods. All material comes from his own observation or from records, correspondence, journals, or extended interviews. The interviews were taped and corrected by the subjects. About reconstructed conversations, he is unusually candid: "I have assumed that if any individual recalled what was said and this recollection was confirmed by a second individual and there was no obvious advantage to be gained from a depiction of the conversation as recalled, then a reconstruction using the dialogue as remembered might be accepted as true" (p. 7). Bryan concludes the note with a modest statement of the book's accuracy as history:

> I suppose one can never be satisfied that one has asked all the questions one might have asked, double-checked all the details one might have double-checked, seen all the people one might have seen. But because all the major people in this story have read the finished manuscript and have expressed their agreement with the incidents as described, I am confident that what I have written is true and that the events, scenes and conversations took place as depicted. (p. 8)

Reconstructed scenes in the book are rendered with a fiction writer's concern for telling detail and emotional effects, and Bryan has no hesitation in breaking chronology for dramatic purposes. The opening chapter reconstructs Michael's last night of leave at the farm and the following morning when the family take him to the local airport to begin the journey to Vietnam—and ends with the disclosure that six months later his casket would be returned to the same airport, and one year after that, his mother would be under surveillance by the FBI for her anti-war activities. But the book's strong novelistic quality does not overwhelm Bryan's intention to write contemporary history. The two seem wholly complementary, the novelist's skill a device for recalling and bringing to life recent events. The truth of those events remain central for reader and writer.

*

But *Friendly Fire* does not remain a detached work of literary nonfiction in the manner of *In Cold Blood* or *Honor Thy Father*. Finally Bryan injects himself into the story, turning the book's focus on himself and his relation to the Mullens; and when this happens, the shift seems a natural and necessary development in light of the book's overall design. Bryan enters the story at the moment when he in fact entered it, on an April day in 1971, a little more than a year after Michael's death. He explains that a return visit to the University of Iowa where he taught from 1967 to 1969 brought the Mullens to his attention. A fellow writer and his wife thought they might make a good story. A year later Bryan decided to write the story, prompted by a speech at Kansas State University in which President Nixon said, "The heart of America is sound. . . . The heart of America is good!" (pp. 247-8)

Bryan believed otherwise. He believed that the "heart of America was broken over the deaths of its young in Vietnamese jungles" and that there "had to be some way to articulate the people's discontent, their estrangement from their government, their increasing paranoia and distrust" (p. 248). He telephoned Peg Mullen, explained what he wanted to do—at first a magazine article—and was invited to the farm. With his appearance at the farm, the book becomes a first-person account.

Bryan describes five days spent with the Mullens and his surprise at the intensity of their indignation, their sense of betrayal by the government, their loss of confidence in the nation's purpose and leaders. He also makes the disturbing discovery that Peg Mullen's various accounts of her experiences since Michael's death tended to vary, the truth "slightly embroidered." He writes: "I wondered why she had felt this necessary. The truth was offensive enough. I came to understand that the truth was no longer adequately outrageous to Peg" (p. 261). When he left the farm, Bryan had a new aim, to find out for himself what had happened to Michael.

In July 1971, the Mullens found that Lieutenant Colonel Schwarzkopf was in Washington at Walter Reed Army Medical Center on a year's convalescent leave. They went to talk with him, considering him the figure responsible for Michael's death. The interview, as the Mullens recounted it to Bryan, left him unconvinced, certain the Mullens had distorted it. He writes: "I suspected . . . that Peg and Gene had become, like the United States government which so enraged them, no longer able to listen to what they didn't want to hear." Bryan also was troubled by his own role. When Gene Mullen had told him about locating Schwarzkopf, he had said, "I've got an ending for your book!" Bryan says he did not want the Mullens to fall into the "corruption" of creating a "perfect ending" for him. (pp. 286, 287) To spare them this, he felt he had to find out for them exactly what had happened to Michael. Moreover, he felt that he and they already knew, they *had* been told, but had resisted the truth because it was not what they wanted to hear.

Bryan turns the account to Schwarzkopf's military background, his experiences as a much-decorated field commander in Vietnam, and to the two days he himself spent talking with him in his Virginia home after his release from Walter Reed. Bryan found Schwarzkopf likable and convincing. The officer described Michael's death as the result of an error in artillery procedures and insisted there was no cover-up of the investigation or any conspiracy directed against the Mullens. Bryan believed him and was struck by how sharply his account of his meeting with the Mullens differed from theirs. The officer's final words to Bryan summed up his feelings about Michael's death and his meeting with the Mullens—and also expressed Bryan's own feelings, what he had come to believe was the truth of the matter:

> "I'll just finish off by saying it's a terrible thing that happened to Michael Mullen . . . a terrible, *terrible* tragedy. . . . He was a very fine young man, and his death was a tremendous loss. It's terrible that any young man should lose his life in such a violent way. And I guess that is what your book is about.
>
> "But it's an even more terrible thing that has happened to the Mullens themselves." (p. 318)

After meeting Schwarzkopf, Bryan contacted others who were there the night Michael was killed—five men in all, including the company commander and a young rifleman who lost his leg in the same "friendly fire" that killed Michael. The men added to Bryan's conviction that Schwarzkopf was telling the truth. Bryan now felt that "Inasmuch as any man can know another's death, I now knew Michael's." So a year after he first met the Mullens, he returned to La Porte City to tell them what he had learned. He thought he would be able to relieve their anguish because of his belief "that the truth, inevitably, would set them free" (p. 320).

But it did not. Bryan reconstructs a painful scene as they sit around the kitchen table of the farm house, he trying to tell the Mullens what took place the night Michael was killed and why the Army had handled the information the way it had, the Mullens resisting, believing that Schwarzkopf was protecting himself by his account and insisting that there had been an official cover-up. Peg becomes upset, Gene angry. For Bryan there is sadness and disappointment. He realizes that for the Mullens, he too has become part of the conspiracy to mask the truth, part of the enemy plot. This is not the case, but in separating himself from their version of the story, he becomes part of their general estrangement from the country. He becomes part of their loss, and in turn experiences the loss himself. He writes: "They, like their son, like the nation itself, had become casualties of the war. And my sadness lay in knowing nothing I could say or write could change that, just as nothing they could say or do could bring back their son" (p. 330).

Bryan leaves the Mullens on pleasant terms but with the edge of different views between them. Gene weeps and asks, "Are we crazy? *Are we?*" Peg asks, "How in the hell can you live a lifetime of being angry? How can you?" (p. 335) There are no answers. And at last, on the day that is the second anniversary of Michael's death, Gene and Bryan go off to visit his grave in a country cemetery, their friendship seemingly intact but the differences between them unresolved.

The book ends with a forty-page section called "The Mission" in which Bryan reconstructs, through the recollections of the men who were there, the action that brought Michael Mullen's unit to night position on a jungle hill where the overhead detonation of an artillery shell sent a piece of shrapnel through Michael's heart, killed another soldier, and wounded six others. The account, given in a flat and impersonal manner, dramatizes the details of the truth about Michael's death as Bryan came to believe it. It is what the Mullens wanted to know and finally could not accept. It is that thing—the simple truth—that in Bryan's view must be added, together with the list of casualty statistics that close the book, to the losses of the war.

Notes

1. DeMott, "In and Out of Universal City," pp. 277, 279.

2. DeMott, "In and Out of Universal City," p. 279.

3. Jo Durden-Smith, *Who Killed George Jackson?* (New York: Knopf, 1976). pp. xiv, xv. Hereafter, page references appear in the text.

4. C.D.B. Bryan, *Friendly Fire* (New York: Putnam's, 1976), p. 65. Hereafter, page references appear in the text.

Conclusion: A Queer Genre

But *is* Bryan's account of the death of Michael Mullen the simple truth?

At least one reviewer of *Friendly Fire* had doubts. Diane Johnson found the first two-thirds of the book carefully and compassionately done, but questioned the part where Bryan enters himself to find out what happened to Michael Mullen. What troubled the reviewer was Bryan's confidence in the military version of the truth given him by Schwarzkopf and his dismissal of the Mullens' claims of cover-up and conspiracy. When Bryan presented his conclusions to the Mullens, Gene had said, "Well, I don't buy it. I don't buy Schwarzkopf, and I don't buy the military" (p. 331). Neither did the reviewer, and for the same reason that little about military accounts of reality in recent years inspires confidence.

But beyond ingrained doubts about the military, the reviewer also felt Bryan had not subjected Schwarzkopf's account of Michael's death to enough scrutiny. More was needed than follow-up interviews with the men of Michael's company and the company commander. Without additional investigative reporting on Bryan's part, the reviewer found "The Mission" section at the end of the book "only a very accomplished fiction," plausible, readable, but leaving her, as he had the Mullens, unreconciled and feeling that Bryan had switched allegiance in the book when he turned from a sympathetic portrayal of the Mullens' protest to a sympathetic defense of the military.[1]

Bryan responded to the review by insisting on the adequacy of his reporting. "The Mission" section had been sent for correction to all the people mentioned, just as the entire manuscript had been corrected by the

Mullens and Schwarzkopf; rather than an accomplished fiction, it was "what happened on the night Michael died."[2] Bryan also insisted that his acceptance of the military version of Michael's death did not lessen his compassion for the Mullens. That the reviewer thought it did, just as the Mullens had, indicated how deeply the war had split the society and caused everyone to choose sides. The truth for Bryan was that Gene Mullen and Norman Schwarzkopf were *both* fine men, that neither the military nor the Mullens had been all right or all wrong. This was exactly the sort of complexity the war had obscured.

There is no way of dealing here with the reviewer's objections to *Friendly Fire*, nor Bryan's defense, beyond simply noting them. Such objections can be addressed to any work of literary nonfiction, and frequently are. They are serious objections that point to a fundamental problem with the form, the inevitable skepticism about accuracy caused by the application of literary devices and the personal voice to factual materials.

The first task of the writer of literary nonfiction, whether he works within the forms of fiction or the journalistic report or some combination of the two, is always to convince the reader that his work is adequate as history. He does this by his reporting and research, by asking all the questions that can be asked and reading all the documents and evaluating all his material with the usual means of verification. And to my mind he strengthens his credibility by including within the finished work some account of how he went about this effort. His primary task, at any event, is always to persuade the reader that he has indeed come to sufficient terms with what Michael Arlen called "the actuality, the nonstorybook element in life."[3]

To present his material in a literary manner and draw from it literary effects is a second step. It is not any easy step to take, for it forces the writer into a second role, maker as well as recorder, and he must keep the roles separate yet exploit each as fully as he can. Nor is the step easy for the reader. He is asked to experience such accounts as both the truth of history and, at least to some extent, the truth of art, to experience both history's correspondence and something of art's coherence. Literary nonfiction is surely, as Diane Johnson said of Bryan's book, a "queer genre" in which a tension of opposed aims is a fundamental characteristic.[4]

That such tension can be managed—not resolved, but held together in harmonious counterpoint—seems to me clear enough from the evidence of some of the works discussed in this book. And of these works, *Friendly Fire* seems to me a fully realized example of the form and one of the most striking achievements in recent literary nonfiction. Unlike Diane Johnson, I find the book convincing as history. That Bryan should have talked with more people or inspected more documents or been more skeptical of his military informants is of course arguable, but I detect no particular lapse in his methods both as they are summarized in the author's note and revealed in the text. He talked with the men who were present in the field the night Michael died, some of whom no longer had military careers to protect, and they were able to read and correct his reconstruction of their accounts. Likewise, the Mullens and Schwarzkopf read and corrected his version of the material they gave him.

Other readers can choose to prefer the Mullens' version of the truth because that version is adequately present in the book. That Bryan himself finds Schwarzkopf's account more in accord with reality does not erase the Mullens' beliefs or render them any less sympathetic. Indeed, Bryan's decision to enter the book himself and offer his conclusions as just that, his conclusions, seems to me an exactly appropriate shift in the book at the end. It is an attempt by the writer revealed, asking questions and wrestling with answers, to perceive the truth of events as fully as one man can and to state that truth, and argue for it, as his own. "The Mission" section is done in the manner of the recording angel but only after the angel has first revealed himself and shown his methods.

At one point late in the book, Bryan breaks off an account of his argument with the Mullens about Schwarzkopf to say that he had originally meant to write only a journalist's book—meaning an "unbiased, dispassionate" account of what happened to a single family as result of the war. (p. 330) But he came to see that in trying to encompass the tragedy of the war through a single experience, he was acting more like a novelist than a journalist. Through his absorption in what happened to the Mullens and his reconstruction of those events as a dramatic narrative, he tried to reach beyond them and endow them with a larger meaning. His book was not simply "reconstructed history," as Noel Behn said of his nonfiction thriller *Big Stick-Up at Brinks!*, but reconstructed history laced through with a fiction writer's tissue of significances.[5]

If, as Saul Bellow said, the function of art is the giving of weight to the particular, the tendency to invest the particular with resonant meanings, then surely *Friendly Fire* as well as *Who Killed George Jackson?*, *Coming into the Country, Blood and Money, In Cold Blood, The Electric Kool-Aid Acid Test*, and other examples of literary nonfiction are works of art as well as works of history. They have in their varied ways implications that reach beyond the factual events they reconstruct—implications that cannot be verified as history but felt and known as art. To say this is not to imply that literary nonfiction is a superior kind of history and certainly not that it is a superior kind of literature. All such talk about rivalry was an unfortunate byproduct of the renewal of interest in the form that took place in the sixties and continued through the seventies. It is quite enough to say that some of the books discussed in the preceding pages are works of historical reconstruction and imaginative writing, fact books that yield something of literature's resonant meanings. As such, they are simply another available resource for the writer and an unusually compelling reading experience for the reader.

Notes

1. Diane Johnson, "True Patriots," *New York Review of Books*, 5 August 1976, p. 43.
2. C. D. B. Bryan, Letter to the *New York Review of Books*, 14 October 1976, p. 52.
3. Arlen, "Notes on the New Journalism," p. 254.
4. Johnson, "True Patriots," p. 42.
5. Noel Behn, *Big Stick-Up at Brinks!* (New York: Warner Books, 1977), Prologue.

Appendix: Literary Nonfiction at the Decade's End

In 1979 literary nonfiction was drawing nearly as much attention as it had in the middle sixties with the appearance of *In Cold Blood*. During the year Norman Mailer, Thomas Thompson, and Tom Wolfe published ambitious new works that quickly made the best-seller lists and sent the authors on rounds of television talk shows. *Esquire* carried a "nonfiction short story" by Truman Capote and installments of Gay Talese's forthcoming study of sexual mores in America, *Thy Neighbor's Wife*. A television adaptation of *Friendly Fire* received considerable acclaim and late in the year work was completed on a television film of *A Time to Die*.

Mailer's *The Executioner's Song* and Thompson's *Serpentine* followed Capote's lead in turning to murder as a subject of perennial importance. Both writers utilized as well Capote's detached, recording-angel methods, though Mailer—surprisingly—carried them to a more rigorous extreme. Both writers also spoke about the factual accuracy of their books in ways that skirted full clarity. *Serpentine* "is, in essence, a true story," Thompson said, but he did not explain the qualification beyond noting that some names had been changed.[1] *The Executioner's Song* "does its best to be a factual account," Mailer said, and he called the work—in a variation on the nonfiction novel—a "true life novel"; at the same time, he insisted that the work should be understood simply as a novel—and so on the best-seller lists it was placed in the category of fiction.[2] In their comments, in other words, both writers did little to dispel the inevitable doubts about accuracy that accompany literary nonfiction.

In *The Right Stuff* Wolfe turned to what many considered an unpromising subject, the origins of the American space program, but managed to find in it material that seemed startlingly fresh. Once again he sought to capture the subjective reality of his characters, but it was his extensive reporting and research that received most notice, with the result that the book met with little of the critical resistance that marked his earlier work. It seemed clear that *The Right Stuff* was a major effort of factual reconstruction and Wolfe's claims to accuracy were not casually dismissed.

I

The central characters of *Serpentine* and *The Executioner's Song* have some things in common: both are intelligent, both spend large parts of their lives in jails, both kill, and both become subjects of popular books. But beyond these broad matters there are striking differences between the two.

Thompson's Charles Sobhraj is sophisticated, cosmopolitan, darkly handsome. Of Indian and Vietnamese extraction, he lives for many years in France and thinks himself French, but most of his criminal career takes place in the East where the police are less aggressive and he easily loses himself in the great masses. He dresses stylishly, neither smokes nor drinks, speaks several languages, and moves easily through the best hotels of Istanbul, Tehran, Bangkok, Hong Kong, and Bombay, often with an attractive woman in tow. When arrested and jailed, he immediately sets about escaping—and often succeeds; when finally tried for murder in India—one of at least twelve that police believe he committed—he plays every legal and extra-legal card he can find. In 1978 Sobhraj is convicted of a lesser murder charge and given a modest sentence, one that allows him to be free in a few years if not tried for other murders.

Mailer's Gary Gilmore is tall, gaunt, painfully provincial. His background is Utah, Mormon, hard-scratch working class; Provo, Salt Lake City, and various prisons make up his world. He is awkward out of prison, poor with women, inclined to wear comic hats and mismatched clothes; he drinks too much, takes too many pills, commits crimes impulsively, and is easily caught. When sentenced to death for two murders, he demands the State of Utah promptly carry out the sentence. Normal appeals would have put off his death for years or reduced the sentence; but he does nothing to save himself and resists the efforts of others. In 1977 Gilmore is executed by a firing squad, the first execution in the country in more than a decade.

In reconstructing the facts of Sobhraj's life Thompson attempts, as he did in *Blood and Money*, to explore true events as meaning—but with less success. He slips into the sensationalism and overheated prose that marred the earlier book, but finally it is a heavy concentration on fate that limits the impact of *Serpentine*. The epigraph, an inscription on a Hindu temple, informs us that "Coincidence, if traced far enough back, becomes inevitable." Coincidence becomes the book's recurring theme; repeatedly Thompson shows the innocent lives of tourists and wanderers merging with the life of Sobhraj, with destructive results. Life within the covers of the book is meant to seem serpentine and darkly fated. It is a theme that might have deeply bound together and illumined the various stories Thompson tells; but finally it seems too little, only a gloss of meaning applied to a complicated effort of reporting. One sighs at the end for unlucky people but does not sufficiently experience the rude chanciness of life that, in retrospect, appears destiny.

Thompson's most strenuous efforts go into the manipulation of time sequences to build suspense. He opens the book with a brief scene on the day an Indian judge is about to hand down his decision after the year-long trial of Sobhraj and Marie-Andrée Leclerc, his love-starved accomplice. The narrative then abruptly switches to one of Sobhraj's more daring jewel thefts, seven years before. Before this story is concluded Thompson turns to an account of Sobhraj's youth and to the stories of three women who will eventually become his victims (one of them Marie-Andrée); finally he returns to the comic conclusion of the jewel theft before setting off on the long account of Sobhraj's murder binge. The book ends with the judge—500 pages intervening—at last revealing his verdict.

It is a grimly fascinating story, but little more than that. Thompson ends the book's opening scene with the comment that the judge's verdict, whatever it was, would not answer the more important question of "Why did these deaths occur? Why did these lives collide?" (p. xii) Thompson does not deeply ponder such questions either, beyond providing the literal answer of showing how several lives collided with Sobhraj's. We never learn why Sobhraj suddenly turned from what Interpol called a "drug and rob" man, a small-time con artist who drugged his victims before taking their passports, money, and jewelry, into a thief who killed his victims and burned many of the bodies. In the book a handwriting expert speculates about Sobhraj: "He was hurt as a young person. He experienced great trouble. And he wants revenge on the world" (p. 422). This familiar formulation is about as much as Thompson offers by way of explanation.

What dominates his attention is what happened, and it was no mean feat to track it all down. But this is where murder comes to the aid of the nonfiction novelist—or seems to. If murder is an enduring subject, it also is a subject in which a good deal of the reporting is ready-made in the form of police and court reports. If the case is an important one there are news stories to draw on as well and principal figures get drawn across the line from private to public lives, used to journalists asking questions and seeing themselves in print. There is nothing wrong with this, of course; the point is simply that the writer has a good deal of raw material handed to him. The temptation must be strong to rely on it, dramatizing, rearranging, highlighting, but finally depending on the power of the material itself to carry the work. The result is work that makes few claims on our attention beyond those of curiosity.

The Executioner's Song is a better book than *Serpentine*. It is more interesting in structure, in its use of language, even in its fact-gathering; it seems to carry documentary journalism to a logical conclusion, dredging up every detail, giving voice to every figure remotely connected to the story. The book also is of considerable interest in that it reveals Mailer's virtuosity as a maker of nonfiction narratives. He is not, as one would expect, in the book himself. He avoids even veiled references to his own presence and there is no fussing with the notion that since everything comes to us through the author we must see and know him if we are to adequately judge his reporting. There is, seemingly, little selection or arrangement or emphasis in the book; even a distinct point of view is lacking. We are left with the incredible story itself.

Mailer divides the book into two parts of equal length, "Western Voices" and "Eastern Voices." In both the narrative method is the same: people who knew Gilmore or were involved with him, and Gilmore himself, are presented in brief scenes, some no more than a few sentences, the material printed in short paragraphs with extra spacing between. The method allows quick shifts among the characters and creates a narrative of massive mosaiclike quality. The language is flat, though slightly tuned to the idioms and rhythms of the characters. The point of view of each scene is that of the character telling his story to an interviewer or into a tape recorder and recalling his thoughts and what was said.

The characters brought forth in the two sections, however, tend to be different. In "Western Voices" the main figures are family members who gather around Gilmore when he is released from a federal penitentiary and returns to Provo, his eventual victims, and Nicole Baker. If Gilmore's life is bleak, his girlfriend's matches it. When they meet Nicole is 19, has been in and out of mental hospitals, is twice divorced, and has two children. Immediately they fall in love; he has her name tattooed on his arm, she has his on her ankle. It is that kind of affair, sudden, passionate, and ruinous— right out of the Johnny Cash records Gilmore admires. When Nicole breaks off with him, Gilmore thinks about killing her. His anger at the loss of Nicole, together with a heavy load of alcohol and drugs, becomes what explanation there is for the senseless killing of a gas station attendant and a motel manager after petty robberies.

With Gilmore's demand that Utah carry out the death sentence, Mailer shifts attention to the "Eastern Voices" of lawyers and media types who crowd into the story. Out of the clamor comes Lawrence Schiller, a veteran of checkbook journalism with earlier stories on Susan Atkins and Jack Ruby, who buys up exclusive rights to the recollections of the key figures.

Schiller tirelessly fends off the competition, passes out a few morsels to the media to build interest in the case, and labors through taped prison interviews with Gilmore, hoping he will not be executed before his story is fully recorded. When last seen in the book Schiller has flown Nicole to California for interviews that bring out much of the book's most intimate material.

In its portrayal of Gilmore's victims and the family figures who try to help Gilmore and steel themselves against the coming blowup, "Western Voices" is the most moving part of the book. But "Eastern Voices" is intriguing in its revelations of the selling of a true-life story. The Gilmore case was special in the attention it drew, but Mailer nonetheless brings to light what is usually hidden in nonfiction accounts of celebrated murders— the payoffs for exclusive rights or legal releases. (Sobhraj sells his story to a Bangkok firm and spends time during his trial dictating to a writer.) Mailer is remorseless in his portrait of Schiller as capable of any exploitation for the sake of the story; there are fine comic moments when we see him troubling over whether he is the journalist he wants to be or the crass hustler others consider him. But Mailer stops short of showing his own role in making the big book Schiller wanted from the story (and whose copyright he shares); in an afterword—helpful in giving the reader some sense of the reporting behind the book and the liberties taken in writing it— Mailer mentions his collaboration with Schiller, but the narrative itself takes no account of it. It is a notable omission. Since Mailer brings up the matter, one wishes to know how he views his own role.

But that would require that he bring himself into the story, and the whole effort of the book is to keep himself out of it, both as direct presence and as behind-the-scenes arranger. There is surely more selection and shaping in the book than meets the eye, and Gilmore is so treated as to emerge in a generally sympathetic light. But Mailer wishes to give the impression of presenting his material with little manipulation and devoid of comment; it is as if the book came straight from the tape recorder, with only a little tidying up here and there and the various stories interwoven for dramatic effect. Depending on one's response to Mailer's earlier nonfiction, the method can seem refreshing; the dust-jacket copy happily announced that this time Mailer "has not predigested his material and imposed a point of view." The work can be admired, in other words, as an example of the "notational nonfiction novel" Mas'ud Zavarzadeh calls for, a work that simply transcribes experience.

To me, however, this suggests the weakness of *The Executioner's Song* as a work of literary nonfiction: there is too little of Mailer in it. The vitality of Mailer's journalism is located in his rarely settling for what he calls the "chores" and "bondage" of ordinary journalism; he has taken to himself the task of the "private eye inquiring into the mysteries of a new phenomenon" or the "good working amateur philosopher" who insists on giving both the events and an interpretation of events. But in *The Executioner's Song* the familiar private eye hot in pursuit of various mysteries is entirely absent—and missed. The story Mailer tells is staggering in its richness; no one could invent characters better than Gilmore, Nicole, and Schiller, nor minor figures better than the dozens that move in and out of the book. But there are mysteries one would like to see Mailer turn to, or turn to more directly—among them the Mormon background out of which Gilmore and Nicole come and Gilmore's developing belief in reincarnation that allows him to meet death with total calm, not even clenching his fists as the count begins for the firing squad.

In an interview Mailer had this to say about Gilmore's attitude toward death:

> . . . what fascinated me about Gilmore was here was a man who obviously had this belief that this life is one of several continuing lives and who also believes that the way in which you die is therefore immensely important: you can die well or you can die badly and it will affect your karma incredibly. This man had this passionate belief so he worked concertedly to be executed by the state rather than be sent to jail for 20 or 30 years, as if his karma would be spoiled irreparably if his soul had had to slowly expire in jail.

It is a line of inquiry Mailer would have leaped upon in the past. But the method of the book permits him to pursue Gilmore's belief in reincarnation only obliquely, through the reflections of others, and to suppress his own speculations. The private eye chooses to do his limited work out of sight, and in this instance and others the work is not enough to give the story the depth of meaning and implication that stamps it in mind and spirit, a memory that refuses to let go.

Elsewhere in the same interview Mailer put in a good word for the novel as "complete fiction" as against true-life fiction:

> For me there's nothing more beautiful than a marvellous novel. I love the idea of a novel; to me a novel is better than a reality. I mean as good as this book may become—and I hope it becomes a very, very good book—it can never be as good as a novel, to my mind. It could be better than a novel in a lot of ways but it could never be as good.[3]

The Executioner's Song is better than many novels: richer in character, in talk, in plot. So is *Serpentine*. Pure invention seems to pale before both stories. But the depth of meaning we associate with the novel at its best is missing. The challenge of documentary journalism as art is to remain faithful to the facts yet invest fact with some of the resonant implications of fiction. It is a difficult enough task, but made all the more so when the subject is murder and the facts are so stunning in themselves.

II

The Right Stuff recalls the early days of rocket-plane testing that took place at Edwards Air Force Base in California after the Korean War and, subsequently, the selection and flights of the original seven Mercury astronauts. Just as the early drug experiments of Ken Kesey and the Merry Pranksters in *The Electric Kool-Aid Acid Test* led to the spread of the drug culture in America, so too the rocket pilots and Mercury astronauts prepared the way for the triumphant moon landings of the Apollo program. And just as Wolfe was not content merely to describe the beginnings of the drug culture, neither is he content in *The Right Stuff* merely to reconstruct events; he provides a cohesive interpretation as well, one in which the first astronauts, not unlike Kesey and the Pranksters, are men turned to the future, constantly seeking "furthur." The difference is that Kesey led the Pranksters in an illusive inward search for expanded consciousness whereas the astronauts pursue a goal, equally illusive and inward, of merit and distinction within the narrow confines of professional flying.

The method of the book is generally similar to *Acid Test* in that Wolfe again tries to convey the subjective reality of his various characters. The story opens on a day in 1955 during which Jane Conrad awaits news of whether a Navy flier who has just crashed is her husband Pete. Wolfe constructs the scene from her point of view, capturing the fear of sudden and gruesome death with which the fliers' wives must live, but he shifts easily out of her thoughts to supply background material and omniscient comment. The section ends with a leap ahead to a day seven years later and reporters wondering if Jane Conrad is frightened during her husband's flight in space. The questioning is ironic given the years of fear she has lived with. Wolfe writes: " 'Why ask *now?*' she wanted to say. But they wouldn't have had the faintest notion of what she was talking about."[4] Throughout the book Wolfe maintains the method of the opening section, projecting the narrative from inside the mind of his characters, shifting away for information and comment, returning to character. He never, however, attempts an internal point of view at the depth of "The Fugitive" chapter of *Acid Test*, and in this as well as in language and tone the book is a less heated authorial performance than the earlier work.

In Wolfe's view the foremost thing to understand about the first astronauts is that they were pilots—and pilots of a special sort: fighter pilots and test pilots. As such, they conceived of themselves as a breed set apart; they were men who daily risked their lives in the most hazardous forms of flying. They were motivated not only by a passion for flying but by patriotism, by egos that knew few limits, and by a vision of an intangible goal apparent only to those within the profession, what Wolfe calls the

Brotherhood of the Right Stuff. The Brotherhood resembles a pyramid and young pilots begin climbing it at the beginning of their careers. There is nothing written down about the pyramid, but the pilots know exactly what steps are required to reach the top; they know they must reveal to themselves and others that they possess the "right stuff" and so are eligible to rise to the next level of the pyramid, eventually moving through a seemingly infinite series of tests into the elite company of a few pilots at the very top.

The exact nature of the right stuff depends on the particular flying challenge at hand: landing on a carrier, combat flying, testing experimental planes. The only common denominator is the assumption that "a man should have the ability to go up in a hurtling piece of machinery and put his hide on the line and then have the moxie, the reflexes, the experience, the coolness, to pull it back in the last yawning moment—and then to go up again *the next day*, and the next day, and every next day . . ." (p. 24). The only fear the pilots have is fear of being left behind, for to be left behind at any point in the climb up the pyramid is to fail utterly, and so they push themselves to extraordinary feats of daring and bravado—and celebrate themselves with bouts of drinking, mad-cap driving, and womanizing.

Wolfe describes the world of the "fighter jocks" with typical verve, but his aim is broader in that he shows how this narrow and in many ways old-fashioned manly activity influenced later space exploits. The shape of the flying pyramid constantly changes, but in the 1950s it was clear where the top was located and equally clear who the man at the top was. The place was Edwards Air Force Base and the man was a young officer named Chuck Yeager. At Edwards, Yeager flew experimental rocket planes, and in 1947 he had become the first man to break the sound barrier. He also flew rocket planes to the edge of space. Although Yeager's feats were not widely known to the public, they were well known among pilots. Similarly, Yeager's style—laconic, unshakeably cool—set the style for all fighter jocks.

In the beginning, test pilots like Yeager had little interest in space flight. They considered the first space vehicles little more than artillery shells; there would be little for an astronaut to do but ride along, a passenger rather than a pilot. When Yeager was asked why he had not tried to become an astronaut, he said: "I've been a pilot all my life, and there won't be any flying to do in Project Mercury" (p. 127). But despite the reservations of the test pilots, the shape of the flying pyramid began changing with the selection of the Mercury astronauts. The reason had nothing to do with flying but with public response to the astronauts. They became celebrities. *Life* magazine purchased their exclusive stories; they were frequent guests at the White House; and far from least in the eyes of the fighter jocks, they were the objects of eager attention from attractive young women. "From the very beginning," Wolfe notes, "this 'astronaut' business was just an unbelievable good deal" (p. 130).

With the outpouring of public attention after the first Mercury flights of Alan Shepard and John Glenn, the flying pyramid was permanently altered. The astronauts "had *become* the True Brotherhood. They were so dazzling you couldn't even *see* the erstwhile True Brethren of Edwards Air Force Base any longer" (p. 389). As they cut back on medical and scientific tests in space and insisted on more and more control of the capsules, the astronauts also grudgingly came to be recognized by the test pilots as true pilots. As Wolfe puts it, the astronauts finally received what they wanted most of all, the one thing that could not be given by an adoring public: "acceptance by their peers, their true brethren, as *test pilots* of the space age" (pp. 434-5).

In Wolfe's account the Mercury astronauts adjust space exploration from a scientific and technological venture, spurred on by Cold War competition, into status competition within the world of fighter pilots and test pilots. They turn flying in space into the latest chapter in an old story of hottest pilot on the base. The effect of the account is to remove space exploration from grand talk about the new ocean of space and scientific discoveries and radical changes in human life and replace it with familiar thoughts about earthly ambition. *The Right Stuff* brings the space program right back to earth.

Rather than heroic types, the astronauts are portrayed as recognizably human figures—vain, competitive, and no more virtuous than the next person. The public image of them as simple small-town churchgoers and dedicated family men was, Wolfe maintains, largely set by John Glenn. The most articulate member of the astronaut group, Glenn gave the media the kind of pious pronouncements they were looking for and generally conducted himself in a strait-laced manner—all of which struck the other astronauts as unbecoming a fighter jock. The exclusive *Life* contract also protected the astronauts from close media inspection, with the result that they all came to resemble Glenn in the public mind: modest, dedicated, well-scrubbed figures. Wolfe's account restores them to their proper role as self-serving, hard-living fighter jocks.

Wolfe's treatment of the astronauts' experience in space is similarly heavy with return-to-earth qualities. For example, he suggests that the astronauts gave few notable descriptions of their space flights because the flights simply were confirmations of what they had been trained to expect. They had gone through all the procedures hundreds of times in realistic simulations; consequently, the tendency during flights was to contrast real experience with the simulator training, and often conclude that the latter was the more rigorous. Nothing, finally, could be more ironic. The novelty of the first manned American space flights cannot be felt because the preparations have destroyed all sense of novelty. The very point of the training had been to make all eventualities familiar, and so the highest praise for the flights is to say they went just the way they were programmed.

The Right Stuff strips space exploration of any sense of new-world mystery and brings it tumbling back to familiar earth. But whatever the loss of an earlier awe, there is a clear gain in understanding. We come to see what we never quite saw before. In Wolfe's hands the early years of the space age take on a gritty yet satisfying human dimension and the men who rode the rockets appear for the first time as full-bodied human beings.

Notes

1. Thomas Thompson, *Serpentine* (Doubleday, 1979), Author's Note. Hereafter, page references appear in the text.

2. Norman Mailer, *The Executioner's Song* (Little, Brown, 1979), p. 1,051.

3. "A Murderer's Tale: Norman Mailer Talking to Melvyn Bragg," *The Listener*, 15 November 1979, p. 662.

4. Tom Wolfe, *The Right Stuff* (Farrar, Straus and Giroux, 1979), p. 20. Hereafter, page references appear in the text.

Bibliographical Note

I am aware of two full-length critical studies devoted to what I call literary nonfiction: John Hollowell's *Fact and Fiction: The New Journalism and the Nonfiction Novel* (Chapel Hill: University of North Carolina Press, 1977) and Mas'ud Zavarzadeh's *The Mythopoeic Reality: The Postwar American Nonfiction Novel* (Urbana: University of Illinois Press, 1976). I have found both books useful, although Hollowell's is limited to a discussion of Capote, Mailer, and Wolfe while Zavarzadeh's seems to me seriously mistaken in its emphasis on the anti-interpretive nature of recent nonfiction. Other books that touch on the subject are *The Magic Writing Machine*, ed. Everette E. Dennis (Eugene: University of Oregon School of Journalism, 1971); *Other Voices: The New Journalism in America*, by Everette E. Dennis and William Rivers (San Francisco: Canfield Press, 1974); *The New Journalism: The Underground Press, The Artists of Nonfiction, and Changes in the Established Media*, by Michael Johnson (Lawrence: University Press of Kansas, 1971); *The New Journalism*, ed. Marshall Fishwick (Bowling Green, Ohio: Popular Press, 1975); and *Liberating the Media: The New Journalism*, ed. Charles C. Flippen (Washington: Acropolis Books, 1974). *Bright Book of Life: American Novelists and Storytellers from Hemingway to Mailer*, by Alfred Kazin (Boston: Little, Brown, 1973), contains a perceptive chapter on Capote's and Mailer's nonfiction. One of the few critics to give serious attention to Wolfe's *The Electric Kool-Aid Acid Test* is Tony Tanner, *City of Words: American Fiction, 1950-1970* (New York: Farrar, Straus and Giroux, 1971). Thomas R. Kendrick's introduction to *Writing in Style*, ed. Laura

Longley Babb (Washington: The Washington Post Co., 1975), treats the new interest in nonfiction writing from a journalist's perspective. I have collected a number of critical articles and interviews that deal in one way or another with literary nonfiction in *The Reporter as Artist: A Look at the New Journalism Controversy* (New York: Hastings House, 1974). An obvious starting point for anyone wishing to read other examples of recent literary nonfiction is Tom Wolfe's *The New Journalism, with an Anthology Edited by Tom Wolfe and E. W. Johnson* (New York: Harper & Row, 1973). Whatever its merits, Wolfe's essay in this book is a central statement of the aims and methods of the New Journalism. Wolfe's views are amplified in an interview printed in *The New Fiction: Interviews with Innovative American Writers*, by Joe David Bellamy (Urbana: University of Illinois Press, 1974).

Index